Grammar and Style Guide

**The World Book
Desk Reference Set**

Grammar and
Style Guide

Published by

World Book, Inc.
a Scott Fetzer company

Chicago

Staff

Publisher
William H. Nault

Editorial

Editor in chief
Robert O. Zeleny

Executive editor
Dominic J. Miccolis

Associate editor
Maureen M. Mostyn

Staff editor
Karen Zack Ingebretsen

Editors
Susan Blum
Louisa M. Johnston
Mary D. Shell

Adviser
Dr. Geraldine E. La Rocque
Professor of English and English Education
University of Northern Iowa
Cedar Falls

Art

Executive art director
William Hammond

Art director
Roberta Dimmer

Assistant art director
Joe Gound

Cover design
David Doty

Photography director
John S. Marshall

Product production

Executive director
Peter Mollman

Manufacturing
Joseph C. La Count

Research and development
Henry Koval

Pre-press services
Jerry Stack, director
Lori Frankel
Randi Park

Research and library services
Mary Norton, director

Contents

Introduction

Though almost everyone uses language everyday—and quite effectively—there are not many people who have a precise knowledge of how the basic principles of language work. These principles include those of *grammar,* or the study of the forms and uses of words in sentences; and of *style,* which refers to the way a person chooses to express thoughts, either in writing or in speaking. These principles of grammar and style can be baffling, as any student who has struggled with identifying a gerundive or writing a sonnet could attest.

When the parts of speech all start looking the same, or when a bibliography cannot wait any longer to be typed, it is useful to have one source that presents all the principles of English grammar and style needed to get along in everyday school, work, or home life. The World Book *Grammar and Style Guide* has been prepared to provide this type of source. A look at the contents shows how much this source has to offer.

The guide offers many devices to help you make your way to proper grammar and style. There are discussions that will open your eyes to the flexibility, beauty, and tradition of the English language; there are illustrations to model your writing against; and there are guidelines to letter-perfect spelling and flawless capitalization and punctuation. You will even find advice on when to bend the "rules," to greater effect than if you had followed them. Tables of common word parts will help you figure out definitions for words when a dictionary is not at hand. The key to all this information is the extensive index found at the end of the book. With it, you can find the topic that you seek, whether it is irregular verbs, the difference between farce and satire, or the proper form for a business letter.

The *Grammar and Style Guide* puts the principles of English in one place—near you. Reach out and use this guide anytime you want to make language work well.

Looking at our language

Whether you are a child, a teenager, or an adult, whether you spend your days in school or at work, you have at your command a powerful tool—the English language. You use this tool for many purposes, such as inquiring about the world around you, communicating your feelings, and sharing your thoughts. Doesn't it make sense to learn all you can about how this powerful tool works and how you can make it work for you?

That is what this book is all about. It will answer your questions about the structure of the English language and give you some guidelines about how to use English correctly and effectively in speech and in letters, reports, and creative writing. It will outline the rules underlying the language and indicate when it is acceptable—and, sometimes, even desirable—to break those rules.

To begin, let's take a closer look at the English language—its rules, its history, and some explanations of its grammar.

Reasons for the rules

Some rules serve specific purposes. For instance, a rule against swimming in a particular river may protect the public health. Other kinds of rules, such as the rules of a language, develop over hundreds of years. As times change, the rules may gradually change as well, and new patterns of speech may be accepted as normal, natural, or correct.

To know when to follow a particular principle of grammar or usage, it is necessary to consider whether your choice of language is appropriate to the situation at hand. In other words, is a formal tone or style equally right in a business speech and a conversation with friends? Is it just as right to use informal language when writing to a senator as when writing to your cousin?

Knowing how to use the right language at the right time in the right circumstances enables you to harness the power of language. The more control you have over language, the more you can make it work for you. Rules or principles of grammar and usage are guides that can maximize language's power potential.

Even people who think they know little about grammar and usage really know a great deal. They use it all the time and have done so since they began to talk in sentences. If English is their native language, then English grammar and usage is natural for them. If English is not their native language, then in learning English they had to learn how English sentences are arranged. In either case—whether English is native or acquired—

learning the principles of grammar and usage in a systematic way helps people understand how the principles work and makes people comfortable with the rules.

Language power

Language is effective only if it accomplishes what the speaker or writer intends. Good intentions, however, do not always guarantee good communication. Sometimes communication breaks down because of the great number of differences among speech patterns, or *dialects,* in the various regions of the English-speaking world.

Where people live and with whom they associate has much to do with their everyday speech patterns. People speak in the way that makes them comfortable, using slang and faddish expressions that come and go. When people talk with their friends, they are usually well understood. But the ability to communicate well with a small, familiar group does not guarantee the same effectiveness with all groups.

Despite the variety of regional dialects, a standard English pattern has developed. This standard English is used to conduct the major social, political, educational, religious, and business affairs in English-speaking countries. People tend to expect to hear standard English from radio announcers, educators, and successful business people and to find standard grammar in newspapers, books, and magazines.

After people have learned the principles of grammar and usage, they readily notice when those principles are not followed. Careless use of language can actually create a false impression. For instance, an English professor who tells a joke involving slang may be taken for an uneducated person by an unsuspecting passerby.

On the other hand, someone with little formal education who is comfortable with standard English usage may give the impression of being very well educated. The moral? *How* people communicate sometimes says more than *what* they communicate.

When you need to communicate with teachers, employers, or anyone else who is not familiar with your everyday speech patterns, it is helpful to be comfortable with the principles of standard English. You may choose to carry on a conversation with friends in any manner whatsoever. But using standard English in other situations will guarantee that you will communicate effectively.

Because language is the tool of the user and because the user's needs are always changing, language never stays exactly the same. In your own lifetime, there have probably been hundreds of changes in the informal language patterns and vocabulary of English. Slang seems to change every day, and new words appear continually. But the formal grammar of standard English changes far less frequently. Students learning English grammar in school today can be assured that the rules they are learning now will still be acceptable in twenty or thirty years.

Historical facts

The history of the English language is usually divided into three major periods: Old English (or Anglo-Saxon); Middle English; and Modern English.

Old English

Until about A.D. 450, England was not called England, nor was English spoken there. Before that time, the country was called Britain and the people were known as Britons. The Britons spoke Celtic dialects, which included many Latin words because Roman troops occupied Britain from A.D. 43 until the mid-400's.

Around 450, invading Germanic tribes called Angles, Saxons, Jutes, and Frisians conquered Britain. These conquerors all spoke similar dialects of Germanic. The Angles and Saxons occupied a large part of Britain, which took its new name, *England,* from the name of the Angles. From the 500's to 1066, the Anglo-Saxon language, now usually called Old English, became firmly established.

Celtic made only a small contribution to the Old English vocabulary. Except for a few words such as *crag* and *bin,* most Celtic words that remain in English today are place names such as *Avon, Kent, London,* and *Thames.*

Latin had a much stronger influence on early English. Even before the Germanic tribes invaded Britain, the Britons had borrowed many words, such as *camp* and *wine,* from their Latin-speaking rulers. During the 500's, Latin-speaking Celt and Roman missionaries spread Christianity in England, and more Latin words entered the English vocabulary at that time. Most of these words were religious terms such as *bishop* and *mass.* In the 800's, Vikings from Denmark and Norway invaded England and many of these Scandinavians settled in England and intermarried with the English. Many English words have their origin in the Scandinavian languages, among them most words that begin with *sk* (for example, *sky, skill,* and *skirt*). Especially important were the Scandinavian pronouns that replaced English pronouns. *They, them,* and *their* took the place of words that today would probably have been something like *hie, hem,* and *her.*

The following sentence from a document written in 1020 shows what Old English looked like. (The letter þ, called *thorn,* represents the sound spelled *th.*)

Ic nam me to gemynde þa gewritu and þa word, þe se arcebiscop Lyfing me fram þam papan brohte of Rome.
(I have remembered the writs and the words that Archbishop Lyfing brought me from the Pope of Rome.)

Which words in the example do you recognize as exactly the same as words still used today? Which words are slightly different but still recognizable? Notice, too, the arrangement of the words in the example. Translated word for word, the last part would say ". . . that Archbishop Lyfing me from the Pope brought of Rome."

Middle English

In 1066, the Normans invaded Britain, replacing the English people as the chief landholders and church officials. The invaders' language—the Norman dialect of French—became the language of the ruling class. The common people, however, continued to speak English.

Norman-French and English existed side by side until political and social changes began to favor the use of English by all classes. By the end of the Middle English period (1100–1500), English had again established itself as the major language in Britain. But, as a result of the Norman Conquest, thousands of French words had entered the English vocabulary—words such as *air, army, art, blue, chair, color, dinner, government, jolly, judge, justice, mayor, paper, poet, prison,* and *towel.* Words from other languages also became part of English during this period, including words of Dutch origin such as *deck, easel, etch, freight, furlough,* and *stoop.*

The Norman Conquest accelerated changes that had already begun to occur in English grammar and pronunciation patterns. Special word endings, called *inflections,* lost their distinctive meanings, and word order instead of word endings became the key to the meaning of a sentence.

An *inflection* is a variation in the form of a word to show case, number, gender, person, tense, mood, voice, or comparison. Some inflections endure in Modern English. Examples are in the following sentences:

I am happy.	The adjective *happy* is in the positive form.
I am happier.	The adjective *happy* is in the comparative form.
I am the *happiest.*	The adjective *happy* is in the superlative form.

The ending -*y*, the ending -*er,* and the ending -*est* all show meaning. The same meanings can also be conveyed by adding words in a certain order; that is, by using words instead of inflections:

I am happy.	The adjective *happy*, with no accompanying word, is in the positive form.
I am more happy.	The adjective *happy*, preceded by the word *more*, is in the comparative form.
I am the most happy.	The adjective *happy*, preceded by the word *most*, is in the superlative form.

The adjective *happy* has been compared in two ways: by inflection and by word order. After the Middle English period began, word order was used more and more to convey meaning.

The following sentence is an example of Middle English. It comes from a proclamation made by King Henry in 1258. (The letter that looks like a *3* is called *yogh*. It was used as the sound *gh* at the end of a word.)

Henri, þur3 Godes fultume King on Engleneloande, Lhoauerd on Yrloande, Duk on Normandi, on Aquitaine, and Eorl on Aniow, send igretinge to alle hise holde. (Henry, by the grace of God [through God's help], King of England, Lord of Ireland, Duke of Normandy and Aquitaine, and Earl of Anjou, sends greetings to all his subjects.)

Modern English

The Modern English period, starting about 1500, witnessed the standardization of the language. Several factors contributed to establishing standard English spelling and certain forms of usage. Among these factors are the introduction of the printing press into England in 1477, the revival of interest in literature, and the growth of popular education. Since printing allowed books to be created in much greater numbers than handwritten books of previous centuries ever could have been, the spelling and usage within those printed books gained a greater acceptance. The revival of interest in literature, especially in classical Greek and Latin literature, led to attempts to label grammar and some spelling as "right" or "wrong." The coincidental growth of popular education enabled this standardization brought to English through printing and the literary revival to be quickly spread.

From the 1500's through the 1700's, more than 10,000 new words entered the language. Many of these were taken from Latin and Greek by scholars who wanted to replace words earlier adopted from French. More than 25 percent of modern English words come almost directly from classical languages. These words include *conduct, dexterity, extinguish, scientific,* and *spurious.*

Because of these and other borrowings (including borrowings from French, Italian, Spanish, Russian, German, American Indian, and Arabic), English today has a larger and more varied vocabulary than almost any other language.

Sources of some English words

Latin	Greek	French	German
1. anchor	1. apostle	1. captain	1. cobalt
2. butter	2. chlorine	2. castle	2. dachshund
3. chalk	3. church	3. fry	3. delicatessen
4. circle	4. comet	4. horrible	4. hamster
5. data	5. demon	5. juggler	5. nickel
6. education	6. idiosyncrasy	6. jury	6. noodle
7. equal	7. oligarchy	7. magic	7. plunder
8. janitor	8. paper	8. prince	8. poodle
9. kitchen	9. pathos	9. question	9. pretzel
10. library	10. phone	10. royal	10. quartz
11. medium	11. telegram	11. secret	11. waltz
12. orbit	12. xylophone	12. soldier	12. yodel

Dutch	Italian	Spanish	Scandinavian
1. buoy	1. balcony	1. alligator	1. fellow
2. coleslaw	2. balloon	2. barbecue	2. kick
3. cruise	3. broccoli	3. canyon	3. law
4. duffel	4. carnival	4. chocolate	4. rag
5. easel	5. duet	5. guitar	5. rug
6. frolic	6. ghetto	6. mosquito	6. saga
7. landscape	7. opera	7. patio	7. score
8. luck	8. solo	8. rodeo	8. scowl
9. pickle	9. trombone	9. tango	9. ski
10. spool	10. umbrella	10. tomato	10. skin
11. wagon	11. violin	11. tornado	11. skirt
12. yacht	12. volcano	12. vanilla	12. window

Arabic	Celtic	Indian	Oriental
1. algebra	1. bog	1. bandanna	1. chow
2. almanac	2. brogue	2. bungalow	2. geisha
3. candy	3. clan	3. cot	3. judo
4. cotton	4. crag	4. curry	4. ju-jitsu
5. giraffe	5. galore	5. jungle	5. ketchup
6. hazard	6. leprechaun	6. loot	6. kimono
7. magazine	7. plaid	7. pajamas	7. silk
8. mattress	8. shamrock	8. shampoo	8. soy
9. sugar	9. slogan	9. thug	9. tea
10. syrup	10. tory	10. yoga	10. tycoon

Pacific Island	Slavic	African	Semitic
1. bamboo	1. coach	1. banjo	1. amen
2. boomerang	2. czar	2. gorilla	2. cherub
3. gingham	3. goulash	3. gumbo	3. hallelujah
4. kangaroo	4. mammoth	4. jazz	4. jubilee
5. luau	5. paprika	5. rumba	5. kosher
6. parakeet	6. polka	6. samba	6. matzo
7. rattan	7. soviet	7. tote	7. rabbi
8. taboo	8. steppe	8. voodoo	
9. tattoo	9. tundra	9. yam	
10. ukulele			

Editor's note: Some of these words, though ultimately from the given language, entered English via other languages. Also, many English words have come from other languages not mentioned here, such as North and South American Indian languages, Portuguese, Persian, and Turkish.

Modern grammatical explanations

Grammar is a set of principles by which a language functions. Grammar serves as a guide to help people communicate easily and accurately.

There are a number of different ways to describe English grammar. The best-known descriptions are called *traditional grammar, structural grammar,* and *transformational grammar.* Many teachers of English grammar use ideas from several different grammar descriptions to help their students understand how English functions.

Traditional grammar

Traditional grammar treats the *parts of speech* as the building blocks for every sentence. Words are labeled as belonging to one of the eight parts of speech: *nouns, verbs, pronouns, adjectives, adverbs, prepositions, conjunctions,* and *interjections.* Words are labeled as one of the eight parts of speech by looking at their formal features and their function or position in a sentence. For instance, both *table* and *man* are nouns because they show the possessive form *(table's, man's)* and the plural form *(tables, men).* Both table and man can also fill a position or function in a sentence like "The _____ is big."

Nouns, verbs, adjectives, and adverbs can be defined by formal features and function or position. Other parts of speech, such as prepositions and conjunctions, have no formal features. They can be identified by their function or position in a sentence.

Many words can be classified as more than one part of speech, depending on how they are used. See how *yellow* can be one of three parts of speech in the following three sentences:

The room was decorated in *yellow*. (noun)
The *yellow* dress needed pressing. (adjective)
Dry cleaning will *yellow* that fabric. (verb)

Structural grammar

Structural grammar describes how sounds, word forms, and word positions affect meaning. Structural grammar concerns itself with two meanings in each sentence, the *structural* meaning and the *lexical* meaning. The lexical meaning is the dictionary meaning of the words. The structural meaning comes from how the words are formed and where they are positioned in the sentence. To illustrate the difference, look at the following example:

The gorby stils kaded mitly.

Except for *the,* this "sentence" is made up of words with no dictionary meaning. Yet it still reads like a sentence and, according to structural grammar, it has a structural meaning. Why? The words follow a familiar pattern that indicates, "More than one thing acted in some manner."

How do readers recognize this pattern? According to structural linguistics, the word *stils* is recognized as a noun because it has a plural ending, *-s,* and is marked by the article *the. Gorby* is an adjective because it appears between an article and a noun and has a typical adjective ending, *-y. Kaded* is recognized as a verb because it has a position in the sentence that is typical for verbs, and because *-ed* is a common past tense verb ending. *Mitly* is an adverb because it ends in *-ly,* a typical adverb ending, and because it appears in a typical adverb position in the sentence.

Note that the structural meaning emerges from word order and word endings. The "sentence" can be given lexical meaning by substituting dictionary words:

The weary cows walked slowly.

In structural grammar, words such as *weary* (adjective), *cows* (noun), *walked* (verb), and *slowly* (adverb) are called "content" or "form class" words. "Function words" such as *the, might, can, rather, very,* and *somewhat* are used to connect form class words to one another and to show how they relate to one another in a sentence.

Transformational grammar

Transformational grammar attempts to explain how people are able to produce all of the possible sentences of a language—even sentences they may never have heard or read before.

15

In transformational grammar, all sentences are divided into *basic,* or *kernel,* sentences, and sentences that are *transformations.* A kernel sentence is a simple declarative sentence such as "The cans are full." Transformations are the result of adding, deleting, or rearranging the words of a kernel sentence.

As an example, let us take the kernel sentence, "The cans are full." By adding words, this sentence can be transformed to the negative sentence, "The cans are not full." By rearranging words, the sentence can be changed to the interrogative sentence, "Are the cans full?" By deleting words, the sentence can be changed to the imperative sentence, "Fill the cans." Any complicated sentence can be traced to kernel sentences. For example, the sentence, "The tall man who arrived late spoke out," can be broken into the kernel sentences: *The man spoke out. The man was tall. The man arrived. The man was late.*

As mentioned earlier, different grammatical explanations give different perspectives on how English functions. Often, these explanations complement one another, highlighting different aspects of language and strengthening the overall understanding of English.

Working with words

The English language has an awesomely large number of words—over 600,000 of them. Many words belong to very specialized scientific and technical vocabularies. The English words most people usually employ for speaking and writing are general, nontechnical words, of which there are many thousands.

Many English words, both technical and common, have roots that come from the classical languages of Greek and Latin. Knowing these roots can help you understand the meanings of words, as can knowing the many prefixes and suffixes that appear at the beginnings and ends of words.

Many English words have more than one meaning. Through the ages, a word may have come to mean something different from its original definition. Other words have shades of meaning that may express positive or negative attitudes. It is important to understand the attitudes the word suggests, as well as its literal meaning. For example, *careless* and *carefree* at first glance seem to mean the same thing. But the adjective *careless* actually suggests a negative or disapproving attitude. ("Forest fires are often caused by the *careless* use of matches.") The adjective *carefree,* on the other hand, suggests a positive and approving attitude. ("Her *carefree* manner enchanted him.") You can see how different these two similar-seeming adjectives are just by reversing the words in the two sentences.

Different shades of meaning also play an important role in figures of speech. Not to be taken literally, figures of speech make imaginative comparisons that increase the clarity of description and make the English language more beautiful and interesting.

It is important to be able to analyze words both by their structure and by their intended meaning. This means that words are sometimes analyzed internally—by their own parts—and sometimes externally—by their usage in the sentence. This chapter shows how to analyze words both ways.

The structure of words

One way to understand words is to pull them apart to find their meanings. This can be done by learning to recognize and understand the meaning of roots, prefixes, and suffixes.

Roots

A *root* is a word or a word part from which other words can be made. The roots of many English words come from Greek and Latin. Words that are members of the same family of meaning often are formed from the same root. For example, many words dealing with believing and trusting are formed from the Latin root *cred* (believe, trust):

credit, credibility, incredible, incredulous

Knowledge of roots can help you determine the meaning of unfamiliar words. For instance, if you know that the Latin roots *scrib* and *script* have to do with writing, you will have important clues to the meaning of words such as *scribble, scribe, transcribe, describe, manuscript, prescription,* and *scripture.* The more roots a person knows, the better. The following is a list of some words formed from Greek and Latin roots:

Latin *agr(i)* (field) + Latin *cultus* (cultivate) = *agriculture*
Latin *aqua* (water) + Latin *duct* (lead) = *aqueduct*
Latin *bibl(io)* (book) + Greek *graph* (write) = *bibliography*

Greek *tele* (distant) + Latin *vis* (see) = *television*
Greek *thermo* (heat) + Greek *meter* (measure) = *thermometer*

See pages 239–243 for a list of some of the most important roots used in English words.

Affixes: prefixes and suffixes

An *affix* is a syllable or syllables put at the beginning or end of a word or word part to change its meaning. A *prefix* comes at the beginning of a word; a *suffix* comes at the end of a word. Knowing the meaning of these affixes can be a great help in understanding and remembering the meanings of many words. Knowing, for example, that the prefixes *un-, il-, im-, in-,* and *ir-* mean "not," the reader classifies these prefixes under the idea "negative prefixes" and immediately translates the idea of "not" to such words as *unaware, illogical, impossible, insensitive,* and *irresponsible. Appropriate* becomes *inappropriate, happy* becomes *unhappy, legal* becomes *illegal.* Similarly, when the reader knows that the suffixes *-able* or *-ible* mean *can be done,* the meanings of such words as *readable, curable,* and *lovable* become clear.

Many prefixes and suffixes can be categorized and remembered by the way they are used. For example, prefixes that deal with moving forward, coming before, or being in front of are: *pre-, pro-, ante-* (as in *precede, proceed, antecedent*). Prefixes that deal with numbers in a general way are: *poly-, multi-, extra-* (as in *polygon, multicolored, extrasensory*). Suffixes that mean the *person who* are: *-er, -or, -ant, -ent, -ist* (as in *farmer, editor, immigrant, resident, hypnotist*). See pages 244–247 for lists of some of the most important prefixes and suffixes used in English words.

By now, it should be obvious that many English words are formed by combining prefixes, suffixes, and roots. In fact, the English language has grown mainly by the process of combining various meaningful parts into new words. So it makes sense that the more you know the meanings of prefixes, suffixes, and roots, the easier it will be for you to figure out the meanings of unfamiliar words and to remember those meanings once you learn them. Get in the habit of learning what the parts of a word mean when you look the word up in the dictionary.

Here are some examples of how meaningful word parts join together to create new meanings:

ab- (away) + *duct* (lead) = *abduct:* to lead away or to carry off

baros (weight) + *meter* (measure) = *barometer:* an instrument that measures the weight of the air

bi- (two) + *camera* (chamber) = *bicameral:* A bicameral legislature has two chambers, or houses.

bio (life) + *graph* (write) + *-er* (person who) = *biographer:* a person who writes someone's life

in- (not) + *somnus* (sleep) = *insomnia:* the inability to sleep

inter- (between) + *sect* (cut) = *intersect:* to cut or divide by passing through

intra- (within) + *vena* (vein) = *intravenous:* An intravenous injection is given directly in the vein.

kleptes (thief) + *mania* (madness) = *kleptomaniac:* a person with an irresistible urge to steal

manus (hand) + *cur* (care) + *-ist* (one who does) = *manicurist:* a person who cares for hands

micro- (small) + *meter* (measure) = *micrometer:* an instrument that measures very small objects or angles

Finding out *why* words mean what they do is interesting as well as informative. Knowing the meanings of roots, prefixes, and suffixes can turn word study into a fascinating game—a kind of jigsaw puzzle where the meaning of the whole becomes clear as you fit the parts together.

Review exercise

Number your paper from 1 to 15. Read each of the following questions. Using the given definitions of the word parts, determine and write the definition of each word.

Example: If *mono-* means "one" and *gam* means "marriage," what is *monogamy*?

Answer: Monogamy is marriage to only one person.

1. If *peri-* means "around" and *meter* means "measure," what is *perimeter?*
2. If *bronch* means "windpipe" and *-itis* means "inflammatory disease," what is *bronchitis?*
3. If *crypt* means "secret" and *gram* means "written," what is *cryptogram?*
4. If *culp* means "fault" and *-able* means "inclined to," what is *culpable?*
5. If *homo* means "same" and *graph* means "write," what is *homograph?*
6. If *an-* means "without" and *arch* means "chief," what is *anarchy?*
7. If *multi-* means "many" and *lingu* means "tongue," what is *multilingual?*
8. If *em* means "buy" and *-orium* means "place for," what is *emporium?*
9. If *ultra-* means "beyond" and *son* means "sound," what is *ultrasonic?*
10. If *spher* means "ball" and *-oid* means "resembling," what is *spheroid?*
11. If *uni-* means "one" and *cornu* means "horn," what is *unicorn?*
12. If *omni-* means "all" and *sci* means "know," what is *omniscient?*
13. If *choreia* means "dancing" and *graph* means "write," what is *choreography?*
14. If *bi-* means "two" and *enni* means "year," what is *biennial?*
15. If *carn* means "flesh" and *vor* means "eat," what is *carnivorous?*

Diction

Good diction means selecting the appropriate words—the words that convey your intended meanings and attitudes. Although important in all communication, good diction is especially important in writing, where ideas and attitudes must be expressed without the helpful accessories of speech such as facial expressions, tone of voice, and gestures.

You can enhance the power of your diction by following these guidelines:

1. Use the correct word. Beware of confusing words that sound somewhat alike and have related or similar meanings (imply/infer; convex/concave; disinterested/uninterested; emigrate/immigrate). For example, to *imply* means to suggest but not express something. ("His silence *implied* anger.") To *infer* means to deduce or arrive at a conclusion from facts on hand. ("We *inferred* from his tone of voice that he was angry.")

2. Use exact words. Never use a vague word when a more exact word would work better. Words such as *nice, good, bad,* and *attractive* can often be replaced by words that convey a more precise meaning. For example, "Your children are very *nice*" would convey a more precise meaning if the word *nice* were replaced with the word *obedient.*

3. Use appropriate words. Words that are right in one situation may be all wrong in another. For example, *male offspring* is a perfectly acceptable expression in itself, but it would be inappropriate to say, "Carole worried that her *male offspring* would not recover from his illness." In this case, *son* or *little boy* is far more appropriate.

Review exercise

Number your paper from 1 to 13. Read each sentence below and choose one answer from those in parentheses that will best finish each sentence. Write that answer on your paper. Use a dictionary to check any word you are unsure about.

Example: The novel I am reading is (interesting, enthralling, funny).
Answer: enthralling

1. Mr. Adams found it necessary to take his (canine, animal, dog) to the vet.
2. (Several, some, five) of my colleagues are coming for dinner tonight.
3. Many (immigrants, emigrants) entered the United States during the nineteenth century.
4. My brother drove up in an old, run-down (car, vehicle, convertible).
5. She had a grand (allusion, illusion) of someday being a millionaire.
6. Ms. Black is a (wonderful, sagacious, superior) businesswoman.
7. The city's skyline was dominated by several towering (structures, buildings, skyscrapers).
8. Please bring several (writing implements, tools, pencils) with you to the examination.
9. The ominous sky told us a storm was (imminent, eminent).
10. Think carefully because your answer to this question is (important, critical, relevant).
11. Jan, Sylvia, and I were best friends as well as (female siblings, sisters, relatives).
12. Tomorrow we will pursue this subject (further, farther).
13. The trio's motives appeared to everyone to be (mean, bitter, malicious).

Denotation and connotation

The *denotation* of a word is its dictionary, or lexical, meaning. The denotations of some words are more specific and definite than the denotations of others. Three classes of words illustrate varying degrees of definiteness.

Concrete words

Proper names—names of people and places—are the most specific words of all. They refer to one person or place and to no other. Almost as exact as proper names are words that refer to actual objects. *Automobile,* for example, has a definite basic meaning because it refers to a specific kind of vehicle. Different styles or makes may come to mind upon hearing or reading the word *automobile*, but the idea of an automobile has a core of meaning for anyone who has ever seen one.

Relative words

Relative words are often descriptive and have shades of meaning. Often, as in a color word such as red, qualifiers are needed to establish definite meaning. *How* red is *red*? Is orangy-red red? Is pinkish-red red? In a family where the tallest member is 5'6", a person 5'10" is considered *tall*. In another family, the shortest person is 5'10". The word *tall*, then—as well as words such as *poor, heavy, thick, pretty, ugly,* or *rough*—are relative terms.

Abstract words

Abstract words are difficult to use accurately. They do not refer to specific objects and have definite meaning only because of their accepted usage. Words such as *labor, culture, education,* and *art* mean different things to different people.

The connotation of a word is the complex of ideas and emotions that the word evokes. Connotations give language much of its color, breadth, and interest. But connotations also can make communication a delicate business.

This is so because many connotations are personal. Say, for example, that you have a violent aversion to bananas. In that case, you will probably have an unpleasant mental—or physical—reaction whenever you hear anyone say the perfectly harmless word *banana.* Or take the case of the word *doctor.* One person, drawing on his memories of booster shots, may give a negative connotation to the word. But another, remembering how a doctor saved his life in an emergency operation, may give the word a very different connotation.

When two people use the same word but give it different personal connotations, confusion, misunderstanding, or even anger may result. There is no way to avoid this communication problem entirely. But by speaking and writing as clearly and precisely as possible, and by paying close attention to the other person's reactions in conversation, you can minimize the dangers of misunderstanding.

Many words have specific connotations that are understood by everyone. Often, words that are synonymous in terms of their denotations have very different connotations. For instance, *famous* and *notorious* both mean "well known." But *famous* has a positive connotation, while *notorious* has a negative one. *Slender* and *skinny* are two other words that mean just about the same thing but communicate two very different attitudes. Other such pairs include *average/mediocre; politician/statesperson; unmarried woman/spinster; unmarried man/bachelor; childlike/childish.*

Figures of speech

A figure of speech uses words or phrases in an imaginative rather than a literal way. Two of the most common figures of speech are the *simile* and the *metaphor*.

A simile (sim′ə lē) is a comparison between two different things and is introduced by the words *like* or *as*. In a simile, the objects compared are different in most respects, but for the writer's or speaker's purpose have one striking resemblance. For instance, "She ate like a pig" is a simile. Note, however, that "A brownie is like a piece of fudge cake" is not a simile, but rather a literal statement of likeness.

A metaphor (met′ə fər) also makes a comparison between two different things, but it does not use the words *like* or *as*. "She was a pig at the table" is an example of a metaphor.

Analogy (ə nal′ə jē) is another form of figurative language. An analogy extends and elaborates on the implied or expressed comparisons of the metaphor or simile. Here is an example of an analogy:

> Education is like a game in which more than one person takes part and each person has a position to play. Your teachers are responsible for the game plan, and you are largely responsible for learning.

Metonymy (mə ton′ə mē) is a common figure of speech in both formal and informal usage. In metonymy, something that is closely associated with a second thing takes the place of the second thing's name. For example, "You've got to have *heart*" means that it is important to have compassion. Likewise, "The *White House* announced a press conference" actually means that the President or the President's staff announced a conference.

Synecdoche (sin ek′də kē) is a figure of speech that names a part when the whole is meant. "The foreman hired six more *hands* for the roundup" is an example of synecdoche. The part, hands, stands for the whole, persons. Synecdoche may also name a whole when a part is meant, as in "*Chicago* won the Stanley Cup."

Two kinds of figurative language that point up the degree to which a statement is emphasized are *exaggeration* (hyperbole) and *understatement* (litotes). Hyperbole (hī pėr′bə lē) is used to emphasize or intensify a situation. "I told you a million times to close the refrigerator door" and "My new friend is just perfect" are examples of hyperbole.

Litotes (lī′tə tēz) are expressions that make a positive statement by expressing the negative of the contrary. In this way, "Mom's not a bad cook" actually means "Mom's a great cook."

To summarize, figures of speech are used to compare, contrast, or make associations:

Comparison. Simile and metaphor are two kinds of figurative language that compare.

Contrast. Hyperbole, litotes, and irony are three kinds of figurative language that contrast.

Association. Metonomy and synecdoche are two kinds of figurative language that express association.

Answer Key

Page 19

1. Perimeter is the measured boundary of an area.
2. Bronchitis is an inflammation of the bronchial tubes or "windpipe."
3. A cryptogram is a message written in a secret code.
4. Culpable means deserving blame.
5. A homograph is one of two or more words that are spelled the same but have different meanings.
6. Anarchy is a state of political disorder due to the absence of a government ruler.
7. Multilingual means able to use several "tongues" or languages.
8. An emporium is a store that carries a variety of merchandise.
9. Ultrasonic means having a sound frequency beyond the human ear's ability to hear.
10. A spheroid is a figure resembling a ball.
11. A unicorn is an imaginary animal having one horn in the middle of the forehead.
12. Omniscient means having complete knowledge.
13. Choreography is the composition or arrangement of dances, especially for ballet.
14. Biennial means occurring every two years.
15. Carnivorous means eating or feeding on animal tissues.

Page 21

1. dog	5. illusion	8. pencils	11. sisters
2. five	6. sagacious	9. imminent	12. further
3. immigrants	7. skyscrapers	10. critical	13. malicious
4. convertible			

Spelling guidelines

Spelling words correctly is an important part of writing. Misspelled words on letters, reports, and papers create an impression of carelessness and detract from a composition's effectiveness.

All writers need to check their spelling from time to time. Even common words that are used frequently can sometimes give people trouble, and spelling demons—words that are commonly misspelled—plague almost everyone.

Mispronunciation

Mispronunciation is one cause of spelling difficulties. A person who mispronounces a word by rearranging, adding, or deleting sounds will very likely spell that word incorrectly. The list below shows words that are often mispronounced and, as a result, misspelled.

antarctic, not antartic
athlete, not athalete
barbarous, not barbarious
burglar, not burgaler
candidate, not canidate
divide, not devide
divine, not devine
drowned, not drownded
escape, not excape
evidently, not evadently
February, not Febuary

government, not goverment
hungry, not hungery
jewelry, not jewlry
kindergarten, not kindygarten
library, not libary
mischievous, not mischievious
nuclear, not nucular
perform, not preform
perspire, not prespire
poem, not pome

practically, not practicly
probably, not probly
quantity, not quanity
similar, not similiar
sophomore, not sophmore
studying, not studing
surprise, not suprise
temperament, not temprament
temperature, not temprature

Spelling English sounds

Being able to pronounce a word properly is no guarantee that you will be able to spell it properly, because many English sounds can be spelled several different ways. For example, look at the following three words:

bene*f*it   *ph*rase   enou*gh*

Each word contains a letter or group of letters that represents the *f* sound, but the spelling of the sound is different in each case.

Although there are no rules to tell you how a given sound will always be spelled in any particular case, it is still helpful to know the possible ways a sound *may* be spelled. The following table shows some possible spellings for many English sounds.

Spellings of English sounds

The sound	as in	may be spelled	as in
short *a*	h*a*t	*ai*	pl*ai*d
		au	l*au*gh
long *a*	*a*pe	*ai*	*ai*d
		ay	pl*ay*
		ea	br*ea*k
		ei	*ei*ght
		ey	th*ey*
short *e*	s*e*t	*a*	m*a*ny
		ai	s*ai*d
		ay	s*ay*s
long *e*	sh*e*	*ae*	C*ae*sar
		i	mach*i*ne
		ie	bel*ie*ve
short *i*	h*i*m	*ee*	b*ee*n
		o	w*o*men
		u	b*u*sy
		y	h*y*mn
long *i*	*i*ce	*ai*	*ai*sle
		ei	h*ei*ght
		y	st*y*le
short *o*	l*o*t	*a*	w*a*tt
long *o*	*o*pen	*ew*	s*ew*
		oa	m*oa*t
		oe	h*oe*
		oo	br*oo*ch
		ou	s*ou*l
		ow	sl*ow*
short *u*	c*u*p	*o*	c*o*me
		ou	d*ou*ble
yü	*yu*le	*eu*	f*eu*d
		ew	f*ew*
		u	*u*se
		ue	c*ue*
f	*f*un	*gh*	enou*gh*
		ph	*ph*oto
g	*g*o	*gh*	*gh*ost
		gu	*gu*e
		gue	ro*gue*
j	*j*ar	*dg*	ri*dg*e
		g	fra*g*ile
m	*m*e	*lm*	ca*lm*
		mb	cli*mb*

26

The sound	as in	may be spelled	as in
n	*n*o	*gn* *kn* *pn*	*gn*at *kn*ow *pn*eumonia
ng	thi*ng*	*n*	thi*n*k
r	*r*un	*rh* *wr*	*rh*yme *wr*ong
s	*s*ay	*c* *ce* *ps*	*c*ent ri*ce* *ps*ychology
sh	*sh*e	*ch* *ci* *ti*	ma*ch*ine spe*ci*al na*ti*on
t	*t*ell	*ed*	dropp*ed*
z	*z*oo	*s* *sc* *ss* *x*	de*s*ert di*sc*ern de*ss*ert *x*ylophone

Spelling rules

Spelling rules can help answer many of your spelling questions. The table that follows presents some of those spelling rules. Do not attempt to memorize all the rules; that is a virtually impossible task. The best strategy is to become as familiar as possible with the rules, and then to refer back to the table whenever you have a specific question or wish to refresh your memory. Remember, too, that there are exceptions to almost every spelling rule, and be sure to pay as much attention to the exceptions as to the rules.

Table of spelling rules

Problems	Rule	Some exceptions
Words with *i*'s and *e*'s: *believe, deceit*	Use *i* before *e* except after *c* or when sounded like *a* as in *neighbor* and *weigh.*	*ancient, financier, counterfeit, either, foreign, height, leisure, seize, weird*
Words ending in *cede: precede*	The root *cede* is always spelled this way except in four words and their various forms.	*supersede, exceed, proceed, succeed* and their other forms *(superseded, exceeding, proceeds, succeeder)*

Problems	Rule	Some exceptions
Words ending in c: *traffic*	Insert *k* when adding an ending that begins with *e*, *i*, or *y: trafficked*.	*arced*
Words ending in soft *ce* or *ge: peace, advantage*	Retain the final *e* before adding *able* or *ous: peaceable,advantageous*.	
Words ending in silent *e: desire*	Drop the final *e* before suffixes beginning with a vowel: *desirable*.	*mileage*
Words ending in silent *e: love*	Retain the final *e* before suffixes beginning with a consonant: *lovely*.	*acknowledgment, argument, duly, judgment, ninth, wholly*
Words ending in *ie: tie*	Change *ie* to *y* when adding *ing: tying*.	
Words ending in *oe: hoe*	Retain the final *e* before a suffix beginning with any vowel except *e: hoeing* but *hoed*.	
Words ending in *y* preceded by a consonant: *occupy*	Change *y* to *i* before a suffix unless the suffix begins with *i: occupies* but *occupying*.	
Adjectives of one syllable ending in *y: dry*	Retain *y* when adding a suffix: *drying*.	
Words of one syllable and words accented on the last syllable, ending in a consonant preceded by a vowel: *glad, repel, occur*	Double the consonant before a suffix beginning with a vowel: *gladden, repelled, occurred*.	*crocheting, ricocheted, filleted, transferable* (but *transferred*). Also, if the accent shifts to the first syllable when a suffix is added, the final consonant is not doubled: *preferred*, but *preference*.
Words ending in a consonant preceded by more than one vowel: *boil, reveal*	Do not double the consonant before a suffix beginning with a vowel: *boiled, revealing*.	
Words ending in more than one consonant: *work, conform*	Do not double the final consonant: *worked, conforming*.	

Problems	Rule	Some exceptions
Words not accented on the last syllable: *benefit*	Do not double the final consonant: *benefited.*	
Words ending in *l: horizontal*	Retain the *l* before a suffix beginning with *l: horizontally.*	Words ending in *ll* drop one *l* before the suffix *ly: hilly, fully.*
Prefixes and suffixes ending in *ll: all-, -full*	Omit one *l* when adding these to other words: *almost, grateful.*	
Prefixes *dis-, il-, im-, in-, mis-, over-, re-, un-*	Do not change the spelling of the root word: *dissimilar, illegal, immoral, innumerable, misspell, overrun, reedit, unnerve.*	
Words ending in a double consonant: *possess, enroll*	Retain both consonants when adding suffixes: *possessor, enrolling.*	
Nouns ending in *f* or *fe: handkerchiefs*	Form the plural by adding *s: handkerchiefs.*	Some nouns ending in *f* or *fe* form the plural by changing the *f* or *fe* to *ve* and adding *s: knives, elves, halves, leaves, loaves, shelves, wives.*
Nouns ending in *y* preceded by a consonant: *lady*	Form the plural by changing *y* to *i* and adding *es: ladies.*	Proper nouns ending in *y* form the plural by adding *s:* "Three *Garys* work in my office."
Nouns ending is *ch, sh, s, x, z: gas, church, brush, glass, fox, topaz*	Form the plural by adding *es: gases, churches, brushes, glasses, foxes, topazes.*	
Nouns ending in *o* preceded by a vowel: *cameo*	Form the plural by adding *s: cameos.*	
Nouns ending in *o* preceded by a consonant; *potato*	Form the plural by adding *es: potatoes.*	*dittos, dynamos, silos.* For some nouns, either *s* or *es* is correct: *buffalos* or *buffaloes, volcanos* or *volcanoes.*

29

Problems	Rule	Some exceptions
Compound nouns: *major general, notary public, sister-in-law*	Make the modified word plural: major *generals, notaries* public, *sisters*-in-law.	
Nouns ending in *ful: cupful*	Form the plural by adding *s* to *ful: cupfuls.*	
Letters, numbers, dates, signs, and words referred to as words	Form the plural by adding *'s:* six *b's*, two *5's,* the *1970's, %'s, but's.*	

Finding words in the dictionary

Whenever you are unsure about how to spell a word, you may turn to a good dictionary for the answer. When a word has more than one acceptable spelling, the dictionary will list them all.

Dictionaries are organized so that words can be found as quickly as possible. The words are listed alphabetically and are usually listed in boldface type for easy identification. Entries may be single words, compound words, or phrases. Compound words are listed alphabetically according to the first word. (*Bank account*, for instance, would be listed alphabetically in the "B" section.)

At the top of each dictionary page are one or more guide words to help you find the word you are looking for. Some dictionaries provide two guide words on each page; others provide one guide word per page. Dictionaries with two guide words per page indicate the first and last word found on each page. Dictionaries with one guide word per page indicate the first and last words on facing pages (the left- and right-hand pages of an open book).

Suppose, for instance, that the guide words on facing pages are *solar eclipse* and *solid.* That would indicate that all the words on the two facing pages fall alphabetically between those two words. Thus, you would know that you could find *soldier, solemn, solicit,* and *sole* on those two pages. But you would have to look on following pages for *solve, solitude,* and *solo.*

Many people believe they must know how to spell a word before they can look it up in the dictionary. But it *is* possible to use the dictionary to find out how to spell a word correctly. The trick is to decide exactly what you need to know.

For instance, if you want to spell the word *separate,* but cannot remember whether an *a* or an *e* follows the *p,* all you need do is check *sepa-.* If you want to spell the word *wagon,* but cannot remember whether to use one *g* or two, look up *wag-* and see what you find.

Your greatest problems will be in words that have a combination of letters that do not look like the sounds they represent—the *a* sounds of *plaid* and *laugh,* for example, or the silent letters that begin *gnat, know,* and *pneumonia.* Before you look up these words in the dictionary, check the table of spellings of English sounds in this book. It will help you find the words you cannot spell.

Common misspellings

Homonyms

Many misspelled words are *homonyms*—words that have the same pronunciation but different meanings and different spellings. Writers must know which spelling is correct for their intended meaning. The list below shows some of the most common homonyms. If there are any words you do not understand, you should look them up in a dictionary.

aisle, isle	faze, phase	scene, seen
altar, alter	forth, fourth	shone, shown
arc, ark	foul, fowl	sole, soul
ascent, assent	hear, here	stake, steak
bare, bear	heard, herd	stationary, stationery
berth, birth	hoarse, horse	steal, steel
brake, break	hole, whole	straight, strait
buy, by	lead, led	suite, sweet
capital, capitol	lessen, lesson	tail, tale
ceiling, sealing	meet, mete	their, there, they're
cereal, serial	passed, past	threw, through
cession, session	peace, piece	throne, thrown
chord, cord	plain, plane	to, too, two
cite, sight, site	principal, principle	vain, vane, vein
coarse, course	rain, reign, rein	waist, waste
dear, deer	right, rite, write	way, weigh
die, dye	ring, wring	weak, week
dying, dyeing	role, roll	which, witch

Spelling demons

Spelling demons are words that are commonly misspelled either because the rules for their spellings are difficult to remember or because their spellings do not follow any particular rules. Following is a list of 300 of the most common spelling demons.

absence	accidentally	accomplish	achievement
accessible	accommodate	ache	acknowledgment

acquaintance
acquire
acquitted
advice
affidavit
aggravate
aghast
all right
ally
already
amateur
analysis
anesthetic
angel
angle
annual
answer
apparent
appetite
appropriate
approximately
ascend
ascertain
assistant
auxiliary
awkward
bachelor
because
beggar
believe
benefit
bicycle
bouillon
boundary
bulletin
bureau
business
cafeteria
calendar
cancellation
captain
career
ceiling
cemetery
changeable
characteristic
chauffeur

chocolate
colonel
column
coming
commercial
committee
community
conceivable
confidence
conscience
controversial
convenience
convertible
copyright
counterfeit
courageous
courteous
dealt
debt
deceased
deceive
definite
description
desperate
despise
develop
disappear
discipline
disease
doctor
ecstasy
efficient
eighth
elementary
eligible
embarrass
eminent
emphasize
enforceable
enough
envelope
environment
exaggerate
exceed
excellent
exhilarating
exhort

existence
expedition
expense
experience
extraordinary
facsimile
familiar
fascinating
fasten
February
fiery
forehead
foreign
forfeit
freight
friend
fulfill
gauge
genius
ghost
grammar
grateful
guarantee
guerrilla
guess
gypsy
handsome
hangar
happening
harass
height
heinous
history
huge
hygiene
illiterate
imitate
immediately
impossible
incidentally
indictment
indispensable
inevitable
innocent
inoculate
interfere
iridescent

irrelevant
itinerary
knowledge
laboratory
legitimate
leisure
liaison
license
lieutenant
lightning
likely
liquefy
literature
livelihood
magnificent
maintenance
maneuver
marriage
mathematics
maybe
medicine
millionaire
miniature
minuscule
miscellaneous
mischief
misspell
mortgage
muscle
mystery
necessary
nickel
niece
night
ninety
ninth
noisily
noticeable
obstacle
occasionally
occurrence
often
omitted
operate
optimistic
ordinarily
origin

original	pursue	scurrilous	thorough
pageant	quiet	secretary	tragedy
paralleled	quite	seize	tranquillity
parliament	raise	semester	twelfth
pastime	realize	sentence	typical
peculiar	receipt	separate	vacillate
permanent	receive	sergeant	vacuum
perseverance	recognize	shepherd	variety
personnel	referred	siege	vegetable
Philippines	relevant	significance	vengeance
philosophy	repeat	skein	vilify
picnicking	rescind	skiing	villain
pleasant	reservoir	skillful	warrant
pneumonia	resistance	specimen	wear
politician	resource	statistics	Wednesday
Portuguese	restaurant	strength	weird
possession	rheumatism	strictly	whether
possibility	rhyme	succeed	women
prairie	rhythm	sugar	won't
precede	ridiculous	superintendent	would
prejudiced	roommate	supersede	writer
preparation	sacrifice	surgeon	writing
privilege	sacrilegious	sympathetic	written
procedure	scarcely	synonym	wrote
professor	schedule	temporary	yacht
pronunciation	scissors	therefore	yield

Improving your spelling skills

Just like riding a bike or playing a musical instrument, spelling is a skill that can be improved when approached with dedication and practiced with motivation. No one method is guaranteed to improve your spelling skills. But each of the following suggestions will help you become a more effective speller.

Hit the books. Books are an excellent source of help for poor spellers. These books include standard dictionaries, word list handbooks, and special dictionaries prepared especially for people who have trouble spelling. Be sure to consult these sources whenever you are in doubt about a word.

Use memory aids. Memory "tricks," called *mnemonics,* can make it easier to learn word spellings. Mnemonics can take almost any form. Jingles, rhymes, word games, and word associations are just some of the devices people use to jog their spelling memories. Some mnemonics are well-known and are used by many people; others are based on individual experience and association and work only for the person who has made them up. Many mnemonics are playful, and some are downright silly. Never worry that a mnemonic device may be too far-fetched or nonsensical. If it helps you remember how to spell a word, then it is a mnemonic that works. Here are some examples of mnemonics:

I before *E* except after *C* or when sounded like *A* as in *neighbor* and *weigh*.
There is *a rat* in *separate*.
A *laboratory* is a place where people labor.

Keep word lists. You may find it helpful to keep a list of all the words you misspell, and to review the list frequently. The more you make a commitment to write down *every* problem word, the more you will increase your spelling accuracy.

Proofread all written material. Spelling errors are often only a matter of carelessness or haste. By carefully proofreading all your written work, you will catch many spelling mistakes before anyone else has a chance to see them.

Use your senses. Mobilize as many senses as you can when learning how to spell a word.

1. See the word on paper. Perhaps you looked the word up in the dictionary, or found it in a book, or wrote it down on your word list. Regardless of where it appears, really *look* at that word on paper. See what letters it begins with, ends with, and has in the middle. Then see it as a whole. After you have concentrated on the word printed on paper, visualize it in your mind.

2. Say the word. Make sure you are pronouncing the word correctly. Divide the word carefully into all its syllables and say them all clearly and distinctly. Then spell the word out loud.

3. Write the word. The muscular motion of writing a word is part of the learning process. But for the learning to stick, you should visualize the word as you write it. Writing a word forty or fifty times without thinking about it will be ineffective.

Make the word part of your vocabulary. The more you use a word in writing and speaking, the more its spelling will become automatic. With practice, spelling even the most difficult or unusually spelled words, such as *gnaw, knife, biscuit, mortgage,* and *lieutenant,* will be second nature.

Review exercises

A. Refer to the table of spelling rules on pages 27–30. Number your paper from 1 to 10. Identify and write down the 10 words from the list below that are correctly spelled.

beleive	cupfuls	handkerchiefs	illegal
precede	occupying	gladden	enrolling
peacable	sisters-in-law	benefited	potatos
argument	allmost	driing	
foriegn	mispell	financeir	

B. From the words listed below, identify and write the 10 words that will be found on the facing pages of the dictionary showing the guide words: fervent—fez.

ferry	festoon	fetch	fewer
fertilize	fetlock	fey	fiber
fiancé	few	fever	feud
fettle	festival	fend	ferret

Answer key

Page 34 (Exercise A)	Page 35 (Exercise B)
1. precede	1. fettle
2. argument	2. festoon
3. cupfuls	3. fetlock
4. occupying	4. few
5. sisters-in-law	5. festival
6. handkerchiefs	6. fetch
7. gladden	7. fey
8. benefited	8. fever
9. illegal	9. fewer
10. enrolling	10. feud

Parts of speech

Every word in a sentence has a function. When the function of the word is identified, the word can be named as a *part of speech*. Traditional grammars list eight parts of speech: *nouns, pronouns, adjectives, verbs, adverbs, prepositions, conjunctions,* and *interjections*.

Some words function in only one way. Others may have more than one possible function. For example, the word *down* may function as a noun, a preposition, or an adverb:

The quarterback passed on the third *down.* (noun)
The ball rolled *down* the hill. (preposition)
Is this elevator going *down*? (adverb)

When you read, write, or speak, you probably do not bother to classify individual words as particular parts of speech. There is no reason for you to do so most of the time. But when you want to identify and correct grammatical errors, it is very helpful to understand what the parts of speech are and how they function. This chapter explains the eight parts of speech and shows how to use them correctly.

Nouns

A *noun* is a word that names a person, place, thing, idea, action, or quality.

Common and proper nouns

There are two kinds of nouns: common nouns and proper nouns. A common noun names a type of person, place, or thing. *Boy, animal, city, mountain, pencil, chair, flower, machine,* and *telephone* are all common nouns. A proper noun names a particular person, place, or thing. *John, Fido, San Francisco,* and *Mount Rushmore* are all proper nouns.

Abstract, concrete, and collective nouns

Nouns may be further divided into three groups: *abstract, concrete,* and *collective*.

An abstract noun names intangibles—things that cannot be seen or touched—such as qualities, actions, and ideas. *Courage, cleanliness, loyalty, greed, love,* and *danger* are all abstract nouns. A concrete noun names tangible things—things that can be seen and touched. *Desk, tree, guitar, hand, student, cup,* and *window* are all concrete nouns.

A collective noun names a group of people or things. *Team, flock, panel, audience, gang, class, herd,* and *jury* are all collective nouns.

When a collective noun refers to the group as a unit, any verbs and pronouns related to the noun are in the singular:

The class has gone to the museum.
The flock headed on its southward course in late October.

When a collective noun refers to the individual members of the group, any verbs and pronouns related to the noun are in the plural:

The gang are all going their separate ways.
The panel are submitting their opinions to the chairperson today.

Gender

All nouns have one of four genders: masculine, feminine, common, or neuter. Each noun is classified according to nature. Nouns that name male living creatures are masculine: *John, father, brother, king, rooster.* Nouns that name female living creatures are feminine: *Mary, mother, sister, queen, hen.*

Most nouns that name living creatures give no indication of gender. These nouns are said to have common gender. *Child, animal, parent, relative, singer,* and *cook* are examples of such nouns. All nouns naming nonliving objects are called neuter. *Rock, candle, picture,* and *ribbon* are all examples of nouns with neuter gender.

Noun endings such as *-ess, -trix,* and *-ine* can be added to nouns to make them feminine (poet*ess,* avia*trix*), but these endings are rarely used today. Instead, nouns of common gender such as *poet* and *aviator* are used to refer to both sexes. Some words that are masculine *(fireman, postman, policeman)* have alternatives with common genders *(fire fighter, mail carrier, police officer).* The use of common gender avoids the possibility of sexist interpretation.

Number

A noun's number shows whether the noun names one or more than one person or thing. A noun is singular if it names one person or thing: *child, rock, mouse.* A noun is plural if it names more than one person or thing: *children, rocks, mice.*

Most nouns change their form when they are expressed in the plural: *cat—cats; church—churches.* Most plurals can be formed simply, by adding *-s* or *-es.* The spelling of some nouns changes more markedly to form the plural: *child—children; woman—women; mouse—mice; shelf—shelves;*

foot—feet. The spelling of some nouns does not change at all in the plural: one *sheep*—two *sheep;* one *deer*—two *deer;* one *quail*—two *quail.* Consult your dictionary whenever you are in doubt about how to form the plural of a noun.

Appositives

An appositive is a noun, or a group of words acting as a noun, that means the same thing, explains, or elaborates on the preceding noun.

Carol, my best *friend,* is moving to Toledo. (friend = Carol)
Lou's *neighbor, Chuck Matts,* won a seat on the city council. (Chuck Matts = neighbor)
Harry's long-standing *dream, to visit California,* finally came true. (to visit California = dream)
I enjoy playing two *sports, football* and *soccer.* (football, soccer = sports)

Review exercises

A. Number your paper from 1 to 26. List all the nouns you find in the paragraph below. After each noun, write *P* if it is a proper noun and *C* if it is a common noun. Further identify each common noun as *a* (abstract) or *c* (concrete).

Example: Mary grew a garden of uncommon beauty.
Answer: Mary—P; garden—Cc; beauty—Ca

My sister Rachel is an avid reader. She has had a library card ever since she was five. Every week she faithfully makes a trip to the Oak Valley branch to return the books she has finished and check out new ones. My parents are naturally delighted to have produced such a cultured offspring, but sometimes they worry that Rachel carries her enthusiasm a bit too far. Last June, for example, the whole family vacationed at the Grand Canyon. We were standing at a lookout point, peering down into the canyon, when Father turned to Rachel and gestured toward a particularly breathtaking vista. What did he see when he turned? There was his daughter with her nose in a guidebook! We all laughed—even Rachel—as she shamefacedly put the pamphlet down and looked at the splendor spread out right in front of her.

B. Number your paper from 1 to 20. Write down each of the following nouns and tell its gender and its number. Use your dictionary if you need help.

Example: hen—feminine, singular

1.	aunt	6.	quail	11.	cow	16.	hero
2.	field	7.	teachers	12.	touchdown	17.	hammer
3.	butlers	8.	group	13.	brother	18.	chairperson
4.	cowboys	9.	bottles	14.	deer	19.	hostess
5.	dog	10.	maid	15.	mice	20.	singers

The possessive case

Nouns change their form to show ownership: *Barbara*'s gloves; the *baby's* bottle; the *scouts'* leader. These form changes indicate that the nouns are in the *possessive case*.

All singular nouns form the possessive by adding an apostrophe and *-s:*

> Sally's coat
> My brother's skates

Exception: Singular nouns that end in *-s* form the possessive by adding either an apostrophe and *-s* or an apostrophe only. Both forms of the possessive are considered correct:

> Charles's book
> Charles' book

Plural nouns that end in *-s* form the possessive by adding an apostrophe only:

> The ladies' dressing room
> The boys' gym teacher

Plural nouns that do not end in *-s* form the possessive by adding an apostrophe and *-s:*

> The men's hats
> The children's toys

In cases of joint possession, only the last word shows possession:

> Jack and Barbara's dog
> Mother and Father's car

When two or more persons possess something individually, both words show possession:

>Helen's and Linda's books
>Dorothy Johnson's and David Washington's law firms

In compound nouns (nouns made of more than one word) only the last word shows possession:

>father-in-law's
>editor-in-chief's

Review exercise

Number your paper from 1 to 10. Write the possessive form for each of the following items.

Example: the cat of her aunt
Answer: her aunt's cat

1. the tool kit belonging to his brother-in-law
2. the birthday of her father
3. a car belonging to Tom and Jim
4. a representative of the girls
5. the article by Bob and the article by Jack
6. music by Kim and lyrics by Dick
7. the jeep of the commander-in-chief
8. the store of Bradley and the store of Carmine
9. blouses for women
10. a performance by Frances

Pronouns

A *pronoun* is a word that takes the place of a noun. Pronouns stand for people or things without naming them.

There are five kinds of pronouns: *personal, relative, demonstrative, indefinite,* and *interrogative.*

Personal pronouns

Personal pronouns indicate by their form whether the pronoun refers to the person speaking (first person), the person spoken to (second person), or the person or thing spoken about (third person).

First person
Singular: I; my, mine; me   *Plural:* we; our, ours; us

Second person
Singular: you; your, yours; you   *Plural:* you; your, yours; you

Third person
Singular: *Plural:* they; their, theirs; them
Masculine: he; his; him
Feminine: she; her, hers; her
Neuter: it; its; it

Reflexive pronouns are formed by adding *-self* or *-selves* to the personal pronouns: *myself, yourself, herself, himself, itself, ourselves, yourselves, themselves.* These pronouns are called reflexive because they indicate that the action of the verb is turned back on the subject.

My baby brother just learned how to feed *himself.*

Reflexive pronouns can also be intensive when they give emphasis to the subject.

I *myself* made that table.

Alert: A reflexive pronoun cannot be used alone. It must refer to someone.

Correct: *Todd* looked at *himself* in the mirror.
Incorrect: They asked *myself* and her to join them.

No doubt you have noticed that the personal pronouns take different forms. For an explanation of these forms, see pages 43–46.

Relative pronouns

Relative pronouns introduce adjective clauses. The relative pronouns are *who, whose, whom, which,* and *that.*

Mr. Samuels is the architect *who* designed our new library.
The mystery book, *which* was a gift from Claire's brother, held her spellbound from beginning to end.
The committee *that* formulated this plan has been commended.

(For more information on adjective clauses, see page 108.)

Demonstrative pronouns

Demonstrative pronouns are used to point out or designate particular people, places, or things. The demonstrative pronouns are: *this, that, these,* and *those.*

That is the dog that chased me.
I want *those.*
These are the best.
Is *this* what you asked for?

Indefinite pronouns

Indefinite pronouns refer generally to one or more than one person or thing.
Some indefinite pronouns are:

all	both	everything	nobody	several
any	each	few	none	some
anybody	either	many	no one	somebody
anyone	everybody	most	one	someone
anything	everyone	neither	other	something

Somebody has been here.
Please pass me a *few.*
We had to choose from among *several.*
Is there *anything* I can do?

Interrogative pronouns

Interrogative pronouns are pronouns used to ask questions. The interrogative pronouns are: *who, which,* and *what.*

Who is going to open the door?
Which of these people have you met?
What is happening over there?

You have probably noticed that the same pronoun sometimes falls into more than one category. For instance, *that* may be a relative pronoun or a demonstrative pronoun.

We did not use the route *that* they recommended. (Relative pronoun)
That is the route I want to take. (Demonstrative pronoun)

To decide how to categorize a pronoun, look at the function it serves in the sentence and label it accordingly.

Review exercises

A. Number your paper from 1 to 5. In the sentences below, supply the appropriate pronoun in the blank space.

Example: Have you seen my pen? No, I have not. Try to think where you used *it* last.

1. Mother, Father, and I went on a trip. _____ went by bus.
2. A woman just knocked on the Martins' door. Who can _____ be?
3. The red bicycle belongs to Bob. The blue one belongs to Ted. The bicycles are _____.
4. I have been looking all over for Frank. Do you know where I might find _____?
5. That car in the auto dealer's window is awfully expensive. _____ costs many thousands of dollars.

B. The paragraph below contains 22 pronouns. Write down every pronoun in the paragraph and label it as personal, reflexive, relative, demonstrative, indefinite, or interrogative.

My parents gave me a puppy for my birthday. Rather than presenting me with a dog they had chosen, they let me go to the pet store and pick one out myself. It was a tough choice; every pup was appealing. A few were purebreds but most were mutts. The pooch that I finally settled on was a seven-week-old mongrel, a charmer with a tan body and brown markings. I knew it was the start of a beautiful relationship when the puppy jumped up joyfully as I slapped my knees and asked, "What do you say, Princess? Want to go home?" Princess wagged her tail as if to say, "I like that."

Case

Personal pronouns and the pronouns *who* and *whoever* change their form depending upon how they are used in a sentence. These form changes show the *case* of the pronoun. There are three cases: *nominative, objective,* and *possessive*.

Nominative case

I	we
you	you
he, she, it	they
who, whoever	

Pronouns used as the subject of a sentence are in the nominative case. (For more information on subjects, see pages 101–102.)

I went to the bank.
You look tired.
We students complained about the assignment.
Who knows the answer?

Many people make mistakes when the subject consists of more than one word. Remember: No matter how many nouns or pronouns are in the subject, the subject is always in the nominative case.

He and *I* have been friends for years. (Not: *Him* and *I*)
You and *she* are invited for dinner. (Not: *You* and *her*)
Martin and *he* went to the game. (Not: *Martin* and *him*)

Pronouns used as predicate nominatives are in the nominative case. (For more information on predicate nominatives, see page 58.)

It was *I* who called.
Someone left a book on the desk. Was it *you* or *he*?

Objective case

me	us
you	you
him, her, it	them
whom, whomever	

Pronouns used as the direct object of a verb are in the objective case. (For more information on direct objects, see page 56.)

Does Mark know that Cathy likes *him*?
Mother wants *us* to come home for dinner.
Jim and Sylvia were talking in class until Mr. Martin asked *them* to stop.
Whom will you invite to your party?

Pronouns used as indirect objects are in the objective case. (For more information on indirect objects, see page 56.)

Uncle Charles and Aunt Sarah sent *me* a lovely birthday card.
Would you please tell *us* a story?
Cindy was happy when Dad gave *her* the car keys.
When the Wilsons moved we gave *them* a party.

Pronouns used as the object of a preposition are in the objective case. (For more information on the object of a preposition, see page 86.)

Deliver the package directly to *me,* please.
Father is driving to the supermarket. Do you want to go with *him?*
To *whom* do you wish to speak?
Why doesn't anyone ever listen to *us* kids?

Many people make mistakes when the direct object, indirect object, and object of a preposition consist of more than one word. Remember: No matter how many nouns or pronouns form the direct object, indirect object, and object of a preposition, they are *all* in the objective case.

If you want to know the answer, just ask *Jack* and *me.*
(*Not: Jack* and *I*)
The store never sent *Mother* and *me* the items we ordered.
(*Not: Mother* and *I*)
Martha requested that all the survey responses be sent directly to *John* and *her.*
(*Not: John* and *she*)

A good way to test yourself in cases like these is to separate the noun and pronoun. Repeat the sentence using only the pronoun to see which pronoun sounds best. For example, ". . . just ask *me*" sounds much better than ". . . just ask *I.*" Therefore, *Jack and me* is correct.

Pronouns used in incomplete constructions take either the objective or the nominative case, depending on the meaning of the sentence:

My cousin is taller than *I.* (Full construction: taller than *I* am)
Sally likes Margaret better than *me.* (Full construction: better than she likes *me*)
Sally likes Margaret better than *I.* (Full construction: better than *I* do)

Possessive case

my, mine	our, ours
your, yours	your, yours
his, her, hers, its	their, theirs
whose	

Possessive pronouns indicate ownership. Possessive pronouns can be used as predicate nominatives. In that case, they use the forms *mine, ours, yours, theirs, its, his, hers, whose.*

This book is *mine.*
The yellow sweater is *yours.*

Possessive pronouns can also be used adjectivally. In that case, they take the form *my, our, your, his, her, its, their, whose.* (For more information on pronomial adjectives, see page 50.)

This is *my* book.
Whose coat is that?

Alert: Never use an apostrophe with possessive pronouns.

The next move is *yours.*
(*Not:* your's)

The wind shifted *its* direction.
(*Not:* it's, which means *it is*)

That new speedboat is *ours.*
(*Not:* our's)

Whose dog was barking last night?
(*Not:* who's, which means
who is)

Theirs is the first house on the left.
(*Not:* their's)

Review exercises

A. Number your paper from 1 to 10. A pronoun is used in each of the following sentences. Identify the pronoun and name its case.

Example: Please tell me the answer.
Answer: me—objective

1. Alice lost her black sweater.
2. We saw the parade on television.
3. The Lawsons lent us some gardening tools.
4. The loud music is coming from their house.
5. Joan gave him a new pencil.
6. Today is not a good day to visit them.
7. You have not finished drying the dishes.
8. Their marching band sounds out of tune.
9. I like to sleep late on Saturdays.
10. The room at the end of the hall is mine.

B. Number your paper from 1 to 10. Some of the following sentences contain pronouns that are used incorrectly. Identify the incorrect sentences, rewrite them correctly, and tell why they were incorrect. Write "Correct" next to the number of any sentence that is correct.

Example: Her and I are best friends.
Answer: *She* and I are best friends. (Both pronouns are part of the subject and so should be in the nominative case.)

1. The teacher gave him and I an extra credit assignment.
2. The ship sailed to it's next port.
3. Judy and he were the only ones who attended the meeting.
4. The test was very difficult for we students.
5. Who will you invite to the party?
6. Was it you or she who left the message?
7. Timmy told Dad and I that dinner was ready.
8. The part-time job is yours.
9. The store owner gave Cindy and me some cheese samples.
10. The winners were Tom and me.

Agreement

The noun a pronoun stands for is called its *antecedent.* A pronoun always agrees with its antecedent in person (first, second, or third person), number (singular or plural), and gender (masculine, feminine, or neuter). In the examples below, antecedents are marked (A), and pronouns are marked (P).

(A)   (P)
Sally gave **her** crayons to Judy.
(Third person, singular, feminine)

(A)   (P)
The **boy** bought **his** own lunch.
(Third person, singular, masculine)

(A)   (P)
Rick and Edna practiced **their** skating routine.
(Third person, plural)

(A)   (P)
I am having a hard time with **my** homework tonight.
(First person, singular)

When the antecedent is a collective noun, use either a singular or a plural pronoun, depending upon the meaning of the sentence.

The jury are in the next room casting *their* votes.
(Each member of the jury is casting an individual vote.)
The jury met to reach *its* decision.
(The jury, acting as a unit, met in order to reach a decision.)

The indefinite pronouns *anybody, anyone, each, either, everybody, everyone, neither, nobody, no one, one, somebody,* and *someone* are singular.

Each girl had *her* own gym locker.
Neither boy took *his* turn at bat.

Many people make mistakes when plural nouns come between these indefinite pronouns (which serve as antecedents) and the pronouns that stand for them. Remember: These indefinite pronouns are singular no matter what words follow them.

One of the women lost *her* gloves.
Neither of the men took *his* vacation this year.

Formerly, when the antecedent of the pronoun referred to both men and women or when the gender of the antecedent was unknown, the masculine singular pronoun was used.

Everyone will get *his* turn to be class monitor.
Each person entering the theater had to show *his* ticket.

However, today, many groups and individuals are reluctant to follow this rule because they feel it arbitrarily assigns roles or characteristics to people on the basis of sex, fostering "sexism" in society. The National Council of Teachers of English (NCTE) has issued guidelines for all NCTE publications and correspondence to help ensure the use of nonsexist language. Among other solutions, the NCTE and other concerned organizations suggest using the plural pronoun. ("Each person entering the theater had to show *their* ticket.") But this solution breaks the traditional rule of pronoun/antecedent agreement. Another solution is to use "his or her" or "his/her." ("Each person entering the theater had to show *his or her (his/her)* ticket.") However, this solution can be awkward. Perhaps the best solution is to rewrite the sentence so that the problem disappears: "All the people entering the theater had to show *their* tickets."

Review exercise

Number your paper from 1 to 10. Each of the sentences contains an underlined pronoun. If the underlined pronoun agrees with its antecedent, write "Correct." If the underlined pronoun does not agree with its antecedent, write the correct form of the pronoun or rewrite the sentence.

Example: Every boy in the class wears their hair short.
Answer: his

1. The flock of geese set out on their yearly flight south.
2. Everybody tried to park their car in the lot closest to the theater.
3. Anyone may buy his ticket at the door.

4. Neither of the boys matched <u>their</u> own record.
5. The band were wearing <u>their</u> new uniforms.
6. If a person wants to succeed <u>you</u> must work hard.
7. The audience showed <u>its</u> approval by clapping and cheering.
8. Each rock in my collection seems to have <u>their</u> own special character.
9. One of the girls left <u>their</u> books in the lunchroom.
10. Everyone is doing the best <u>they</u> can.

Adjectives

An *adjective* **is a word that modifies a noun or a pronoun.**

That is, it is a word that makes the meaning of a noun or pronoun more specific by describing it or limiting it in some way. There are two types of adjectives: descriptive and limiting adjectives.

Descriptive adjectives

A descriptive adjective indicates a quality or condition of a noun.

The area was covered with *thick* vines.
The plants had *short* roots.
The trees were surrounded by *red* flowers.
High hills rose in the distance.

Limiting adjectives

A limiting adjective points out a noun or indicates its number or quantity. Limiting adjectives can be classified as *numerical adjectives, pronominal adjectives,* or *articles.*

Numerical adjectives

Numerical adjectives give number. There are two kinds of numerical adjectives: *cardinal* and *ordinal.*
Cardinal numbers tell "how many?"

The manuscript contained *ten* pages.
Six people were in the room.
The table seats *eight* persons.

Ordinal numbers tell "in what order?"

>Our team came in *third.*
>The *second* step is broken.
>The *fifth* carbon copy is hard to read.

Pronomial adjectives

Many pronouns can be used as adjectives, in which case they are called pronomial adjectives. There are four kinds of pronomial adjectives: personal, demonstrative, indefinite, and interrogative.

Personal—my, our, your, his, her, their

>Here is *my* garden.
>Welcome to *our* home.
>Where is *your* scarf?
>John was listening to *his* radio.
>Sally lost *her* ring.
>Hank and Phyllis danced to *their* favorite song.

Demonstrative—this, these, those, that

>*That* route is too long.
>*These* colors go well together.
>*Those* people are lost.
>*This* time you've gone too far.

Indefinite—any, few, other, several, somebody

>Select *any* dessert you wish.
>*Few* people are as friendly as Martin.
>*Other* methods will work just as well.
>*Several* questions arose.
>*Somebody* from the group should go.

Interrogative—which, what

>*Which* song is number one?
>*What* day will you be available?

Articles

Some grammarians consider both the definite and indefinite articles to be adjectives.

The doctor came to his office. (definite article)
A number of people complimented me on my baking. (indefinite article)

Placement of adjectives

Adjectives usually precede the noun or pronoun they modify.

She bought the *red* dress.
We sat in the *warm* sun.
The *skinny young* man always ate as much as he wanted.
The *poor* woman wore a *torn, rumpled* coat.

Adjectives may be placed after the noun or pronoun for stylistic variety or special emphasis. In this case, the adjective is said to be in apposition to the noun or pronoun.

The mountain climber, *exhausted,* paused in the shelter.
The dog, *lean* and *alert,* led the search party.
The house, *old* and *neglected,* had stood vacant for years.

Comparison of adjectives

Descriptive adjectives modify nouns and pronouns by indicating their qualities and characteristics. The degree to which nouns and pronouns have the quality or characteristic can be indicated by means of comparison. Adjectives can be compared in ascending (upward) or descending (downward) order.

There are three degrees of comparison: *positive, comparative,* and *superlative.* The positive degree does not actually compare. It expresses the quality or characteristic: *tall, attentive, good.* The comparative degree expresses a degree higher or lower than the positive: *taller, more attentive, better, less tall, worse.* The superlative degree expresses the highest or lowest degree of the quality or characteristic: *tallest, most attentive, best, least tall, worst.*

There are three ways of forming the comparison upward:

1. Some adjectives form the comparative by adding *-er* for the comparative degree and *-est* for the superlative degree. Almost all adjectives of one syllable and some adjectives of two or more syllables form the comparative this way.

Positive	Comparative	Superlative
tall	taller	tallest
short	shorter	shortest
smart	smarter	smartest
tender	tenderer	tenderest

51

2. Most adjectives of two or more syllables form the comparative by using the words *more* and *most*.

Positive	Comparative	Superlative
stubborn	more stubborn	most stubborn
attentive	more attentive	most attentive
reasonable	more reasonable	most reasonable

3. Some adjectives form their comparatives irregularly. The most common of these include:

Positive	Comparative	Superlative
good/well	better	best
bad/ill	worse	worst
many/much	more	most
far	farther	farthest
little	less	least

To indicate comparison downward, all adjectives use the words *less* and *least*.

Positive	Comparative	Superlative
tall	less tall	least tall
stubborn	less stubborn	least stubborn
reasonable	less reasonable	least reasonable

Review exercises

A. Number your paper from 1 to 21. Identify and write all the adjectives from the paragraph below. Then tell whether each adjective is descriptive or limiting.

We traveled for hours along the long, winding road, making few stops to check our simple map. Many roads led to the main highway and we had become confused and weary. No cars passed and the dark, threatening sky seemed to close around us. We were happy to see the bright, yellow glow of a sign with some arrows pointing to the driveway of an old inn. A warm lobby welcomed us when we entered the inn. A genial man came to greet us. The other guests smiled and invited us to join them. What a wonderful end to a trying day!

B. On your paper write the upward and downward comparatives and superlatives of each of the adjectives below.

long	dark	bold	remarkable
attractive	understandable	high	beautiful

Never use "more" and "most" when adding the suffixes -er and -est to adjectives. This is known as a "double comparison" and should be avoided.

Incorrect: Sandra was more smarter than Caroline.
Correct: Sandra was smarter than Caroline.
Incorrect: Harold is the most tallest person I know.
Correct: Harold is the tallest person I know.

Choice of adjectives

Avoid unnecessary, vague, and repetitious adjectives. Adjectives should make descriptions sharper and more interesting. Unnecessary, vague, and repetitious adjectives weaken the descriptive power of your writing and speech.

Unnecessary adjectives: We visited the observation tower on top of the *tall*, 110-story building. (Any 110-story building would be tall. Adding the adjective *tall* gives no additional information.)
Vague adjectives: Debbie is one of the *nicest* people I have ever met. (The sentence gives no information about what makes Debbie so special. Is she kind? Polite? Helpful? Be specific.)
Repetitious adjectives: A *big, huge* truck drove by and splashed water all over my new coat. (Delete *big* or *huge*. They mean almost the same thing.)

Predicate adjectives

A predicate adjective is an adjective that follows a linking verb. Linking verbs include all forms of the verb *to be: am, are, is, was, were.* Other linking verbs include: *appear, feel, grow, look, seem, smell, sound,* and *taste,* among others. They tell about the subject's state of being. They connect the subject to the adjectives or nouns that follow. (See pages 58–59.)

Because many linking verbs can also be used as action verbs (verbs that tell about something that occurs), many people make the mistake of using an adverb after a linking verb. But a modifier following a linking verb is *always* an adjective, *never* an adverb.

Incorrect: That soup tastes *strangely.*
Correct: That soup tastes *strange.*

Incorrect: I feel *badly* when you leave.
Correct: I feel *bad* when you leave.

To test whether to use an adjective or an adverb, ask, "Which word is being modified?" If the verb is being modified, use an adverb. (See pages 79–85.) If the subject is being modified, use an adjective.

The children grew *tall.*
(The adjective *tall* modifies the subject *children.*)
The children grew *quickly.*
(The adverb *quickly* modifies the verb *grew.*)
Mrs. Johnson appeared *worried* when she heard the news.
(The adjective *worried* modifies the subject *Mrs. Johnson.*)
Mrs. Johnson appeared *suddenly* from behind the house.
(The adverb *suddenly* modifies the verb *appeared.*)

Common errors

This/that, kind/sort—These/those, kinds/sorts

The pronomial adjective always agrees in number with the noun it modifies:

This (singular) *kind* (singular) of weather
That (singular) *sort* (singular) of book

Those (plural) *kinds* (plural) of songs
These (plural) *sorts* (plural) of exercises.

Alert: Do not use "a" after kind and sort.

Incorrect: That sort of a cake.
Correct: That sort of cake.

Few/fewer—little/less

Few and *fewer* answer the question, "How many?" (Can you count them?)

I have a *few* errands to run. (You can count the errands.)
Marcy has *fewer* records than Tracy. (You can count the records.)

Little *and* less *answer the question, "How much?"* (These you cannot count.)

Mrs. Marks has *little* patience with students who talk in class.
My sister has *less* time to spend with me now that she has a part-time job.

Review exercises

A. Number your paper from 1 to 11. For each sentence choose the correct word in the parentheses.

Example: Johnny seemed _____ (happy, happily).
Answer: happy

1. The hamburgers smell _____ (deliciously, delicious).
2. Ann looked _____ (carefully, careful) for her lost purse.
3. The referee appeared _____ (prompt, promptly) at five.
4. My city's water tastes _____ (good, well).
5. Sandy kept her room _____ (neat, neatly) for an hour.
6. The bread remained _____ (fresh, freshly) in the plastic bag.
7. I feel _____ (bad, badly) about missing your birthday.
8. The sea turned _____ (rough, roughly).
9. The lion turned _____ (quick, quickly).
10. The children remained _____ (quietly, quiet).
11. Your theory proved _____ (correct, correctly).

B. Number your paper from 1–9. In place of each blank, write the appropriate word: *this, those, these, fewer,* or *less.*

Example: Fewer than ten people attended the meeting.

Grass houses are common in the tropics. (1) kind of house is just right for warm weather because there are (2) rooms to block air movement. Because of the climate, (3) insulation is needed. The houses are built with plants that grow in the area. (4) kinds of materials are abundant and easy to work with. (5) than three people can build one of (6) kind of house in (7) than a day. (8) kind of house is easy to repair, too. All in all, there are (9) problems with tropical housing than there are with houses built in a cold climate.

Verbs

A *verb* is a word that expresses an action or a state of being.

Action verbs express physical and mental actions. Some examples of action verbs are: *run, talk, sing, make, believe, think, hope, desire. State of being verbs* express a condition or state of being. Some examples of state of being verbs are: *appear, be, become, feel,* and *seem.*

Transitive and intransitive verbs

Transitive verbs

A transitive verb expresses action that is performed on something. Something receives the action. Each of the sentences below contains a transitive verb:

John *hits* the ball.
(The ball receives the hitting.)
Margaret *writes* letters to her cousins.
(The letters receive the writing.)
Mark and Sally *love* their mother.
(Mother receives the loving.)

Direct object. The verbs above are transitive because they take a *direct object.* A direct object names the person or thing that receives the action of the verb. In the first sentence above, the direct object is the noun *ball,* which receives the action of the verb *hits.* In the second sentence, the direct object is the noun *letters,* which receives the action of the verb *write.* In the third sentence, the direct object is the noun *mother,* which receives the action of the verb *love.*

An easy way to find the direct object in a sentence is to find the subject and verb and then ask "What?" or "Whom?" In the first sentence, you would ask, "John hit *what?*" In the second, you would ask, "Margaret writes *what?*" In the third, you would ask, "Mark and Sally love *whom?*" In each case, the noun that answers the question is the direct object.

Indirect object. Transitive verbs may also take indirect objects. An indirect object names the person or thing to whom or for whom the action of the verb is performed. Each of the sentences below contains both a direct object and an indirect object.

John threw a *bone* to the *dog.*
Jennifer sent her *friend* a *letter.*
Martha gave her *mother* some *perfume.*

In the first sentence, the indirect object is *dog* and the direct object is *bone.* (Ask: "John threw *what* to *whom?*") In the second sentence, the indirect object is *friend* and the direct object is *letter.* (Ask: "Jennifer sent *what* to *whom?*") In the third sentence, the indirect object is *mother* and the direct object is *perfume.* (Ask: "Martha gave *what* to *whom?*")

Intransitive verbs

An intransitive verb is a verb that does not take a direct object. Each of the sentences below contains an intransitive verb:

Mark *sings* in the school choir.
Harriet *walks* in the woods.
Our baby brother *sleeps* through the night.

Transitive or intransitive?

Many verbs can be either transitive or intransitive, depending upon how they are used in the sentence. Remember: If a verb takes a direct object, it is a transitive verb. If it does not take a direct object, it is an intransitive verb.

Mary *writes* a letter. (transitive—the direct object is *letter*)
Mary *writes* beautifully. (intransitive—no direct object)
John *walked* his dog. (transitive—the direct object is *dog*)
John *walked* to the store. (intransitive—no direct object)
I *read* three books a week. (transitive—the direct object is *books*)
I *read* quickly. (intransitive—no direct object)

Review exercises

A. Number your paper from 1 to 10. Find the verbs in the paragraph below. Write each verb and tell whether it is transitive or intransitive.

The ancient Pacific sailor made a chart from the ribs of coconut leaves. He used tiny shells for islands. The sailor navigated without a compass. He determined directions from the sun, moon, and stars. In unknown waters he watched the flights of birds, and the birds led him to land. Sometimes he carried the helpful frigate bird in his canoe. When he released the bird, it flew in wider and wider circles until it discovered the direction of the nearest land.

B. Number your paper from 1 to 10. For each sentence, find and label the verb, the direct object, and the indirect object. Beware: Some sentences may not contain all three elements.

Example: My cousin Sarah lent me her record.
Answer: verb—lent; direct object—record; indirect object—me

1. The teacher gave the class a test today.
2. Please send me your latest catalogue.
3. Sheila threw it high.
4. Don built Fido a new doghouse.
5. Grandmother mailed them from Florida.
6. Tim brought the gang a pizza.
7. I saw that!
8. Arnold's neighbor gives him trumpet lessons.
9. Mother baked Dad a birthday cake.
10. Take them outside.

Linking verbs

A linking verb is an intransitive, state of being verb that requires an adjective or a noun or pronoun to complete its meaning. The most common linking verb is the verb *to be* in all its forms: *am, are, is, was, were.* Some other common linking verbs are: *act, appear, feel, grow, look, seem, sound, taste,* and *turn.*

Each of the following sentences contains a linking verb.

Jack *seems* sad.
I *feel* bad.
The chocolate cake baking in the oven *smells* delicious.
That man in the grey hat *is* our lawyer.

Each of the sentences above tells about a state of being. The verbs— *seem, feel, smell, be*—link the subjects of the sentences with the adjectives or nouns that describe them. The adjectives or nouns that follow linking verbs are very closely related to the subjects of the linking verbs; in fact, they describe, define, or explain the subject.

Most linking verbs can also be used as action verbs (verbs that express physical and mental action).

The hour *grew* late. (linking verb)
The children *grew* quickly. (action verb)
Harold *appeared* satisfied with our answer. (linking verb)
Mrs. Robinson *appeared* at the door soon after the mail carrier rang.
(action verb)

Adjectives that follow linking verbs are called *predicate adjectives*. Nouns that follow linking verbs are called *predicate nominatives*.

Joyce looks *pretty*. (predicate adjective)
The radio sounds *funny*. (predicate adjective)
Clarence became a *doctor*. (predicate nominative)
Marsha was a *leader*. (predicate nominative)

(For more information on predicate adjectives, see pages 53–54. For more information on predicate nominatives, see page 44.)

Review exercises

A. Number your paper from 1 to 10. For each sentence, write the linking verb and tell whether it is followed by a predicate adjective or a predicate nominative. Then write the predicate adjective or predicate nominative.

Example: Jenny became chairperson of the Pep Club.
Answer: became—predicate nominative, chairperson

1. Johnny was hungry before bedtime.
2. We felt bad about losing the game.
3. Mr. Tipton was a pilot.
4. Josie looked nervous before her recital.
5. Are you happy about your new puppy?
6. Laurie is the school spelling champion.
7. Andy seemed glad to find his math book.
8. Those trees are evergreens.
9. Sheila grew more and more quiet as the day went on.
10. Maureen is the newest cheerleader.

B. Number your paper from 1 to 10. For each sentence, identify the verb and tell whether it is used as a linking verb or an action verb.

Example: The food looks delicious.
Answer: looks—linking verb

1. Because of the rain, Cora grew anxious.
2. That fish smells old.
3. Taste the soup in the pot.
4. Sunflowers and zinnias grew in our garden.
5. Look both ways at each corner.
6. Rachel acted distant yesterday.
7. Don't you look nice today!
8. Because of my cold, I can't smell anything.
9. The weather turned chilly.
10. Turn left at Elm Street.

Voice

All transitive verbs may have two voices: active or passive. In the active voice, the subject of the verb performs the action. In the passive voice, the subject of the verb receives the action.

John hit the ball. (active voice; subject—John)
The ball was hit by John. (passive voice; subject—ball)

A local company performed the opera. (active voice; subject—company)
The opera was performed by a local company.
(passive voice; subject—opera)

Notice what has happened in these four sentences. *Ball,* the direct object in the first sentence, has become the subject in the second sentence. *Opera,* the direct object in the third sentence, has become the subject in the fourth sentence. Sentences may be transformed from the active voice to the passive voice by turning the direct object into the subject.

The passive voice is formed by using the appropriate form of the verb *to be*, plus the past participle of the principal verb: The ball *is hit;* The ball *was hit;* The ball *will be hit;* The ball *will have been hit,* for example.

Review exercises

Number your paper from 1 to 10. Write whether the sentence is active or passive. Then, rewrite each sentence so that the active sentences become passive and the passive sentences become active.

Example: Alice wrote the class play.
Answer: Active
          Passive: The class play was written by Alice.

1. Tim sang the national anthem.
2. The mountain was climbed easily by the Scout troop.
3. The lost earrings were found by the salesclerk.
4. Abby carried the injured dog to the pet hospital.
5. Mrs. Jennings was given a blue ribbon by the judges for her pie.
6. The Bartons' car crushed our flower bed.
7. The charcoal was supplied by the park rangers.
8. Rebecca planted a vegetable garden.
9. A large fine was paid by the guilty party.
10. Mr. Powers repaired my typewriter.

Mood

The mood of a verb indicates the attitude or viewpoint behind the verb's expression. There are three moods: *indicative, imperative,* and *subjunctive.*

The indicative mood indicates a statement or question of fact:

That man is my uncle.
Ned knows how to tapdance.
Did you see the beautiful antique cars on display?

The imperative mood indicates a request or a command:

Take it easy.
Come here, please.
Finish your homework before you go out.

The subjunctive mood indicates that the action or state of being is doubtful, conditional, unreal, or improbable:

If I were you, I would be more careful.
Should you care to reconsider, Mr. Brown will be happy to speak with you.

Review exercises

Number your paper from 1 to 10. Read each sentence and identify the mood being expressed: indicative, imperative, or subjunctive.

Example: Jack missed the last train.
Answer: indicative

1. The President threw the ceremonial first pitch at the World Series.
2. Please sit down.
3. Would they come if we were to invite them?
4. That movie was wonderful!
5. Are you going to the band concert?
6. Step to the rear of the elevator.
7. The garage needs cleaning.
8. I wish my singing voice were better.
9. Please move your car, Jane.
10. If there were enough time, we could talk about it now.

Person and number

The *person* of a verb indicates whether the verb refers to the person speaking (first person), the person spoken to (second person), or the person spoken about (third person).

First person	Second person	Third person
I go	you go	he goes
I walk	you walk	she walks
we see	you see	it sees

The *number* of a verb indicates whether the verb refers to a singular or a plural subject.

Singular	Plural
I go	we go
you go	you go
he goes	they go

In almost all verbs, only the third person singular changes form to indicate person and number.

Review exercises

Number your paper from 1 to 20. Identify each of the following by number and person.

Example: We ride
Answer: first person plural

1. They call
2. You found
3. She waits
4. I like
5. They will swim
6. You cooked
7. It falls
8. We fly
9. He sees
10. They vary
11. I pass
12. She won
13. It looks
14. We carry
15. You fought
16. He tried
17. You blame
18. She drives
19. It seems
20. We finished

Tense

The tense of a verb indicates the time of the verb's action. There are three major divisions of time: *past, present,* and *future.* In each of these time frames, the action may be considered as simple (simply occurring at the particular moment) or perfect (the action is completed or "perfected").

There are thus six tenses in English: *present, present perfect, past, past perfect, future,* and *future perfect.*

The present tense
—indicates action occurring in the present:

> I see my sister playing in the schoolyard.
> The fire fighters hear the alarm and spring into action.

—indicates habitual or customary action:

> Jim walks his dog every morning before school.
> My brother talks in his sleep.

—indicates unchanging conditions, facts, or beliefs:

> One plus one equals two.
> Congressional elections are held every two years.
> When it rains it pours.

—indicates action completed in the past (This is called the historical present and is used when the writer or speaker wants to make an especially vivid impression.):

Then, on December 16, about 45 Bostonians dressed as Indians raid three British ships and throw 340 chests of tea into Boston Harbor. The Revolutionary War in America is coming closer now. It finally begins on April 19, 1775. This time, the place is Lexington, Massachusetts.

—indicates action that will occur:

> She flies to Houston tomorrow.
> He signs the contract next week.

The present perfect tense
—indicates action begun in the past and completed by the present moment:

> Jerry has taken all the required courses.
> I have seen the play that was recently reviewed in the *Daily Chronicle.*

—indicates action begun in the past and continuing up to or through the present moment:

> Cynthia has been my friend since the first day she moved to town.
> Harry has been shooting baskets for at least half an hour.

The past tense
—indicates action completed in the past:

> We went to the movies yesterday.
> I enjoyed meeting your cousin.

The past perfect tense
—indicates an action that occurred in the past prior to another past action or event:

> Mark had finished drying the dishes by the time Sam arrived.
> I had heard good things about you long before I met you.

The future tense
—indicates an action that will occur in the future:

> They will call you later this afternoon.
> Martin will visit his aunt next month.

The future perfect tense
—indicates an action that will be completed at some future time:

> Sandra will have finished two years of college by the time you see her this summer.
> We will already have left for our vacation before Saturday.

Review exercises

Number your paper from 1 to 20. For each sentence, identify and write the tense of the verb.

Example: Doug will wash the car.
Answer: future

1. The whole family went to the library this morning.
2. The leaves had fallen by the end of October.
3. I take a piano lesson every Saturday.
4. The class graduates in June.
5. We have always enjoyed fresh raspberries.
6. Tom had finished the plowing by lunchtime.
7. The sick cattle will not survive the winter.
8. You know how to behave in school.
9. I will have been in this town ten years next month.
10. Max feels much better today.
11. The Carsons have moved away.
12. We played two sets of tennis this morning.
13. Our team will win for sure!
14. The cats had run away several times before.
15. Ms. Stein dictates the spelling lesson every day.
16. The monarch butterflies will have migrated by August.
17. The debating team has won the trophy again.
18. Fish breathe with gills.
19. We had asked the minister to dinner several times.
20. You will find that book on the very top shelf.

Verb phrases

Frequently, two or more verbs are required to indicate tense, voice, and mood. (I *will go* to the store this afternoon; The game *was enjoyed* by all; I *might decide* not to go.)

These groups of two or more verbs are called *verb phrases*. Verb phrases consist of a form of the principal verb plus one or more auxiliary, or "helping," verbs.

The principal verb

In verb phrases, the principal verb usually takes the form of the present participle or the past participle. The present participle of a verb ends in *-ing;* for example, *seeing; hearing; speaking.* The past participle of a verb ends in *-d, -ed, -t, -en,* or *-n;* for example, *walked; left; stolen.*

Auxiliary verbs

The most common auxiliary or "helping" verbs are: *be, can, could, do, have, may, might, must, shall, should, will,* and *would.* (The verbs *be, do,* and *have* can also function as principal verbs. For instance: "I am a student;" "You do your best;" "We have three books." The other auxiliary verbs, such as *could, might, should,* and *would,* are sometimes called "modal verbs.") Note: The entire verb phrase is considered to be the verb. For example, in the sentence, "I have seen the Grand Canyon," the verb is *have seen.* In the sentence, "I will have finished my book report by Friday," the verb is *will have finished.* Word placement has no effect on what constitutes the verb. In the sentence, "I will certainly have decided by Friday," the verb is *will have decided.*

Review exercises

Number your paper from 1 to 15. For each sentence, identify and write the verb phrase.

Example: We are driving into town today.
Answer: verb phrase: are driving

1. We had always gone to the Rocky Mountains to ski.
2. The children will enjoy camping overnight in the back yard.
3. You could not have predicted that snowfall.
4. The army may build a new training center in our town.
5. Would you please look at the rear left tire?
6. Those people must really love to fish!
7. I have been thinking about you since we met.
8. The helicopters are landing behind the hospital.
9. We should try harder to keep in touch.
10. I can hardly read that old letter.
11. The dogs were not trained to hunt.
12. I am studying music at the conservatory.
13. Was Mother baking all afternoon?
14. The back fence has been repaired at last.
15. We do not know very many people here.

Principal parts

Every verb has three principal parts: the present infinitive (usually called "the present"), the past indicative (usually called "the past"), and the past participle. Regular verbs form the past and the past participle by adding -d or -ed to the present infinitive:

Present	Past	Past participle
walk	walked	walked
look	looked	looked
dance	danced	danced
close	closed	closed

Verbs that form the past tense and/or the past participle in any other way are called irregular verbs:

Present	Past	Past participle
eat	ate	eaten
sit	sat	sat
speak	spoke	spoken
write	wrote	written
mean	meant	meant

Most dictionaries give the principal parts of irregular verbs. The principal parts of regular verbs are not listed. Following is a list of the principal parts of some of the most common irregular verbs:

Present	Past	Past participle
be	was	been
beat	beat	beaten
become	became	become
begin	began	begun
bend	bent	bent
bind	bound	bound
blow	blew	blown
break	broke	broken
bring	brought	brought
build	built	built
burn	burned/burnt	burned/burnt
buy	bought	bought
catch	caught	caught
choose	chose	chosen
come	came	come
dive	dived/dove	dived
do	did	done

Present	Past	Past participle
draw	drew	drawn
drink	drank	drunk
drive	drove	driven
eat	ate	eaten
fall	fell	fallen
fight	fought	fought
flee	fled	fled
fly	flew	flown
forbid	forbade	forbidden
freeze	froze	frozen
get	got	got/gotten
give	gave	given
go	went	gone
grow	grew	grown
hang (suspend)	hung	hung
hang (execute)	hanged	hanged
hide	hid	hidden/hid
hold	held	held
know	knew	known
lay (put or place)	laid	laid
lead	led	led
lend	lent	lent
let	let	let
lie (recline; remain in position)	lay	lain
lie (tell a lie)	lied	lied
lose	lost	lost
make	made	made
mean	meant	meant
pay	paid	paid
quit	quit	quit
ride	rode	ridden
ring	rang	rung
rise	rose	risen
run	ran	run
say	said	said
see	saw	seen
set (put or place)	set	set
shake	shook	shaken
shrink	shrank/shrunk	shrunk/shrunken
sing	sang	sung
sink	sank	sunk
sit (remain in upright position)	sat	sat
sling	slung	slung
sow	sowed	sown/sowed

Present	Past	Past participle
speak	spoke	spoken
spring	sprang	sprung
steal	stole	stolen
sting	stung	stung
swear	swore	sworn
swim	swam	swum
swing	swung	swung
take	took	taken
teach	taught	taught
tear	tore	torn
throw	threw	thrown
wake	woke/waked	waked/woken
wear	wore	worn
weave	wove	woven
wring	wrung	wrung
write	wrote	written

Review exercises

Number your paper from 1 to 20. For each sentence, write the correct past or past participle form of the verb in parentheses.

Example: Most people had _____ by the time we arrived. (go)
Answer: gone

1. Steve _____ to the basketball game with the team. (ride)
2. The old rowboat had _____ in the storm. (sink)
3. I _____ my dog how to open the kitchen door. (teach)
4. The people had been _____ by the earth tremor. (shake)
5. Sir Gawain _____ an oath of loyalty to King Arthur. (swear)
6. The boys _____ away from the raft. (swim)
7. The eggs were _____ with a fork. (beat)
8. Mrs. Little _____ harshly to the noisy children. (speak)
9. Those lazy campers have _____ in their sleeping bags long enough. (lie)
10. We _____ the table before dinner. (set)
11. Do not go out on the pond until it has thoroughly _____. (freeze)
12. I _____ a thank you note to Grandmother. (write)
13. The principal has _____ our art display. (see)
14. Willie _____ to the park with his sled. (go)
15. John and Sue have _____ their parents to the ball game. (take)
16. The chorus _____ in the first five rows. (sit)
17. The window was _____ by accident. (break)
18. The rest of the guests _____ after midnight. (leave)
19. My parakeet _____ all around the house. (fly)
20. Dinner will be _____ on the back porch. (eat)

Conjugation

The conjugation of a verb is the orderly presentation of all its forms to indicate tense, voice, mood, number, and person. All the forms of a verb can be derived from its three principal parts (present, past, and past participle) combined with any necessary auxiliary verbs. For example, examine the complete conjugation of the active voice of the verb *to see*.

Indicative mood

Singular	Plural	Singular	Plural
Present tense		**Present perfect tense**	
I see	we see	I have seen	we have seen
you see	you see	you have seen	you have seen
he, she, it sees	they see	he, she, it has seen	they have seen
Past tense			
I saw	we saw	**Past perfect tense**	
you saw	you saw	I had seen	we had seen
he, she, it saw	they saw	you had seen	you had seen
Future tense		he, she, it had seen	they had seen
I shall see	we shall see		
you will see	you will see	**Future perfect tense**	
he, she, it will see	they will see	I shall have seen	we shall have seen
		you will have seen	you will have seen
		he, she, it will have seen	they will have seen

Subjunctive mood

Singular	Plural	Singular	Plural
Present tense		**Present perfect tense**	
(if) I see	(if) we see	(if) I have seen	(if) we have seen
(if) you see	(if) you see	(if) you have seen	(if) you have seen
(if) he, she, it sees	(if) they see	(if) he, she, it has seen	(if) they have seen
Past tense			
(if) I saw	(if) we saw	**Past perfect tense**	
(if) you saw	(if) you saw	(if) I had seen	(if) we had seen
(if) he, she, it saw	(if) they saw	(if) you had seen	(if) you had seen
Future tense		(if) he, she, it had seen	(if) they had seen
(if) I should see	(if) we should see		
(if) you should see	(if) you should see	**Future perfect tense**	
(if) he, she, it should see	(if) they should see	(if) I should have seen	(if) we should have seen
		(if) you should have seen	(if) you should have seen
		(if) he, she, it should have seen	(if) they should have seen

Imperative mood

(you) See—singular and plural

	Present	Past	Perfect
Infinitive forms:	to see		to have seen
Participles:	seeing	seen	having seen
Gerunds:	seeing		having seen

(For a discussion of verbals [infinitive forms, participles, and gerunds] see pages 72–74.)

A synopsis of a conjugation is a presentation of a verb's conjugation in one person and one number. Following is a synopsis of the passive voice of the verb *to see*, using the the first person singular.

Indicative mood

Present tense:	I am seen
Past tense:	I was seen
Future tense:	I shall be seen
Present perfect tense:	I have been seen
Past perfect tense:	I had been seen
Future perfect tense:	I shall have been seen

Subjunctive mood

Present tense:	(if) I be seen
Past tense:	(if) I were seen
Future tense:	(if) I should be seen
Present perfect tense:	(if) I have been seen
Past perfect tense:	(if) I had been seen
Future perfect tense:	(if) I should have been seen

Imperative mood

(You) Be seen—singular and plural

	Present	Past	Perfect
Infinitive forms:	to be seen		to have been seen
Participles:	being seen	seen	having been seen
Gerunds:	being seen		having been seen

All the conjugations shown above are called *simple conjugations*. One other important conjugation should be mentioned—the *progressive conjugation*, which shows continuous action. Following is a synopsis of the progressive conjugation of the verb *to see* in the active voice. The synopsis shows the conjugation in the first person singular.

Indicative mood

Present tense:	I am seeing
Past tense:	I was seeing
Future tense:	I shall be seeing
Present perfect tense:	I have been seeing
Past perfect tense:	I had been seeing
Future perfect tense:	I shall have been seeing

Subjunctive mood

Present tense:	(if) I be seeing
Past tense:	(if) I were seeing
Future tense:	(if) I should be seeing
Present perfect tense:	(if) I have been seeing
Past perfect tense:	(if) I had been seeing
Future perfect tense	(if) I should have been seeing

Imperative mood
(You) Be seeing—singular and plural

Alert: Do not confuse verb phrases in the progressive conjugation with the present participle used as an adjective.

I *am singing*. (verb phrase in progressive conjugation) The *singing* bird nested in the tree. (present participle used as an adjective)

Review exercise

On a piece of paper, write the following conjugations.

1. Conjugate the verb *walk* in the present tense, indicative mood, active voice.
2. Conjugate the verb *come* in the future tense, indicative mood, active voice.
3. Conjugate the verb *carry* in the past tense, indicative mood, passive voice.

4. Conjugate the verb *elect* in the past perfect tense, indicative mood, active voice.
5. Conjugate the verb *choose* in the present perfect tense, indicative mood, passive voice.

Verbals

Verbals are verb forms that function as parts of speech other than verbs while retaining some characteristics of verbs. There are three kinds of verbals: *infinitives, participles,* and *gerunds.*

The infinitive

The infinitive, the basic form of the verb, is often preceded by the preposition *to: to walk, to go, to see.* It is in this form that the infinitive acts as a verbal.

An infinitive may be used as a noun, as an adjective, or as an adverb.

As a noun:
To err is human.
(Infinitive used as the subject of a sentence)

I want *to go.*
(Infinitive used as a direct object)

Her main goal, *to win,* is unrealistic.
(Infinitive used as an appositive)

As an adjective: Here is a book *to read.*
(Infinitive used to modify the noun *book*)

Our vacation was a time *to relax.*
(Infinitive used to modify the predicate nominative *time*)

As an adverb:
That is easy *to say.*
(Infinitive used to modify the predicate adjective *easy*)

John played *to win.*
(Infinitive used to modify the verb *played*)

Notice that although the infinitive functions as a noun and is the subject of the sentence in the following examples, it retains some of the characteristics of a verb. For instance, it can take a direct object

To play the piano was his greatest desire.
(infinitive: *to play;* direct object: *piano*)

or it can be modified by an adverb

To run quickly is difficult.
(infinitive: *to run;* adverb: *quickly.*)

The participle

Every verb has two participles: a past participle and a present participle. The past participle usually ends in *-ed, -d, -t, -en,* or *-n;* for example, *walked, chosen.* The present participle always ends in *-ing;* for example, *singing, dancing.*

Participles have two uses. Sometimes they are used to make verb phrases (for example: I *am singing;* you *had gone*). Sometimes they are used as adjectives. It is when participles act as adjectives that they are classed as verbals:

Carole calmed the *frightened* kitten.
(Past participle used as an adjective)

Do you like *baked* potatoes?
(Past participle used as an adjective)

Burning leaves smell good.
(Present participle used as an adjective)

The *chirping* birds woke us up early.
(Present participle used as an adjective)

Notice that although the past and present participles function as adjectives, they retain some of the characteristics of verbs. For instance, they can take an object

The girl *painting the fence* is my sister.
(present participle: *painting;* direct object: *fence*)

or they can be modified by an adverb

Bowing modestly, the violinist acknowledged the audience's applause.
(present participle: *bowing;* adverb: *modestly*)

The Gerund

A gerund is a verb form ending in *-ing* that functions as a noun.

Swimming is good exercise.
(Gerund acting as the subject)

I enjoy *hiking.*
(Gerund acting as a direct object)

My favorite sport, *fencing,* keeps me in shape.
(Gerund acting as an appositive)

Note that although the gerund functions as a noun, it retains some of the characteristics of a verb. For instance, it can take an object

I enjoy *singing folk songs.*
(gerund: *singing;* object: *folk songs*)

or it can be modified by an adverb

Walking briskly is healthy.
(gerund: *walking;* adverb: *briskly*)

Gerunds and present participles used as adjectives both have -*ing* endings. Be careful not to confuse them when analyzing their function in a sentence.

I like *swimming.*
(gerund used as a noun)
The *swimming* children frolicked in the pool.
(present participle used as an adjective)

Review exercises

A. Number your paper from 1 to 20. Identify the verbal in each sentence and tell if it is an infinitive, a participle, or a gerund.

Example: A twisted branch lay along the path.
Answer: twisted—participle

1. Carly asked Jo to pay for lunch.
2. Curling is a popular Canadian sport.
3. The frightened deer ran into the woods.
4. We all like to get presents.
5. The boy playing the guitar is my cousin.
6. Mother reads to relax.
7. Sarah's hobby is making pottery.
8. Lucy likes jogging better than Bob does.
9. The squawking blackbirds chased the cat away.
10. We asked him to play an encore.
11. The police found the stolen car.
12. Finding the right street was difficult without a map.
13. Here is some chocolate to use for the icing.
14. The player kicking the most goals will receive the trophy.
15. Can you fix that broken door?
16. Johnny sang to please me.
17. Bowling is fun for the whole family.
18. Jean, tired after the race, slept through dinner.

19. Do you plan to go?
20. I like driving snowmobiles.

B. Number your paper from 1 to 10. Identify the participle in each sentence and tell if it is *past* or *present.*

Example: No one could comfort the crying child.
Answer: crying—present

1. The bird flying alone lives in our yard.
2. He erased the scribbled notes.
3. Crossing the street, I found a wallet.
4. Mother, searching every cupboard, finally found the popcorn.
5. The borrowed books must be returned immediately.
6. The whistling tea kettle signaled that the water was ready.
7. We repaired the broken window.
8. The student selling the most subscriptions will receive an award.
9. A letter written by the President is very valuable.
10. The quarreling children were sent to their rooms.

C. Number your paper from 1 to 10. In each of the following sentences, tell if the underlined word is a gerund or a present participle.

Example: Tending a garden takes patience.
Answer: gerund

1. Walking along the path, I noticed some rare flowers.
2. Driving defensively is always a good idea.
3. Everyone in our group enjoys taking photographs.
4. Just look at that beautiful, sparkling lake.
5. Have you ever considered singing in the choir?
6. The violinist's virtuoso playing impressed the concertgoers.
7. The prairie was full of crackling campfires.
8. John, studying for his finals, stayed up late all last week.
9. We heard the thunder rumbling in the distance.
10. This task demands clear thinking.

Agreement

Verbs agree in person and number with their subjects.

Harry runs a mile a day.
(Third person singular subject: *Harry*
Third person singular verb: *runs*)

We go to the store after school.
(First person plural subject: *We*
First person plural verb: *go*)

Singular verbs are used with the following indefinite pronouns: *anybody, anyone, each, either, every, everybody, everyone, neither, nobody, no one, one, somebody, someone.*

Each apartment *has* its own separate heating unit.
Neither boy *wants* to run the errand.

Alert: Singular verbs are used with these pronouns even when the pronouns and the verbs are separated by phrases or clauses containing plural nouns:

Each of the apartments *has* its own separate heating unit.
Neither of the boys *wants* to run the errand.

Compound subjects (two or more nouns used as the subject) usually take a plural verb.

Melissa and Charles plan to be married in June.
Mother and Father go out every Saturday night.

When the parts of a compound subject are thought of as one unit, they take a singular verb.

Peanut butter and jelly is my favorite sandwich spread.
The hustle and bustle of traffic *is* getting on my nerves.

Compound subjects joined by the words *or, either . . . or,* and *neither . . . nor* take a singular verb unless the second subject is plural.

Either Becky or Linda *wins* every prize.
Neither Harry nor Cathy *wants* to dry the dishes.
Sam or Kevin *has* the key.
Jenny or the boys *have* the car.

Consistency of Tense

Be sure that the tenses of all verbs in a sentence are consistent with one another. All actions occurring at the same time should be in the same tense.

Incorrect: John walked into study hall and starts complaining about his grade on the spelling test.
Correct: John walked into study hall and started complaining about his grade on the spelling test.

Sometimes sentences describe a number of actions occurring at different times. Make sure the tenses represent the sequence of events correctly.

Incorrect: He already left by the time I arrived.
Correct: He had already left by the time I arrived.
Incorrect: Elaine has promised to call when she got home.
Correct: Elaine has promised to call when she gets home.

Transitive and intransitive verb pairs

A number of verb pairs sound similar to each other and have similar—but not identical—meanings. Be careful not to confuse these verbs.

Lay/Lie

Lay is a transitive verb. It means "to put or place something." Its principal parts are: *lay, laid, laid.* (Its present participle is *laying.*)

> *Lay* the cloth on the table, please.
> Sam *laid* the sails on the beach to dry.
> Mother couldn't remember where she had *laid* her keys.
> I was *laying* the tablecloth when the phone rang.

Lie is an intransitive verb. It means to "rest or recline." Its principal parts are: *lie, lay, lain.* (Its present participle is *lying.*)

> I'm sleepy. I think I'll *lie* on the sofa and take a quick nap.
> There are dog hairs all over the sofa. I guess Rover *lay* down on it.
> You have *lain* in the sun too long and will probably get a bad burn.
> The zebras were *lying* about in the tall grass, enjoying the sun.

Notice that a special problem in dealing with *lie* and *lay* is that the past tense of lie is the same as the present tense of lay.

Set/Sit

Set is a transitive verb. It means "to put or place something." Its principal parts are: *set, set, set.*

> *Set* that heavy package on the chair by the door.
> Chuck *set* the bowl securely on the counter.
> Margie had *set* the plant in the entryway before the party began.

Sit is an intransitive verb. It means "to rest in an upright position." Its principal parts are: *sit, sat, sat.*

After a few hours of shopping, all I want to do is *sit* for a while in a comfortable chair.
Father *sat* near home plate so he could watch the catcher.
The doorbell rang as soon as we had *sat* down to dinner.

Raise/Rise

Raise is a transitive verb. It means "to move something upward" by an agent. Its principal parts are: *raise, raised, raised.*

That dress will look more stylish if you *raise* the hem a few inches.
The soldiers saluted when the lieutenant *raised* the flag.
We noticed that the grocer had *raised* the price of butter.

Rise is an intransitive verb. It means "to go up" by itself. Its principal parts are: *rise, rose, risen.*

Our family likes to *rise* early in the morning.
Everyone *rose* when the judge entered the courtroom.
The water level *has risen* at least two inches since yesterday's storm.

Review exercises

A. Number your paper from 1 to 10. Choose the verb that agrees with the subject in the following sentences.

Example: John and Jack (take, takes) the mail to the post office.
Answer: take

1. Neither boy (was, were) given first prize.
2. Both Toby and Jan (dances, dance) with the folk club.
3. Each of the houses (is, are) painted a different color.
4. Nobody in our family (was, were) going to the park.
5. Everybody who served on the committees (was, were) given a certificate of appreciation.
6. (Is, Are) Jack and Tom on the football team this year?
7. Neither Becky nor Cindy (plans, plan) to come.
8. Harry and Lisa (shops, shop) for their mother.
9. None of the kids in our club (wants, want) to arrange the party.
10. One of my favorite records (is, are) missing.

B. Number your paper from 1 to 5. Choose the correct verbs for use in the following sentences.

Example: Her hopes (rose, raised) as the campaign (rose, raised) more funds.
Answer: rose, raised

1. She wanted to (sit, set) near the table where the trophy had been (sit, set).
2. She wanted to (lay, lie) the scarf on the chair where the cat was (laying, lying).
3. The audience (rose, raised) as the stagehand (rose, raised) the curtain.
4. He (lay, laid) the blanket on the seat where the baby was (laying, lying).
5. You can (sit, set) that on the shelf while the group (sits, sets) in the living room.

Adverbs

An *adverb* **is a word that modifies a**
verb, an adjective, or another adverb.

Types of Adverbs

Adverbs usually answer the questions How? When? Where? or To what extent?

Mark walked *slowly.*
(Slowly modifies the verb *walked* and tells *how.)*
I will leave *soon.*
(Soon modifies the verb *leave* and tells *when.)*
Let's go *out.*
(Out modifies the verb *go* and tells *where.)*
Sally is *not* late.
(Not modifies the adjective *late* and tells *to what extent.)*
The elderly man moved *quite* gingerly.
(Quite modifies the adverb *gingerly* and tells *to what extent.)*

Adverbs that tell *how* are called *adverbs of manner.* Some examples are: *beautifully, energetically, happily, quickly, fast.*
Adverbs that tell *when* are called *adverbs of time.* Some examples are: *now, soon, then, before, later.*
Adverbs that tell *where* are called *adverbs of place.* Some examples are: *in, out, near, up, down, forward, there.*

Note that some adverbs of place can also function as prepositions:

Let's climb *up.* (adverb)
The kitten climbed *up* the tree. (preposition)

Adverbs that tell *to what extent* are called *adverbs of degree.* Some examples are: *very, extremely, rather, somewhat, quite, almost.*

The above terms (adverbs of manner, time, place, and degree) classify adverbs according to their meaning. Another way to classify adverbs is by their function.

Interrogative adverbs introduce questions. Some examples are: *why, when, where,* and *how.*

When did you go?
Where have you been?

Relative adverbs introduce subordinate clauses. Some examples are: *when, where, why.*

I will meet you *when* classes are over.
Do you know *why* Max was so angry?

Conjunctive adverbs (sometimes called *transitional adverbs*) join two independent clauses or two sentences and modify one of them. Some examples are: *hence, however, moreover, nevertheless, otherwise, still, therefore, thus.*

We followed the recipe; *however,* the casserole was not so good as we'd hoped.
Sarah liked the dress; *nevertheless,* she did not buy it.

Independent adverbs have no grammatical function in the sentence or clause. Some examples are: *yes, no.*

No, I don't think I'll join you.
Yes, you did leave your gloves at the skating rink.

Comparison of Adverbs

Adverbs of manner (adverbs that tell *how*), like adjectives, may be compared upward and downward in three degrees: *positive, comparative,* and *superlative.* And, like adjectives, adverbs can be compared upward by two different methods.

1. Most adverbs are compared upward by using "more" for the comparative degree and "most" for the superlative degree.

Positive	Comparative	Superlative
happily	more happily	most happily
quickly	more quickly	most quickly
accurately	more accurately	most accurately

2. A few adverbs are compared upward by using -er for the comparative degree and -est for the superlative degree.

Positive	Comparative	Superlative
soon	sooner	soonest
near	nearer	nearest
early	earlier	earliest

All adverbs are compared downward by using "less" for the comparative degree and "least" for the superlative degree.

Positive	Comparative	Superlative
early	less early	least early
happily	less happily	least happily
quickly	less quickly	least quickly
accurately	less accurately	least accurately

Some adverbs are compared irregularly.

Positive	Comparative	Superlative
badly	worse	worst
far	farther	farthest
	further	furthest
little	less	least
much	more	most
well	better	best

Review exercises

A. Number your paper from 1 to 21. The following paragraphs contains 21 adverbs. Identify and write all the adverbs in the paragraphs.

The climbers rose at dawn and moved quickly up the slope to the base camp. "Where did they go?" asked a reporter who was extremely upset to find that the party had moved out without him. It was hard for him to reach the climbers, who were moving fast in the morning hours. The reporter hoped to join them when they stopped for a break. Did he meet them? No, he did not. He climbed steadily; however, he was not skilled enough to overtake them.

On the mountain, the climb progressed beautifully in its early hours. Later, climbing became somewhat difficult. How could the group continue? The wind tore at their clothing when they tried to move forward. They struggled to go on; nevertheless, the wind held them down. They could not go onward. The climbers rested at the second camp before attempting a final push to the top.

B. Number your paper from 1 to 10. Copy the adverb(s) in each of the following sentences and identify them as adverbs of degree, manner, place, or time.

1. She grinned *happily* as she crossed the finish line.
2. Had you ever met him *before?*
3. All the seniors were instructed to step *forward.*
4. Our upstairs neighbors came *down* to visit last night.
5. The audience recognized that the group performed extremely well.
6. The glider performed *beautifully* and then descended *quickly.*
7. The stalled bus must arrive *sooner* or *later.*
8. He is *there* on the field near the 40-yard line.
9. She was *somewhat* late and missed the train.
10. His score was *exceptionally* high and he was *extremely* pleased with the results.

Adverb or adjective?

Many words that end in *-ly* are adverbs *(surely, strongly, sharply)*. However, some words that end in *-ly* are adjectives *(lovely, manly, friendly, cowardly)*. And some adverbs do not end in *-ly (here, there, far, soon, fast).*

Some words can be used either as adverbs or adjectives.

Word	Adverb	Adjective
deep	Dig *deep* to find water.	We dug a *deep* well.
far	We walked *far* into the forest.	He came from a *far* country.
hard	Mark hit the ball *hard.*	It was a *hard* choice.
little, long	The world will *little* note nor *long* remember. . .	He had *little* feet and *long* legs.
near	The horse came *near.*	It was a *near* escape.
right	Turn *right* at the stop sign.	That was the *right* way to turn.
straight	He drew his lines *straight.*	He walked a *straight* line.

Other words that can be used either as adverbs or adjectives include: *close, daily, first, hard, high, late, only, tight.*

To test whether a word is an adverb or an adjective, look at how it is used in the sentence. If it modifies a noun, it is an adjective. If it modifies a verb, adjective, or other adverb, it is an adverb.

There goes Marsha on her *daily* trip to the store.
(*Daily* is an adjective modifying the noun *trip.*)

Marsha goes to the store *daily*.
(*Daily* is an adverb modifying the verb *goes*.)

Some words have two closely related adverb forms:

cheap—cheaply	near—nearly
deep—deeply	quick—quickly
hard—hardly	right—rightly
high—highly	slow—slowly
late—lately	tight—tightly

In some cases, usually in short commands, the two forms have the same meaning and can be used interchangeably. The shorter form is considered to be more informal.

Go *slow* around that curve.
Go *slowly* around that curve.

In other cases, the two forms have different meanings and cannot be used interchangeably.

Sam hit the ball *hard*.
Nancy *hardly* had time to catch her breath before she had to go out and pinch hit.
Come sit *near* me.
You *nearly* missed that turnpike exit.

Well/Good

Well can be used as both an adverb and an adjective. As an adverb, *well* means "capably or successfully."

Richard did *well* on the math test.

Alert: *Good* is only an adjective and should never be used adverbially as a synonym for *well*.

Incorrect: Margaret played *good*.
Correct: Margaret played *well*.

As an adjective, *well* means "in good health" or "satisfactory."

You look *well*.   All is *well*.

Bad/Badly

Badly is used only as an adverb.

I did *badly* on my spelling test.

Bad is used only as an adjective (in this case, as a predicate adjective).

I feel *bad.*

Placement of Adverbs

Since adverbs may modify verbs, adjectives, and other adverbs, they may appear in many different positions in a sentence. The meaning of a sentence may vary depending on where the adverb is placed. For example:

Jack *almost* caught a dozen fish this morning.
(Twelve times, Jack came very close to catching a fish.)
Jack caught *almost* a dozen fish this morning.
(Jack caught somewhat fewer than twelve fish.)
I *just* spoke with Sally.
(I spoke with Sally only a few minutes ago.)
I spoke *just* with Sally.
(Sally was the only person with whom I spoke.)

Be especially careful about the placement of adverbs such as *almost, only, just, even, hardly, scarcely, merely,* and *nearly.* Place these adverbs as close as possible to the words they modify.

Review exercises

A. Write two sentences for each of the following words. In the first sentence, use the word as an adjective. In the second sentence, use the word as an adverb.

Example: long
Answer: Shirley has *long* hair. (adjective)
Harry was not gone *long.* (adverb)

1. late   2. early   3. only   4. fast   5. well

B. Rewrite each of the following sentences two or three times using the adverb in parentheses. Place the adverb in a different position each time to give each sentence a different meaning.

Example: I met all the members of Ruth's family. (almost)
Answer:　I almost met all the members of Ruth's family.
　　　　　　I met almost all the members of Ruth's family.

1. Jane runs for exercise. (just)
2. Mark likes burned cookies. (even)
3. Kevin wrote the class play. (only)
4. Karen seems interested in reading. (often)
5. We stopped here to get a sandwich. (merely)

Prepositions

A *preposition* is a word or group of words that shows the relationship of a noun or pronoun to some other word in the sentence.

The fish swam *in* the tank.
(The preposition *in* shows the relationship between the noun *tank* and the verb *swam.*)

The boy running *with* his dog slipped and fell.
(The preposition *with* shows the relationship between the noun *dog* and the participle *running.*)

Sandra hung her coat *on* the hook.
(The preposition *on* shows the relationship between the noun *hook* and the noun *coat.*)

We were talking *about* you.
(The preposition *about* shows the relationship between the pronoun *you* and the verb *were talking.*)

Following is a list of some of the most frequently used prepositions.

about	behind	for	throughout
above	below	from	to
across	beneath	in	toward
after	beside	in spite of	under
against	between	of	until
around	by	off	up
at	down	on	with
because of	during	out	
before	except	over	

Object of the Preposition

The object of the preposition is the noun or pronoun that follows the preposition and whose relationship to another word is shown by the preposition.

What do you think about his *idea?*
(The noun *idea* is the object of the preposition *about.*)

Harold loves hamburgers broiled on the *grill.*
(The noun *grill* is the object of the preposition *on.*)

Come sit beside *me.*
(The pronoun *me* is the object of the preposition *beside.*)

Preposition or adverb?

Many words that function as prepositions can also function as adverbs. For example:

The cat ran *out* the door.
(*Out* functions as a preposition, taking the object *door.*)

The cat ran *out.*
(*Out* functions as an adverb, modifying the verb *ran.*)

We stumbled *down* the hill.
(*Down* functions as a preposition, taking the object *hill.*)

We stumbled *down.*
(*Down* functions as an adverb, modifying the verb *stumbled.*)

The smoke drifted *up* the chimney.
(*Up* functions as a preposition, taking the object *chimney.*)

The smoke drifted *up.*
(*Up* functions as an adverb, modifying the verb *drifted.*)

In cases like these, to tell whether the word functions as a preposition or an adverb, test to see if it takes an object. If it does, it functions as a preposition. If it does not, it functions as an adverb.

Review exercises

A. Number your paper from 1 to 10. For each of the sentences below, identify and write the preposition(s) used. Then write their objects.

Example: Please put the dry dishes in the cupboard.
Answer: preposition: in
              object: cupboard

1. The soldiers had gone to war.
2. My cat jumped off the chair.
3. Mice hide in holes.

4. We live next door to the new house.
5. I saw the girl on the porch.
6. The one with the green hat lives by the church.
7. Grandmother worked on her sewing project throughout the day.
8. The secretary ran to the drugstore during his coffee break.
9. Would you consider using this material for the curtains?
10. You should have kept the secret to yourself.

B. Number your paper from 1 to 10. In each sentence below tell whether the italicized word functions as a preposition or as an adverb.

Example: Cindy's horse can jump *over* the wall.
Answer: preposition

1. Please see who is *at* the door.
2. The children have a later bedtime *during* the summer.
3. I am sure we have met *before*.
4. The puppy hid *beneath* the bed.
5. Mark lives in the apartment *above* mine.
6. Can you come *over*?
7. *After* the snowfall, the girls built a fort.
8. I'm eager to go *out* tonight.
9. The favorite horse is trailing far *behind* the others.
10. Look out *below!*

Which preposition to use?

Specific prepositions are often closely associated with other nouns, adjectives, and verbs. For instance:

account for	foreign to	sensitive to
argue with	happy about	similar to
capable of	independent of	sympathize with
confide in	inseparable from	tamper with
desirous of	obedient to	
envious of	protest against	

The same word may sometimes be associated with several different prepositions. In this case, each preposition provides a slightly different shade of meaning:

angry at	careless of	part from
angry with	concerned for	part with
apply for	concerned with	quarrel over
apply to	free from	quarrel with
careless about	free of	

In a good dictionary, the principal word entry will explain the subtle differences in meaning created by using different prepositions. When two or more words associated with different prepositions appear before one object, do not delete any of the prepositions:

Charlie was interested *in* and curious *about* local politics.

When two or more words associated with the same preposition appear before one object, all but the last preposition may be deleted:

Charlie was interested and involved *in* local politics.

Between/Among

Between is used for two persons or items.

John interrupted a private discussion *between* Patty and me.

Among is used for three or more persons or items.

The guitar players strolled *among* the diners in the Spanish restaurant.

Ending a sentence with a preposition

In the past, grammarians frowned upon ending a sentence with a preposition. Today, some teachers still enforce the rule forbidding a preposition at the end of a sentence. Others, however, believe that it is permissible to end a sentence with a preposition, especially when it would be awkward not to do so.

What are you crying about?
Whom is she waiting for?
Whom is Tom going with?

(For more information on this question, see pages 145–146.)

Review exercise

In the following sentences, some words are correctly or incorrectly associated with one preposition or with two different prepositions. Identify the correct sentences. Rewrite the incorrect sentences adding the missing prepositions.

Example: Tim was curious and attracted to the pinball machine.
Answer: Tim was curious *about* and attracted to the pinball machine.

1. Gregory is sensitive but careless about his sister's feelings.
2. The neighborhood protested and argued over the new law.
3. The campaign workers were committed and devoted to the candidate.
4. Mr. and Mrs. Martin are inseparable yet independent of each other.
5. Jim was feeling jealous and angry with his brother.
6. A person can alternately confide and then quarrel with his best friend.
7. As children, we are sometimes obedient yet annoyed with our parents.
8. Our newest employee is both capable of and concerned with superior output.
9. We sympathize and are concerned for you.
10. I am happy and envious of your new job assignment.

Conjunctions

A *conjunction* joins words, phrases, clauses, or sentences.

There are three kinds of conjunctions: coordinating, subordinating, and correlative.

Coordinating conjunctions

Coordinating conjunctions join sentence elements that have the same grammatical value—words with words; phrases with phrases; clauses with clauses; and sentences with sentences. The most common coordinating conjunctions are *and, but, for, or, nor, yet,* and *so.*

Words with words: Samantha will play basketball *or* baseball.
(The coordinating conjunction *or* joins the two nouns *basketball* and *baseball.*)

Phrases with phrases: Andy sat on the bench strumming his guitar *and* humming a tune.
(The coordinating conjunction *and* joins the two participial phrases *strumming his guitar* and *humming a tune.*)

Subordinate clauses with subordinate clauses: That is the woman who works in the bakery *but* who hates sweets.
(The coordinating conjunction *but* joins the two subordinate clauses *who works in the bakery* and *who hates sweets.* See further explanation below under "Subordinating conjunctions.")

Sentences with sentences: Our team members vowed to win the trophy. *Yet* they failed.
(The coordinating conjunction *yet* joins the two sentences *Our team members vowed to win the trophy* and *They failed.*)

Subordinating conjunctions

Subordinating conjunctions connect subordinate clauses to main clauses. The most common subordinating conjunctions include:

after	before	so that	when
although	how	that	where
as	if	though	while
as if	in order that	till	why
because	since	unless	

> We will meet for practice on the field tomorrow *unless* it rains. (The subordinating conjunction *unless* connects the subordinate clause, *unless it rains,* to the main clause.)
>
> You must finish your homework *if* you want to go out. (The subordinating conjunction *if* connects the subordinate clause, *if you want to go out,* to the main clause.)

Correlative conjunctions

Correlative conjunctions are two coordinating conjunctions used as a pair. Some common correlative conjunctions are:

both . . . and	not only . . . but also
either . . . or	whether . . . or
neither . . . nor	

> Marsha had *neither* the time *nor* the patience to listen to Judy's complaints.
> We couldn't decide *whether* to stay *or* to go.

Review exercises

Number your paper from 1 to 10. In place of each blank, write the appropriate conjunction. Use each conjunction from the list once.

and, because, before, but, either, nor, or, unless, when, whether

1. I like to listen to jazz _____ rock.
2. Neither Mother _____ I have finished our needlepoint.
3. They will not go back to work _____ you agree to their terms.
4. Carl is athletic _____ his brother is not.
5. Sally earned an *A* in driver's education _____ she tried hard.
6. Mrs. Bailey asked _____ Sam could stay for dinner.
7. It is _____ sleet or wet snow.
8. He will send for you _____ he is ready.
9. It makes no difference to me if you go _____ stay.
10. He left _____ I could apologize.

Placement of correlative conjunctions

Place correlative conjunctions so that they clearly join the words you wish to connect.

Unclear: Mark both likes Monica and Sandy.
Clear: Mark likes both Monica and Sandy.
Unclear: Randy not only got A's in math but in English, too.
Clear: Randy got A's not only in math but in English, too.

Elements joined by correlative conjunctions

Correlative conjunctions should join sentence elements that are similar—nouns with nouns, adjectives with adjectives, prepositional phrases with prepositional phrases, and so forth.

Incorrect: Rita is both talented and makes friends easily.
Correct: Rita is both talented and likeable.
Incorrect: We went not only to the bank but also grocery shopping.
Correct: We went not only to the bank but also to the grocery store.

Review Exercise

Number your paper from 1 to 10. Rewrite the following sentences changing the placement of correlative conjunctions to make the sentences clearer, or rewriting the elements joined by correlative conjunctions so that they are similar.

Example: Plants that receive a lot of light not only grow taller but also fuller.
Answer: Plants that receive a lot of light grow not only taller but also fuller.

1. I will neither ask for your cooperation nor your help.
2. Johnny spends almost all his free time either working on his model airplanes or he watches TV.
3. Sally hasn't decided whether to attend the lecture or if she will go to the movies.
4. My Uncle Joe not only raises chickens but cows, too.
5. Janet is a student who both does well in math and science.
6. Jack will go to college next year whether on scholarship or paying his own way.
7. We enjoy living in the city both for its cultural attractions and because it is very convenient.
8. Either you may come with us or stay home.
9. Ralph gave a speech that not only was rousing but convincing.
10. Pat had neither the will to succeed nor was she very skilled.

Interjections

An *interjection* is a word or phrase that expresses emotion.

Interjections have no grammatical connection with the other words in a sentence. Interjections that express strong emotion are set off by an exclamation point. Interjections that express mild emotion are set off by a comma. Commonly used interjections include: *bravo, hurrah, oh, ouch,* and *whoops.*

Watch out! You almost drove through a stop sign.
Oh, never mind.

Interjections are used more frequently in spoken than in written language. When using interjections in your writing, do so sparingly. Too many interjections will dull the very impact you are trying to create.

Review exercises

Copy the following sentences. Add the punctuation for each interjection. Add capital letters where necessary.

Example: Oh I think I should have turned left.
Answer: Oh, I think I should have turned left.
Example: Wow he cleared that hurdle with a foot to spare.
Answer: Wow! He cleared that hurdle with a foot to spare.

1. Well I think we can close the office now.
2. Whew that foul ball almost hit me.
3. Oh excuse me.
4. Hurrah it's the last day of school.
5. Ouch you stepped on my foot.

Answer key

Page 38 (Exercise A)

1.	sister—Cc	10.	offspring—Cc	19.	Rachel—P
2.	Rachel—P	11.	Rachel—P	20.	vista—Cc
3.	reader—Cc	12.	enthusiasm—Ca	21.	daughter—Cc
4.	card—Cc	13.	June—P	22.	nose—Cc
5.	week—Cc	14.	family—Cc	23.	guide book—Cc
6.	trip—Cc	15.	Grand Canyon—P	24.	Rachel—P
7.	branch—Cc	16.	point—Cc	25.	pamphlet—Cc
8.	books—Cc	17.	canyon—Cc	26.	splendor—Ca
9.	parents—Cc	18.	Father—P		

Page 38 (Exercise B)

1. aunt—feminine, singular
2. field—neuter, singular
3. butlers—masculine, plural
4. cowboys—masculine, plural
5. dog—common, singular
6. quail—common, singular or plural
7. teachers—common, plural
8. group—common, singular or plural
9. bottles—neuter, plural
10. maid—feminine, singular
11. cow—feminine, singular
12. touchdown—neuter, singular
13. brother—masculine, singular
14. deer—common, singular or plural
15. mice—common, plural
16. hero—masculine, singular
17. hammer—neuter, singular
18. chairperson—common, singular
19. hostess—feminine, singular
20. singers—common, plural

Page 40

1. his brother-in-law's tool kit
2. her father's birthday
3. Tom and Jim's car
4. the girls' representative
5. Bob's and Jack's articles
6. Kim's music and Dick's lyrics
7. the commander-in-chief's jeep
8. Bradley's and Carmine's stores
9. women's blouses
10. Frances's performance or Frances' performance

Page 43 (Exercise A)

1. We   2. she   3. theirs   4. him   5. It

Page 43 (Exercise B)

1. my—personal
2. me—personal
3. my—personal
4. me—personal
5. they—personal
6. they—personal
7. me—personal
8. one—indefinite
9. myself—reflexive
10. It—personal
11. few—indefinite
12. most—indefinite
13. that—relative
14. I—personal
15. I—personal
16. it—personal
17. I—personal
18. What—interrogative
19. you—personal
20. her—personal
21. I—personal
22. that—demonstrative

Page 46 (Exercise A)

1. her—possessive
2. We—nominative
3. us—objective
4. their—possessive
5. him—objective
6. them—objective
7. You—nominative
8. Their—possessive
9. I—nominative
10. mine—possessive

Page 46 (Exercise B)

1. The teacher gave him and *me* an extra credit assignment. (The correct form of the pronoun is *me*, as the objective case is used for indirect objects.)
2. The ship sailed to its next port. (Apostrophes are never used with a possessive pronoun.)
3. Correct
4. The test was very difficult for us students. (The correct form of the pronoun is *us*, as the objective case is used for objects of prepositions.)
5. Whom will you invite to the party? (The correct form of the pronoun is *whom*, as the objective case is used for direct objects.)
6. Correct
7. Timmy told Dad and me that dinner was ready. (The correct form of the pronoun is *me*, as the objective case is used for indirect objects.)
8. Correct
9. Correct
10. The winners were Tom and I. (The correct form of the pronoun is *I*, as the nominative case is used for a predicate nominative.)

Page 48

1. its (agrees with *flock*, which is singular)
2. his or her; his/her (Or: All the drivers tried to park their cars in the lot closest to the theater.)
3. Correct
4. his (agrees with *neither*, which is singular)
5. Correct
6. he or she; he/she (Or: If people want to succeed they must work hard.)
7. Correct
8. its (agrees with each, which is singular)
9. her (agrees with one, which is singular)
10. he or she, he/she (Or: All involved are doing the best they can.)

Page 52 (Exercise A)

1. long—descriptive
2. winding—descriptive
3. few—limiting
4. simple—descriptive
5. Many—limiting
6. main—descriptive
7. confused—descriptive
8. weary—descriptive
9. No—limiting
10. dark—descriptive
11. threatening—descriptive
12. happy—descriptive
13. bright—descriptive
14. yellow—descriptive
15. some—limiting
16. old—descriptive
17. warm—descriptive
18. genial—descriptive
19. other—limiting
20. wonderful—descriptive
21. trying—descriptive

Page 52 (Exercise B)
long—longer, longest; less long, least long
attractive—more attractive, most attractive; less attractive, least attractive
dark—darker, darkest; less dark, least dark
understandable—more understandable, most understandable; less understandable, least understandable
bold—bolder, boldest; less bold, least bold
high—higher, highest; less high, least high
remarkable—more remarkable, most remarkable; less remarkable, least remarkable
beautiful—more beautiful, most beautiful; less beautiful, least beautiful

Page 54 (Exercise A)

1.	delicious	5.	neat	9.	quickly
2.	carefully	6.	fresh	10.	quiet
3.	promptly	7.	bad	11.	correct
4.	good	8.	rough		

Page 55 (Exercise B)

1.	This	6.	this
2.	fewer	7.	less
3.	less	8.	This
4.	Those or These	9.	fewer
5.	Fewer		

Page 57 (Exercise A)

1.	made—transitive	6.	led—transitive
2.	used—transitive	7.	carried—transitive
3.	navigated—intransitive	8.	released—transitive
4.	determined—transitive	9.	flew—intransitive
5.	watched—transitive	10.	discovered—transitive

Page 57 (Exercise B)
1. verb—gave; direct object—test; indirect object—class
2. verb—send; direct object—catalogue; indirect object—me
3. verb—threw; direct object—it
4. verb—built; direct object—doghouse; indirect object—Fido
5. verb—mailed; direct object—them
6. verb—brought; direct object—pizza; indirect object—gang
7. verb—saw; direct object—that
8. verb—gives; direct object—lessons; indirect object—him
9. verb—baked; direct object—cake; indirect object—Dad
10. verb—take; direct object—them

Page 58 (Exercise A)

1.	was—predicate adjective, hungry	6.	is—predicate nominative, champion
2.	felt—predicate adjective, bad	7.	seemed—predicate adjective, glad
3.	was—predicate nominative, pilot	8.	are—predicate nominative, evergreens
4.	looked—predicate adjective, nervous	9.	grew—predicate adjective, quiet
5.	are—predicate adjective, happy	10.	is—predicate nominative, cheerleader

Page 59 (Exercise B)
1. grew—linking verb
2. smells—linking verb
3. Taste—action verb
4. grew—action verb
5. Look—action verb
6. acted—linking verb
7. look—linking verb
8. smell—action verb
9. turned—linking verb
10. Turn—action verb

Page 60
1. active.
   passive: The National Anthem was sung by Tim.
2. passive
   active: The Scout troop climbed the mountain easily.
3. passive
   active: The sales clerk found the lost earrings.
4. active
   passive: The injured dog was carried to the pet hospital by Abby.
5. passive
   active: The judges gave Mrs. Jennings a blue ribbon for her pie.
6. active
   passive: Our flower bed was crushed by the Bartons' car.
7. passive
   active: The park rangers supplied the charcoal.
8. active
   passive: The vegetable garden was planted by Rebecca.
9. passive
   active: The guilty party paid a large fine.
10. active
    passive: My typewriter was repaired by Mr. Powers.

Page 61
1. indicative
2. imperative
3. subjunctive
4. indicative
5. indicative
6. imperative
7. indicative
8. subjunctive
9. imperative
10. subjunctive

Page 62
1. third person plural
2. second person singular or plural
3. third person singular
4. first person singular
5. third person plural
6. second person singular or plural
7. third person singular
8. first person plural
9. third person singular
10. third person plural
11. first person singular
12. third person singular
13. third person singular
14. first person plural
15. second person singular or plural
16. third person singular
17. second person singular or plural
18. third person singular
19. third person singular
20. first person plural

Page 64

1. past
2. past perfect
3. present
4. present—indicates future
5. present perfect
6. past perfect
7. future
8. present
9. future perfect
10. present
11. present perfect
12. past
13. future
14. past perfect
15. present
16. future perfect
17. present perfect
18. present
19. past perfect
20. future

Page 65

1. verb phrase: had gone
2. verb phrase: will enjoy
3. verb phrase: could have predicted
4. verb phrase: may build
5. verb phrase: would look
6. verb phrase: must love
7. verb phrase: have been thinking
8. verb phrase: are landing
9. verb phrase: should try
10. verb phrase: can read
11. verb phrase: were trained
12. verb phrase: am studying
13. verb phrase: was baking
14. verb phrase: has been repaired
15. verb phrase: do know

Page 68

1. rode
2. sunk
3. taught
4. shaken
5. swore
6. swam
7. beaten
8. spoke
9. lain
10. set
11. frozen
12. wrote
13. seen
14. went
15. taken
16. sat
17. broken
18. left
19. flew
20. eaten

Page 71

1. I walk / we walk
   you walk / you walk
   he, she, it walks / they walk
2. I shall come / we shall come
   you will come / you will come
   he, she, it will come / they will come
3. I was carried / we were carried
   you were carried / you were carried
   he, she, it was carried / they were carried
4. I had elected / we had elected
   you had elected / you had elected
   he, she, it had elected / they had elected
5. I have been chosen / we have been chosen
   you have been chosen / you have been chosen
   he, she, it had been chosen / they have been chosen

Page 74 (Exercise A)

1. to pay—infinitive
2. Curling—gerund
3. frightened—participle
4. to get—infinitive
5. playing—participle
6. to relax—infinitive
7. making—gerund
8. jogging—gerund
9. squawking—participle
10. to play—infinitive
11. stolen—participle
12. Finding—gerund
13. to use—infinitive
14. kicking—participle
15. broken—participle
16. to please—infinitive
17. Bowling—gerund
18. tired—participle
19. to go—infinitive
20. driving—gerund

Page 75 (Exercise B)

1. flying—present
2. scribbled—past
3. Crossing—present
4. searching—present
5. borrowed—past
6. whistling—present
7. broken—past
8. selling—present
9. written—past
10. quarreling—present

Page 75 (Exercise C)

1. present participle
2. gerund
3. gerund
4. present participle
5. gerund
6. gerund
7. present participle
8. present participle
9. present participle
10. gerund

Page 78 (Exercise A)

1. was
2. dance
3. is
4. was
5. was
6. Are
7. plans
8. shop
9. wants
10. is

Page 78 (Exercise B)

1. sit, set
2. lay, lying
3. rose, raised
4. laid, lying
5. set, sits

Page 81 (Exercise A)

1. quickly
2. Where
3. extremely
4. out
5. fast
6. when
7. No
8. steadily
9. however
10. enough
11. beautifully
12. Later
13. somewhat
14. How
15. when
16. forward
17. on
18. however
19. down
20. onward
21. before

Page 82 (Exercise B)

1. happily—manner
2. before—time
3. forward—place
4. down—place
5. extremely—degree
6. beautifully—manner
   quickly—manner
7. sooner—time
   later—time
8. there—place
9. somewhat—degree
10. exceptionally—degree
    extremely—degree

Page 84 (Exercise A)

Answers will vary. Example sentences:

1. Dad is taking a *late* train. (adjective)
   Harold turned in his paper *late*. (adverb)
2. We are having an *early* spring. (adjective)
   Please plan to arrive *early*. (adverb)
3. Susie Smith is an *only* child. (adjective)
   Jack *only* has one chance at bat. (adverb)
4. Ben ran a *fast* race. (adjective)
   Frank talks *fast*. (adverb)
5. I am glad John is *well* again. (adjective)
   Nancy did *well* at the tryouts. (adverb)

Page 84 (Exercise B)
1. Just Jane runs for exercise.
   Jane just runs for exercise.
   Jane runs just for exercise.
2. Even Mark likes burned cookies.
   Mark even likes burned cookies.
   Mark likes even burned cookies.
3. Only Kevin wrote the class play.
   Kevin only wrote the class play.
   Kevin wrote only the class play.
4. Karen often (or often Karen) seems interested in reading.
   Karen seems interested in reading often.
5. We merely stopped here to get a sandwich.
   We stopped here merely to get a sandwich.

Page 86 (Exercise A)
1. preposition: to
   object: war
2. preposition: off
   object: chair
3. preposition: in
   object: holes
4. preposition: to
   object: house
5. preposition: on
   object: porch
6. preposition: with
   object: hat
   preposition: by
   object: church

7. preposition: on
   object: project
   preposition: throughout
   object: day
8. preposition: to
   object: drugstore
   preposition: during
   object: break
9. preposition: for
   object: curtains
10. preposition: to
    object: yourself

Page 87 (Exercise B)
1. preposition
2. preposition
3. adverb
4. preposition
5. preposition

6. adverb
7. preposition
8. adverb
9. preposition
10. adverb

Page 88
1. Gregory is sensitive *to* but careless about his sister's feelings.
2. The neighborhood protested *against* (also *about*) and argued over the new law.
3. Correct
4. Mr. and Mrs. Martin are inseparable *from* yet independent of each other.
5. Jim was feeling jealous *of* and angry with his brother.
6. A person can alternately confide *in* and then quarrel with his best friend.
7. As children, we are sometimes obedient *to* yet annoyed with our parents.
8. Correct
9. We sympathize *with* and are concerned for you.
10. I am happy *about* and envious of your new job assignment.

Page 90

1.	and	6.	whether
2.	nor	7.	either
3.	unless	8.	when
4.	but	9.	or
5.	because	10.	before

Page 91

1. I will ask for neither your cooperation nor your help.
2. Johnny spends almost all his free time either working on his model airplanes or watching TV.
3. Sally hasn't decided whether to attend the lecture or to go to the movies.
4. My Uncle Joe raises not only chickens but cows, too.
5. Janet is a student who does well in both math and science.
6. Jack will go to college next year whether on scholarship or with his own funds.
7. We enjoy living in the city both for its cultural attractions and for its convenience.
8. You may either come with us or stay home.
9. Ralph gave a speech that was not only rousing but convincing.
10. Pat had neither the will to succeed nor high skills.

Page 92

1. Well, I think we can close the office now.
2. Whew! That foul ball almost hit me.
3. Oh, excuse me.
4. Hurrah! It's the last day of school.
5. Ouch! You stepped on my foot.

Sentences

The sentence is an important building block of communication. In this chapter, you will learn many facts about sentences. You will discover how to identify the two basic parts of every sentence. You will learn about word groups, called phrases and clauses, that are frequently found in sentences. You will learn that there are different kinds of sentence structures (simple; compound; complex; complex-compound) and different types of sentences (declarative; interrogative; and exclamatory). And you will learn that sentences can be classified by the way they express ideas: sentences can be loose, periodic, or balanced.

Subject and predicate

In traditional grammar, a sentence is a group of related words that contains a subject and a predicate and expresses a complete thought.The *subject* is the part of a sentence about which something is said. The *predicate* is the part of a sentence that says something about the subject.

> I / like strawberries.
> subject / predicate

> The bright summer sun / filtered through the trees.
> subject / predicate

In most cases, the subject precedes the predicate. In some cases, however, the subject follows the predicate.

> Up and away flew / the kite.
> predicate / subject

> In the mailbox was / the letter we'd been waiting for.
> predicate / subject

There are two ways of looking at a sentence's subject and predicate. One way is to look at the *complete* subject and predicate. The other way is to look at the *simple* subject and predicate. The *simple subject* is the noun or pronoun about which something is said. The *complete subject* consists of the simple subject and all the words associated with it.

> The cheerful little girl / played baseball in the park.
> Simple subject: girl
> Complete subject: the cheerful little girl

The tall glass building / reflected the sunlight.
Simple subject: building
Complete subject: the tall glass building

The sticky black mud / covered the sidewalk.
Simple subject: mud
Complete subject: the sticky black mud

When teachers refer to the subject of a sentence, they are usually referring to the simple subject. The *simple predicate* is the verb that says something about the subject. The *complete predicate* consists of the verb and all the words associated with it.

The track team / ran at a slow pace.
Simple predicate: ran
Complete predicate: ran at a slow pace

The eagle / rose from the nest with stately grace.
Simple predicate: rose
Complete predicate: rose from the nest with stately grace

The car / spun out of control on the turn.
Simple predicate: spun
Complete predicate: spun out of control on the turn

Compound subjects

A compound subject consists of two or more nouns that are the subject of the same verb.

Sandra and Jim went to the movies.
Cathy, Max, and I are running for class president.

Compound predicates

A compound predicate consists of two or more verbs that have the same subject.

Richard *danced and sang* in the school play.
The soda *bubbled and fizzed* in the glass.

Complete thought

In addition to containing a subject and a predicate, a sentence must express a complete thought. If it does not, it is called a sentence fragment. Following are some examples of sentence fragments:

the tree along the path
(This is a sentence fragment because it contains no predicate.)

ran toward the lake
(This is a sentence fragment because it contains no subject.)

If I win the contest
(This is a sentence fragment because it does not express a complete thought, even though it contains both a subject and a predicate.)

Review exercises

A. Number your paper from 1 to 5. Identify the simple and complete subject and the simple and complete predicate in each of the following sentences.

Example: The stormy dark clouds whirled rapidly through the sky.
Answer: Simple subject—clouds
Complete subject—the stormy dark clouds
Simple predicate—whirled
Complete predicate—whirled rapidly through the sky

1. A bright red sun hung low in the sky.
2. The twisted old tree fell to the ground with a crash.
3. Forward toward the stage ran the twenty happy winners.
4. A tall grandfather clock tilted precariously in the truck.
5. The tired old dog drank slowly from the water dish.

B. Number your paper from 1 to 10. Identify the following thoughts as complete or incomplete.

Example: The highway was crowded with cars
Answer: Complete

Example: Where he skated
Answer: Incomplete

1. A new actor joined the company
2. Nobody at the movies
3. Slipped on the ice and fell
4. Heavy dew covered the ground
5. The candle flickered in the wind
6. What the Senator said
7. Hurricane winds approached the shore
8. A jagged piece of glass
9. If they reach the peak
10. Crowds of people filled the mall

Phrases

A phrase is a group of two or more related words that do not contain both a subject and a predicate.

Prepositional phrases contain a preposition, its objects, and any modifiers.

> in the sunny garden
> after my arrival
> by the cool fountain

Participial phrases contain a past or present participle, its objects, and any modifiers. (Past participles end in *-ed;* present participles end in *-ing.*)

> working at his sloppy desk
> singing songs
> surprised at the news
> locked from within

Gerund phrases contain a gerund, its objects, and any modifiers. Gerund phrases look exactly like participial phrases; they are formed the same way (see examples above). The difference between participial phrases and gerund phrases has to do with their functions in sentences where they are used. You will learn more about the difference between these phrases below.

Infinitive phrases contain the infinitive, its objects, and any modifiers.

> to live near the ocean
> to play happily
> to try a new tactic

Phrases are used in place of single words in sentences.

Prepositional phrases are used as adjectives or adverbs.

As adjectives:	The man *in the grey hat* is my father.
	(The prepositional phrase modifies the noun *man.*)
	Do you shop at that store *on the corner*?
	(The prepositional phrase modifies the noun *store.*)
As adverbs:	Don't talk *with your mouth full*.
	(The prepositional phrase modifies the verb *talk.*)
	We arrived *after the intermission*.
	(The prepositional phrase modifies the verb *arrived.*)

Participial phrases are used as adjectives:

Do you see that girl *playing in the yard*?
(The participial phrase modifies the noun *girl*.)
Frightened by the horror movie, Fred was unable to fall asleep.
(The participial phrase modifies the proper noun *Fred*.)

Gerund phrases are used as nouns.

Driving on mountain roads demands special concentration.
(The gerund phrase is the subject of the verb *demands*.)
I enjoy *taking long walks in the country*.
(The gerund phrase is the object of the verb *enjoy*.)

Alert: Do not confuse gerund phrases and participial phrases. Gerund phrases are used as nouns; participial phrases are used as adjectives.
Swimming laps takes stamina. (The gerund phrase is the subject of the verb *takes*.)
The girl *swimming laps* is my sister. (The participial phrase modifies the noun *girl*.)

Infinitive phrases are used as nouns, as adjectives, or as adverbs.

I want *to go to the library*.
(The infinitive phrase is the object of the verb *want*.)
To become a pilot was his lifelong dream.
(The infinitive phrase is the predicate nominative.)
This is a meal *to savor slowly*.
(The infinitive phrase modifies the noun *meal*.)
I run *every* day to stay in shape
(The infinitive phrase modifies the verb *run*.)

Dangling modifiers result from improper placement of phrases, which should appear as close as possible to the words they modify and should clearly and sensibly modify those words. Failure to observe these guidelines can result in constructions that are often absurd or amusing, but always incorrect.

Incorrect:	Roasting in the oven, I smelled the turkey.
Correct:	I smelled the turkey roasting in the oven.
Incorrect:	After talking to his teacher, Jack's attitude improved.
Correct:	After talking to his teacher, Jack improved his attitude.
Incorrect:	He grabbed for the book reaching sideways.
Correct:	Reaching sideways, he grabbed for the book.
Incorrect:	I need my coat to go to the library.
Correct:	Before I go to the library, I need to put on my coat.
Incorrect:	Careening around the corner, the pedestrian was hit by a car.
Correct:	Careening around the corner, a car hit the pedestrian
Correct:	A pedestrian was hit by a car careening around the corner.

Review exercises

A. Number your paper from 1 to 10. Indentify the underlined phrase in each of the following sentences as a participial, prepositional, gerund, or infinitive phrase. Then tell whether the phrase acts as an adjective, an adverb, or a noun. Finally, if it acts as an adjective or adverb, tell which word it modifies. If it acts as a noun, tell whether the noun functions as the subject, the object, or the predicate nominative.

| **Example:** | The boat <u>with the red sail</u> is the leader. |
| **Answer:** | prepositional phrase, acts as an adjective modifying the noun *boat* |

1. The woman planned <u>to own a home.</u>
2. <u>Jogging for a mile</u> creates energy.
3. We saw the cheerleader <u>leaping in the air.</u>
4. She jumped <u>at the sound.</u>
5. <u>To play the piano</u> was her ambition.
6. They enjoyed <u>attending concerts in the park.</u>
7. <u>Satisfied with the pizza,</u> Beth did not want to eat any more.
8. The plant <u>with the pink flowers</u> wins the prize.
9. You can sing <u>in the choir.</u>
10. This is a lesson <u>to study carefully.</u>

B. Number your paper from 1 to 5. Rewrite each sentence eliminating the dangling modifier. Answers may vary.

| **Example:** | They watched the concert standing up. |
| **Answer:** | Standing up, they watched the concert. |

1. Resting on the table she saw a vase.
2. To be considered for the prize, your attendance record must be perfect.

3. Looking in the mirror, the crack distorted her image.
4. The boat pulled into port listing badly.
5. Ignored by John, the dance was no fun for Sheila.

Clauses

A clause is a group of words that are related and that contains both a subject and a predicate.

Independent clauses

A clause that expresses a complete thought and can stand by itself is called an *independent clause* or a *main clause*. An independent clause can become a simple sentence merely by adding a period.

The rooster crowed in the barn.
(The clause *the rooster crowded in the barn* is a complete thought and can stand by itself. Thus it is an independent clause.)

An independent clause may be very long or very short:

Rain falls
Roses are red
Twenty people attended the ceremony
The Spanish class visited a Mexican restaurant
The man in the brown hat talking to the train conductor seems very angry about the delay.

Remember: A clause is independent so long as it contains both a subject and a predicate and expresses a complete thought.

Review exercise

Number your paper from 1 to 10. Identify and write the independent clause in each of the sentences below.

Example: The ranch hands repaired the barbed-wire fence after they had found it broken.
Answer: The ranch hands repaired the barbed-wire fence

1. The athletes entered the stadium.
2. His batting average has improved since he became a switch hitter.
3. The peeling paint made the house look neglected.
4. The parade began when the drum major blew his whistle.
5. If it rains tomorrow, the picnic will be postponed.

6. Many students were happy to help clean up the park during spring vacation.
7. I take a sack lunch to school.
8. No one was hurt when the railroad bridge collapsed.
9. The wind blew the sign down during the night.
10. Sue, Bill, and the other members of the committee ordered enough food for the party.

Dependent clauses

A clause that does not express a complete idea and cannot stand by itself is called a *dependent* or *subordinate clause*. A dependent clause depends upon the independent clause in the sentence to complete its meaning. Dependent clauses act as adjectives, adverbs, or nouns.

Adjective clauses

An adjective clause can modify any noun or pronoun in a sentence. Adjective clauses function in sentences exactly as single-word adjectives do. They may be used in several ways.

To modify the subject:

The package *that Sue wrapped* was the prettiest.
(The adjective clause modifies *package*.)

To modify the predicate nominative:

The tall firefighter is the one *who saved my cat*.
(The adjective clause modifies *one*.)

To modify the direct object:

The puppy chased the stick *that his master threw*.
(The adjective clause modifies stick.)

To modify an indirect object:

We sent our classmate *who was sick* a get-well card.
(The adjective clause modifies *classmate*.)

To modify the object of a preposition:

We walked up the hill *where the hut had been built*.
(The adjective clause modifies *hill*.)

Review exercise

Number your paper from 1 to 10. For each sentence, write the adjective clause and tell what it modifies.

Example: The dress that she wore was blue.
Answer: *that she wore*—modifies the subject *dress*

1. The student who runs the best campaign will be elected.
2. The children preferred the cookies that were homemade.
3. Bob refinished the table that he bought at the junk store.
4. Sally stared into the fire that we had built.
5. Lakes where the fishing is good are crowded in the summertime.
6. Bob prefers the math teacher who taught him last year.
7. The sign was posted in front of the lot that we wanted to buy.
8. Sam gave the coach who was leaving a picture of the team.
9. This is the climate that I like best.
10. I am reading my sister a story that I wrote.

Adverb clauses

An adverb clause functions as an adverb. It can modify any verb, adjective, or adverb in a sentence. It may be used in several ways.

To modify a verb:

We ate *when the guests had arrived*.
(The adverb clause modifies the verb *ate*.)

To modify an adjective:

I baked enough cupcakes *so that there is one for each child*.
(The adverbial clause modifies the adjective *enough*.)

To modify an adverb:

The noise of the stereo was so loud *that I could not hear the phone*.
(The adverb clause modifies the adverb *so*.)

To modify a predicate adjective:

Rachel is often cranky *when she first wakes up*.
(The adverb clause modifies the predicate adjective *cranky*.)

Review exercise

Number your paper from 1 to 10. Identify and write the adverb clause in each sentence and tell what word is being modified. Tell if the modified word is a verb, an adjective, or an adverb.

Example: Karen will sit wherever she chooses.
Answer: *wherever she chooses*—modifies the verb *will sit*.

1. While John is setting the table, Gary will slice the bread.
2. Caroline is shorter than I am.
3. Erin missed the school bus because she overslept.
4. The dog whined as though he knew we were leaving.
5. Albert is usually correct when he answers a question.
6. Ducks spend the winter wherever they find a food supply.
7. Whenever Paul and I meet, we talk about old times.
8. I was so sick that I had to miss the party.
9. I went to the store because we ran out of milk and sugar.
10. Until we know the answer, we will not make any decisions.

Noun clauses

A noun clause functions as a noun. It may be used in a sentence in any situation where a noun or pronoun may be used.

As a subject:

What happened at the party surprised everyone.
(The noun clause is the subject of the verb *surprised*.)

As a direct object:

Sarah knew *that her costume was attractive*.
(The noun clause acts as the object of the verb *knew*.)

As an indirect object:

We will give *whoever wants one* a copy of the entire speech.
(The noun clause acts as the indirect object of the verb *give* answering the question, We will give the copy to whom?)

As the object of a preposition:

The campers took nothing except *what they could carry in their packs*.
(The noun clause acts as the object of the preposition *except*.)

As a predicate nominative:

The question is *whether we should build a house or buy one*.
(The noun clause is the predicate nominative after the linking verb *is*.)

As an appositive:

His first thought, *that the noise was a gunshot*, was incorrect.
(The noun clause acts as an appositive of the subject *thought*.)

Review exercise

Number your paper from 1 to 10. Write down the noun clause in each of the following sentences. Tell how each functions (as a subject, a direct object, an indirect object, an object of a preposition, a predicate nominative, or an appositive).

Example: What you see is called a rainbow.
Answer: *What you see*—functions as the subject

1. Hillary brought whatever her sisters forgot.
2. Just drop that package on whatever surface looks clear.
3. The future is usually whatever people make it.
4. Wild Bill sent whoever wrote to him an honorary rodeo certificate.
5. The major's plan, that the tanks be camouflaged, went into effect before the attack.
6. Andrea decided that she needed more exercise.
7. How Lisa looks is important to her.
8. We discussed how we would finance the trip.
9. The contestant announced that she had won.
10. The fact is that the clowns stole the show.

Elliptical clauses

By definition, a clause contains a subject and a predicate. Usually, both of these essential elements are expressed, leaving nothing to be understood. Sometimes, however, part or all of either the subject or the predicate is not expressed but is still understood to be part of the clause. When a clause has an essential element missing, it is called an *elliptical clause.*

Mrs. Jones retired in November; Mr. Jones retired a month later.
(two complete independent clauses)

Mrs. Jones retired in November; *Mr. Jones, a month later.*
(one complete independent clause followed by an elliptical independent clause from which the verb *retired* has been omitted)

While he was listening to the radio, Sam heard an interview with the Senator. (one complete dependent clause followed by one complete independent clause)

While listening to the radio, Sam heard an interview with the Senator. (one elliptical dependent clause, from which the subject *he* and the first word of the verb phrase *was listening* have been omitted, followed by one complete independent clause)

Elliptical clauses make sentences less wordy and add variety to passages that contain many sentences full of clauses.

Restrictive and nonrestrictive clauses

Clauses can be either *restrictive* or *nonrestrictive*. Restrictive clauses are essential to the meaning of the sentence. That is, they restrict the meaning of the sentence by identifying a definite person or thing. Nonrestrictive clauses are not essential to the meaning of the sentence. They merely add description to an already identified person or thing. Nonrestrictive clauses can be omitted without changing the meaning of the sentence.

Nonrestrictive clauses are set off by commas; restrictive clauses are not. *Which* is the relative pronoun used to introduce nonrestrictive clauses; *that* is used for restrictive clauses.

Restrictive: The crowd that was gathered in front of the stage was loud and unruly.

Nonrestrictive: The crowd, which had gathered in front of the stage to hear the concert, turned loud and unruly when the band failed to arrive.

Restrictive: The doctor who treated my sister had graduated from one of the best medical schools in the country.

Nonrestrictive: The doctor, who had graduated from one of the best medical schools in the country, was offered jobs at many excellent hospitals.

Review exercises

A. Number your paper from 1 to 5. Rewrite each sentence changing the underlined clause to an elliptical clause.

Example: Polly vacationed for two weeks; Rose vacationed for a month.
Answer: Polly vacationed for two weeks; Rose, for a month.

1. Amy grew two inches last year; Grace grew one inch.
2. The Reds traded two outfielders; the Padres traded three pitchers.

3. When you are reading, you should have a good light.
4. Aileen and Barb vowed to remain friends while they are competing for the student council seat.
5. After he had been studying for three hours, Greg took a break.

B. Number your paper from 1 to 5. Below are five sentences followed by added information. Rewrite each sentence, inserting the information in clause form (restrictive or nonrestrictive). Use the relative pronouns *who, which,* or *that* to begin the clauses. For nonrestrictive clauses insert commas.

Example: The book from the library is two days overdue.
             (I borrowed the book.)
Answer: The book that I borrowed from the library is two days overdue.
             (restrictive clause—no commas)

1. Ralph's cousin was eager to travel north in the winter to get a glimpse of snow. (Ralph's cousin lives in Florida.)
2. Grandmother received the flowers. (Bill and I sent the flowers.)
3. Connect part A to the base of part B. (Part A comes pre-assembled.)
4. Mary is an athlete. (Mary excels in baseball and basketball.)
5. The citizens protested the highway. (The planning commission had proposed the highway.)

Sentence Structure

Sentences may be classified in several different ways. One way of classifying sentences is by their structure. The four kinds of sentence structure are *simple, compound, complex,* and *compound-complex.*

Simple sentences are made up of one independent (main) clause and no dependent (subordinate) clauses. A simple sentence may contain a compound subject or a compound verb, or both a compound subject and a compound verb.

The boy ate the apple.
The windows are small.
A man and his son came to the store.
The pianist bowed to the audience and sat down at the piano.
My brother and sister love to swim and ski.

Compound sentences contain two or more independent clauses and no dependent clauses. The clauses in a compound sentence are joined by coordinating conjunctions (*and, but, so,* and so forth), conjunctive adverbs (*however, nevertheless,* and so forth), or simply by a semicolon.

Carole made the lemonade and *Harry mixed the punch.*
We don't like horror movies; nevertheless, *we stayed to the end of the film.*
The guests have no way to get here; someone must pick them up.

Complex sentences contain one independent clause and one or more dependent clauses.

dependent   independent

Although Harry was late, we let him join the game.

dependent   independent   dependent

After I finished my homework, I went to the store *that you told me about.*

Compound-complex sentences contain two or more independent clauses and one or more dependent clauses.

dependent

When the house gets cold in the winter, Father lights

independent   independent

a fire in the fireplace and mother makes some hot chocolate.

dependent   independent

If Sally can come to visit tomorrow, we'll go to the park;

dependent   independent

if she can't, I'll stay home and read.

Review exercise

Number your paper from 1 to 10. Identify each of the following sentences as simple, compound, complex, or compound-complex. Then write each clause and tell if it is dependent or independent.

Example: When the bell rings, the teacher takes attendance.
Answer: complex—when the bell rings (dependent)
the teacher takes attendance (independent)

1. The dog was hungry, but he wouldn't eat.
2. The little girl helped the old woman cross the street.

3. Sylvia likes to cook, but Joan cooks only when she is in the mood.
4. This is the man who repaired the car.
5. Billy and Sam argued about politics during lunch.
6. We played for two hours, and the score remained tied.
7. The mayor approves of the tax cut, but he won't vote for it until he is sure it will work.
8. The ball went in the basket before the whistle blew.
9. Allen writes well, but his stories are too short.
10. Ginny plans to find a job as soon as she graduates.

Sentence Types

Sentences may also be classified according to what they do and how ideas are presented in them.

What sentences do

A sentence can state a fact or make an assertion; ask a question; give a command or make a request; or express strong feeling.

A sentence that states a fact or makes an assertion is a *declarative sentence*. Declarative sentences end with a period. Most of the sentences you write are declarative sentences.

The boy is tall.
The new factory provided jobs for many people in the community.
The tag at the back of Kim's blouse scratched her neck when she moved.

A sentence that asks a question is an *interrogative sentence*. Interrogative sentences end with a question mark.

Is there a shorter route to take to the mall?
What time is it?
Do you like Mexican food?

A sentence that gives a command or makes a request is an *imperative sentence*. *You* is the understood subject of imperative sentences. Commands may be followed by a period or an exclamation point; requests end with a period.

Please take out the garbage. (request)
Go away! (command)
Bring the paper with you when you come in. (command)

115

A sentence that expresses strong feeling is an *exclamatory sentence*. Exclamatory sentences end with an exclamation point.

You should be ashamed of yourself!
I disagree completely!

Review exercise

Number your paper from 1 to 10. Following the direction given, write an appropriate sentence beside each number.

Example: Write an exclamatory sentence about a fire.
Answer: Call the fire department!

1. Write a declarative sentence about how something tastes.
2. Write an interrogative sentence about the zoo.
3. Write an exclamatory sentence about the weather.
4. Write an imperative sentence that might be said by someone who wants to borrow money from a friend.
5. Write a declarative sentence about an action you might see.
6. Write an exclamatory sentence about an accident.
7. Write an interrogative sentence about how to get from one place to another.
8. Write an imperative sentence that might be said by someone in a hurry.
9. Write a declarative sentence about more than one person.
10. Write an exclamatory sentence that expresses surprise.

How ideas are arranged in sentences

Ideas may be arranged in sentences in a number of ways.
Loose sentences present a complete idea first and then add details later to strengthen the statement.

The people gathered at the country house were all related either by blood, marriage, or adoption.
The new team was a strong one, with a combination of enthusiastic rookies and seasoned athletes.

Loose sentences are direct and easy to follow, and they help the reader grasp the main idea quickly. However, too many loose sentences in succession can be boring.
Periodic sentences place the main thought or idea at the close of the sentence.

If the bank is insured, depositors will be able to get their money back
   after a robbery.
At the very end of his speech, Raymond Jackson announced that he
   had decided to run for Congress.

Periodic sentences can provide variety, and often create a sense of drama
by keeping the main idea until the end. When loose and periodic sentences
are used together, writing gains added pace and interest.
Balanced sentences use the same or similar forms to present thoughts and
ideas to be compared or contrasted.

To write is difficult, to have written is joy.
It is harder to watch defeat in silence than to experience defeat in action.

Balanced sentences have a definite beat. Used occasionally, they have
a dramatic effect, but overuse may create a stiff and stilted tone.

Review exercises

A. For each of the five topics, write a loose sentence.

Example: a picnic
Answer: The picnic was a huge success because everyone showed up
            and the weather was perfect.

1. a pet show   4. a trip to the mountains
2. a carnival   5. a new bike
3. a spring flood

B. Rewrite the following loose sentences as periodic sentences.

Example: It rained hard for an hour while we waited on the porch.
Answer: While we waited on the porch, it rained hard for an hour.

1. The entire population of the town attended the parade to honor the
    astronauts.
2. No women would work until jobs were given to the entire group.
3. Three members came late because of heavy traffic on the highway.
4. The coach repeated what the manager said, using the same words
    and rough manner.
5. The catcher is the most important player on a baseball team, accord-
    ing to Andy.

C. Rewrite the following unbalanced sentences as balanced sentences.

Example: Youth is a time to explore while enjoyment comes with age.
Answer: Youth is a time to explore; age is a time to enjoy.

1. The summer brings grass and flowers; with winter come ice and snow.
2. When you are here, I enjoy being with you, but I miss you when you are gone.
3. Numbers are the language of math, and the language of grammar is words.
4. To err is human but it is divine to forgive.
5. It is better to have loved someone and then to have lost that person than never to have loved at all.

Answer Key

Page 103 (Exercise A)
1. Simple subject—sun
   Complete subject—a bright red sun
   Simple predicate—hung
   Complete predicate—hung low in the sky
2. Simple subject—tree
   Complete subject—the twisted old tree
   Simple predicate—fell
   Complete predicate—fell to the ground with a crash
3. Simple subject—winners
   Complete subject—the twenty happy winners
   Simple predicate—ran
   Complete predicate—forward toward the stage ran
4. Simple subject—clock
   Complete subject—a tall grandfather clock
   Simple predicate—tilted
   Complete predicate—tilted precariously in the truck
5. Simple subject—dog
   Complete subject—the tired old dog
   Simple predicate—drank
   Complete predicate—drank slowly from the water dish

Page 103 (Exercise B)

1. Complete
2. Incomplete
3. Incomplete
4. Complete
5. Complete
6. Incomplete
7. Complete
8. Incomplete
9. Incomplete
10. Complete

Page 106 (Exercise A)

1. infinitive phrase, acts as a noun functioning as the object of the verb *planned*
2. gerund phrase, acts as a noun functioning as the subject of the verb *creates*
3. participial phrase, acts as an adjective modifying the noun *cheerleader*
4. prepositional phrase, acts as an adverb modifying the verb *jumped*
5. infinitive phrase, acts as a noun functioning as the subject
6. gerund phrase, acts as a noun functioning as the object of the verb *enjoyed*
7. participial phrase, acts as an adjective modifying the proper noun *Beth*
8. prepositional phrase, acts as an adjective modifying the noun *plant*
9. prepositional phrase, acts as an adverb modifying the verb *sing*
10. infinitive phrase, acts as an adjective modifying the noun *lesson*

Page 106 (Exercise B)

1. She saw a vase resting on the table.
   On the table, she saw a vase resting.
2. To be considered for the prize, you must have a perfect attendance record.
   You must have a perfect attendance record to be considered for the prize.
3. When she looked in the mirror, the crack distorted her image.
   The crack distorted her image when she looked in the mirror.
4. The boat, listing badly, pulled into port.
   Listing badly, the boat pulled into port.
5. Ignored by John, Sheila did not have fun at the dance.
   The dance was no fun for Sheila, whom John ignored.

Page 107

1. The athletes entered the stadium
2. His batting average has improved
3. The peeling paint made the house look neglected
4. The parade began
5. The picnic will be postponed
6. Many students were happy to help clean up the park during spring vacation
7. I take a sack lunch to school
8. No one was hurt
9. The wind blew the sign down during the night
10. Sue, Bill, and the other members of the committee ordered enough food for the party

1. *who runs the best campaign*—modifies the subject *student*
2. *that were homemade*—modifies the direct object *cookies*
3. *that he bought at the junk store*—modifies the direct object *table*
4. *that we had built*—modifies *fire,* the object of the preposition *into*
5. *where the fishing is good*—modifies the subject *lakes*
6. *who taught him last year*—modifies the direct object *teacher*
7. *that we wanted to buy*—modifies *lot,* the object of the prepositional phrase *in front of*
8. *who was leaving*—modifies the indirect object *coach*
9. *that I like best*—modifies the predicate nominative *climate*
10. *that I wrote*—modifies the direct object *story*

1. *While John is setting the table*—modifies the verb *will slice*
2. *than I am*—modifies the adjective *shorter*
3. *because she overslept*—modifies the verb *missed*
4. *as though he knew we were leaving*—modifies the verb *whined*
5. *when he answers a question*—modifies the predicate adjective *correct*
6. *wherever they find a food supply*—modifies the verb *spend*
7. *Whenever Paul and I meet*—modifies the verb *talk*
8. *that I had to miss the party*—modifies the adverb *so*
9. *because we ran out of milk and sugar*—modifies the verb *went*
10. *Until we know the answer*—modifies the verb *will make*

1. *whatever her sisters forgot*—functions as a direct object
2. *whatever surface looks clear*—functions as the object of the preposition *on*
3. *whatever people make it*—functions as a predicate nominative
4. *whoever wrote to him*—functions as an indirect object
5. *that the tanks be camouflaged*—functions as an appositive
6. *that she needed more exercise*—functions as a direct object
7. *How Lisa looks*—functions as a subject
8. *how we would finance the trip*—functions as the direct object
9. *that she had won*—functions as a direct object
10. *that the clowns stole the show*—functions as a predicate nominative

1. Amy grew two inches last year; Grace, one inch.
2. The Reds traded two outfielders; the Padres, three pitchers.
3. When reading, you should have a good light.
4. Aileen and Barb vowed to remain friends while competing for the student council seat.
5. After studying for three hours, Greg took a break.

Page 113 (Exercise B)
1. Ralph's cousin, <u>who lives in Florida</u>, was eager to travel north in the winter to get a glimpse of snow.
2. Grandmother received the flowers <u>that Bill and I sent</u>.
3. Connect part A, <u>which comes pre-assembled</u>, to the base of part B.
4. Mary is an athlete <u>who excels in baseball and basketball</u>.
5. The citizens protested the highway <u>that the planning commission had proposed</u>.

Page 114
1. compound—the dog was hungry (independent)
   he wouldn't eat (independent)
2. simple—the little girl helped the old woman cross the street (independent)
3. compound-complex—Sylvia likes to cook (independent)
   Joan cooks (independent)
   only when she is in the mood (dependent)
4. complex—this is the man (independent)
   who repaired the car (dependent)
5. simple—Billy and Sam argued about politics during lunch (independent)
6. compound—we played for two hours (independent)
   the score remained tied (independent)
7. compound-complex—the mayor approves of the tax cut (independent)
   he won't vote for it (independent)
   until he is sure it will work (dependent)
8. complex—the ball went in the basket (independent)
   before the whistle blew (dependent)
9. compound—Allen writes well (independent)
   his stories are too short (independent)
10. complex—Ginny plans to find a job (independent)
    as soon as she graduates (dependent)

Page 116
Answers will vary. Some examples are:
1. This cake tastes delicious.
2. Is the zoo open on Sunday?
3. Look at that lightning!
4. Please lend me a quarter, Sam.
5. The toddler stumbled and fell.
6. That driver completely ignored the stop sign!
7. Is this the road to Albuquerque?
8. Get out of my way!
9. The Browns and the Thompsons are having a joint garage sale.
10. I can't believe it!

Page 117 (Exercise A)
Answers will vary. Some examples are:
1. John's cat won first prize at the pet show with the highest total of points ever awarded.
2. The carnival opened yesterday in that field north of town.
3. The creek flooded the garden this spring, ruining the plants.
4. We camped in the Rockies last summer and plan to return next winter to ski.
5. Lucy loves her new bike, which is her first 10-speed.

Page 117 (Exercise B)
Answers may vary. Some examples are:
1. To honor the astronauts, the entire population of the town attended the parade.
2. Until jobs were given to the entire group, no women would work.
3. Because of heavy traffic on the highway, three members came late.
4. Using the same words and rough manner, the coach repeated what the manager said.
5. According to Andy, the most important player on a baseball team is the catcher.

Page 118 (Exercise C)
Answers may vary. Some examples are:
1. The summer brings grass and flowers; the winter brings ice and snow.
2. I enjoy being with you when you are here; I miss you when you are gone.
3. Numbers are the language of math; words are the language of grammar.
4. To err is human; to forgive, divine.
5. It is better to have loved and lost than never to have loved at all.

Capitalization

Capital letters act as signals to readers. They distinguish proper nouns and adjectives from common nouns and adjectives. They announce new sentences and the beginning of direct quotations. Knowing when to use capital letters and when to use lower-case letters can sometimes be confusing. The following list gives you some general rules to observe for capitalization.

1. Capitalize proper nouns.

> James Smith   San Francisco   Declaration of Independence

2. Capitalize proper adjectives. Proper adjectives are adjectives that are formed from proper nouns, and proper nouns that are used as adjectives.

> American tourist   Shakespearean drama   Chinese art
> Iowa farmers   New England states   Texas chili

3. Do *not* capitalize the following words; even though they are derived from proper nouns, their use is now considered common enough that they are no longer capitalized.

anglicize	french fries	quixotic
arabic numerals	india ink	roman numerals
bohemian life style	japan (varnish)	russian dressing
brazil nut	macadam road	scotch plaid
chinaware	manila envelope	turkish bath
derby hat	pasteurized milk	venetian blinds
dutch oven	plaster of paris	vienna bread
frankfurter (hot dog)	platonic friendship	vulcanize

4. Capitalize the pronoun *I* and the interjection *O*.

> Rejoice, O ye people, for I bring you glad tidings.

5. Capitalize words that show family relationships when they are used instead of a name or as part of a name.

> I asked Mother if Uncle John was coming.

Do *not* capitalize these words when they are preceded by a possessive, such as *my, your, their.*

> My mother and uncle visited your grandfather.

6. Capitalize nicknames and other identifying names.

Babe Ruth   the Sun King   Richard the Lion-Hearted

7. Capitalize special titles when they immediately precede a personal name.

General Patton   Governor Ella Grasso   Pope John Paul II

Do *not* capitalize them when they do not precede the name.

Ella T. Grasso, governor of Connecticut
George S. Patton was a great American general.

8. Capitalize professional titles and their abbreviations when they follow a personal name.

John Smith, M.D.   Jane Doe, Doctor of Philosophy
Maria Ames, R.N.

9. Capitalize personified nouns.

She was called by Destiny to clear a path for Justice.

10. Capitalize brand names.

Comet (cleanser)   Cougar (car)   Rice Krispies

11. Capitalize specific political and geographical locations (and the adjectives derived from them).

Chicago   Cook County   Asia   Asian

12. Capitalize the names of all nationalities, races, and tribes (and the adjectives derived from them).

German   Japanese   Sioux   Nordic   Caucasian

13. Capitalize words of direction when they are used to designate a specific place.

North Pole   Far East   Middle West   the South

Do *not* capitalize *north, south, east,* and *west* when they refer to a direction or a section of a state.

> We live west of Chicago and vacation in northern Michigan.

14. Capitalize the names of specific geographic features and the common nouns that are part of the proper names.

> Mississippi River   Rocky Mountains   Pacific Ocean
>
> But:
>
> the Mississippi and Ohio rivers   the falls of the Niagara

15. Capitalize the names of buildings, monuments, streets, bridges, parks, and other specific locations, and the common nouns that are part of the proper names.

> White House   Grant Park   Statue of Liberty
> Brooklyn Bridge   Fifth Avenue   U.S. Route 34

16. Capitalize the names of organizations, business firms, and institutions.

> League of Women Voters   General Foods Corporation
> Northwestern University   Burnsville High School

17. Capitalize the names of political parties and religious denominations and their members.

> Republican Party   Roman Catholic   Islam
> Democrat   Presbyterian

18. Capitalize the names of sacred writings and of specific creeds, confessions of faith, and prayers.

> the Bible   the Talmud   the Koran
> Apostles' Creed   Hail Mary   the Lord's Prayer

19. Capitalize nouns and pronouns that refer to a specific Supreme Being.

> God   Allah   Jehovah   Lord   Zeus
> Trust in Him for He is good.
>
> But:
>
> The Romans believed in many gods.

20. Capitalize specific cultural and historical events, wars, treaties, laws, and documents.

Reign of Terror	World War II	Treaty of Versailles
Homestead Act	Articles of Confederation	

21. Capitalize the names of historical and cultural periods.

Renaissance   Roaring Twenties   Era of Good Feeling

But:

colonial period   Elizabethan drama

22. Capitalize the names of specific branches, departments, and other divisions of government.

House of Commons	Department of State	Supreme Court
Chicago Park District	Library of Congress	

But:

traffic court   the city council

23. Capitalize the names of specific awards and prizes.

Nobel Peace Prize   Academy Award   Medal of Honor

24. Capitalize the names of specific trains, planes, ships, satellites, and submarines. (These specific names are also italicized or underlined.)

Orient Express	*Spirit of St. Louis*	
Lusitania	*Skylab*	*Nautilus*

25. Capitalize the names of stars, planets, constellations, and other astronomical designations. But lower-case *sun* and *moon*.

Big Dipper	Milky Way	North Star
Mars Ursa	Major Earth	

But:

the earth

26. Capitalize the days of the week, months of the year, and holidays. Lower-case the seasons of the year.

Tuesday	October	Memorial Day	
spring	fall	summer	winter

27. Capitalize the first word of a sentence or a word or phrase that has the force of a sentence.

The children are running across the street.
Stop!   Wow!

28. Capitalize the first word of a direct quotation.

"We're leaving tomorrow," said Mary.
Jane replied, "Have a good trip."

29. Capitalize the first word of a complete statement following a colon (:).

Here is my decision: You will not be promoted.

30. Capitalize the first word in the salutation and the first word of the complimentary close of a letter.

Gentlemen:	Yours truly,
Dear Sir:	Sincerely yours,
My dear Ellen:	With love,

31. Capitalize the first word and all important words in the titles of works of art, books, magazines, newspapers, poems, songs, articles, television shows, plays, reports, and other writing.

The Thinker	*The Last Supper*	*A Christmas Carol*
The Saturday Evening Post	*Sun-Times*	"The Raven"
The Skin of Our Teeth	"The Waltons"	

32. Capitalize the parts of a book when reference is made from one part to another of the same book.

The sources for this information are listed in the Bibliography.

But:

A bibliography is a list of sources.

Review exercise

Number your paper from 1 to 10. In each of the following sentences, find and correctly write all the words that should be capitalized.

Example: my father, david lee, is a spanish teacher at grove school.
Answer: My, David Lee, Spanish, Grove School

1. last winter, john, alice, marilyn, and i went to see epcot center in orlando, florida.
2. one bright sunday morning in august, aunt sally, mother, and i took a drive south along the mississippi river.
3. every day, mayor burns parks her mustang in the parking lot just north of city hall.
4. mrs. rose said, "please run to benson's food mart on first street and buy a box of cheerios and a loaf of french bread."
5. dr. klaus, our family doctor, hails from the middle west but owns a summer home on mirror lake in new england.
6. while touring europe, we visited some famous museums including the louvre in paris where we saw the *mona lisa.*
7. the victorian age is my favorite period of english literature.
8. on memorial day, lieutenant steven sanders and michael brown, a captain in the u.s. army, will be awarded the purple heart.
9. the *chicago tribune* reviewed shakespeare's *romeo and juliet* now being performed at the blackstone theater.
10. after crossing the ogden bridge, turn left on route 41 and drive approximately four miles to faith lutheran church.

Answer key

Page 128
1. Last, John, Alice, Marilyn, I, Epcot Center, Orlando, Florida
2. One, Sunday, August, Aunt Sally, Mother, I, Mississippi River
3. Every, Mayor Burns, Mustang, City Hall
4. Mrs. Rose, Please, Benson's Food Mart, First Street, Cheerios
5. Dr. Klaus, Middle West, Mirror Lake, New England
6. While, Europe, Louvre, Paris, *Mona Lisa*
7. The, Victorian Age, English
8. On, Memorial Day, Lieutenant Steven Sanders, Michael Brown, U.S. Army, Purple Heart
9. The, *Chicago Tribune,* Shakespeare's, *Romeo and Juliet,* Blackstone Theater
10. After, Ogden Bridge, Route, Faith Lutheran Church

Punctuation

Punctuation has one purpose: to make writing clear. The correct use of punctuation makes your writing more effective, expresses your thoughts clearly, and shows the relation of your thoughts to one another. The punctuation marks and their most common uses are presented here.

A period is used—

1. At the end of complete declarative sentences and of commands given without emphasis.

> The sun was shining.
> Please, wash the car.

2. After each number or letter that begins a heading in an outline.

> Why I Like Sports
> I. A way to improve my health
>   A. By exercising indoors
>   1. Weight training

3. After initials, abbreviations, and after each part of some abbreviations.

> E. W. Smith, Inc.   Dr.   ft.   Mrs.   U.S.   C.O.D.

The abbreviations for some organizations and government agencies do *not* use periods.

> FBI   VISTA   ABC   IBM

A question mark is used—

At the end of direct questions, statements ending with a question, or words or sentences that indicate a question.

> Why did you buy that dress?   That was silly, wasn't it?
> You're leaving now?   Why?

An exclamation point is used—

1. After a word, phrase, or sentence expressing strong feeling.

> Yuch! That tastes awful.   What a beautiful day!

2. To emphasize a command or a strong point of view; or to show amusement, sarcasm, or irony.

Go away!
Okay, I'll forget about it!
I'm supposed to fix supper while you read the paper!

A colon is used—
1. After a complete sentence followed by a list.

Executives carry many things in their briefcases: reports, newspapers, and brown-bag lunches.

2. After a statement followed by a clause that further explains the statement.

Working women often find themselves with a double workload: They have an income-producing job and the housework.

3. After the salutation of a business letter.

Dear Sir: Gentlemen: Dear Ms. Williams:

4. To separate hours from minutes, parts of a citation, or parts of a book's title.

6:30 A.M.   Genesis 1:15   *Germany: A Modern History*

A comma is used—
1. To separate long coordinate clauses of a compound sentence.

She could go to college now, but she would rather wait a year.

2. Between words, phrases, or clauses in a series.

Jane carried her coat, hat, and gloves.
I washed the dishes, Joe dried them, and Sam put them away.

3. To set off phrases and dependent clauses preceding the main clause of a sentence.

By taking the tollway, we saved fifteen minutes.
Although the children were tired, they continued playing.

4. To set off phrases, clauses, or appositives that are not essential to the meaning of the sentence.

The nurses, kind as they were, couldn't replace Mother.
Mr. Garcia, the office manager, is well-organized.

5. To set off coordinate phrases modifying the same noun.

Her hair is as long as, but darker than, mine is.

6. Between parts of a sentence suggesting contrast or comparison.

The more time you take now, the less you'll have later.

7. To indicate the omission of one or more words.

The eggs were runny; the bacon, greasy; and the toast, burnt.

8. To separate identical or similar words in a sentence.

Walk in, in groups of three.

9. To separate words that might be mistakenly joined when reading a sentence.

Soon after, the bridge was closed for repairs.

10. To set off words that introduce a sentence *(first, second, yes, no, oh)*; and to set off words that suggest a break in thought *(however, namely, of course)*.

No, I can't do that.   First, write down your name.
The car broke down, of course, before I got to work.

11. To set off the name of a person spoken to.

Kevin, your bicycle is across the street.
Your bicycle, Kevin, is across the street.

12. To set off a short quotation from the rest of the sentence.

"I'll order the drapes today," Mother said.
"I wish," John mused, "that this lecture would end."

13. After the greeting of an informal letter and after the complimentary close of any letter.

Dear Mom and Dad,   With love,   Sincerely yours,

14. Before any title or its abbreviation that follows a person's name.

J. E. Lopez, M.D.   Janet Brown, Dean of Students

15. To separate the parts of a date, an address, or a geographic location.

May 31, 1969   Christmas Day, 1976
We once lived at 5615 Martin Drive, Milwaukee, Wisconsin.
Disneyland is in Anaheim, California.

16. To set off groups of digits in large numbers.

6,780   42,536   103,789,450

17. To separate unrelated numbers in a sentence.

In 1979, 37,000 doctoral degrees were granted.

The semicolon is used—

1. Between parts of a compound sentence when they are not joined by the conjunctions *and, but, for, nor,* or *or.*

I want to finish the report now; I'll go to lunch later.

2. To separate independent clauses when the clauses are long or when the clauses already contain commas.

Because the visibility was good, we planned to visit the observation floor of the Sears Tower; but since the elevators were not working, we toured the lobby.

3. After each clause in a series of three or more clauses.

Lightning flashed; thunder roared; and rain poured down.

If the clauses in the series are short, you may use either semicolons or commas. Your choice depends on how much you want to separate the clauses;

semicolons create a greater pause than do commas. If the clauses are long, it is usually better to use semicolons.

4. Before words like *hence, however, nevertheless, therefore,* and *thus* when they connect two independent clauses.

Today is a holiday; *therefore,* the mail will not be delivered.

5. To separate items in a list when commas are used within the items.

Attending the council meeting were Mr. Sloan, the grocer; Mrs. Bates, the banker; and Mr. Green, the florist.

6. Before explanatory expressions such as *for example, for instance, that is,* and *namely* when the break in thought is greater than that suggested by a comma.

People prefer to own a home for several reasons; *namely,* the privacy of a back-yard, the storage space of a basement or an attic, and the spacious room sizes.

The dash is used—

1. To indicate a sudden change or break in thought.

The best way to finish that—but no, you don't want my opinion.

2. To suggest halting or hesitant speech.

"I—er—ah—can't seem to find it," she mumbled.

3. Before a repeated word or expression.

He was *tired—tired* of running away from himself.

4. To emphasize or define a part of a sentence.

Marge Smith—that well-organized woman in the office—was promoted to assistant manager.

5. Before a summarizing statement introduced by *all, this,* or similar words.

Fame, fortune, and position—*these* are the rewards for hard work.

To indicate a dash, use one line (—) when writing by hand; when typing, two hyphens (--) are used for a dash.

The apostrophe is used—
1. To form the possessive of a noun.

Singular possessive	**Plural possessive**
the tree's leaves	the boys' bicycles
Mary's hat	the Johnsons' car
Charles's book	Tom and Bob's mother

2. To show omission of one or more letters, words, or numbers.

    didn't (did not)   '79 (1979)
    one o'clock (one of the clock)

3. To show plurals of numbers, letters, and words discussed as words.

    two *4*'s   some *B*'s   too many *and*'s

The hyphen is used—
1. When spelling out compound numbers between 21 and 99.

    twenty-three   sixty-one   twenty-ninth

2. When writing out fractions used as modifiers, but *not* when fractions are used as nouns.

  two-thirds majority
  but: Two thirds were counted present.

3. To avoid confusion of words that are spelled alike.

  re-cover the sofa, *but* recover from the loss
  re-lay a carpet, *but* a relay race

4. In some words, to avoid the awkward joining of letters.

    semi-invalid   anti-intellectual
    but cooperate

5. After a prefix when the root word begins with a capital letter.

>   pre-Columbian   anti-American   mid-Victorian

6. After the prefixes *all-, ex-, quasi-,* and *self-* (in most cases).

>   all-inclusive   ex-husband   quasi-legal   self-help

7. Between parts of a compound adjective when it appears before the word it modifies.

>   up-to-date news   hard-working man   well-known person
>   *But:* She is well known.   It is up to date.

8. Between parts of some compound nouns.

>   father-in-law   stay-at-home   great-grandmother
>   *But:* coat of arms   man in white

9. To divide a word at the end of a line.
   You may divide a word only between syllables—but *not* between all syllables in all words. There are some places where you should not divide a word, even where there is a syllable break. Here are some general guidelines for deciding where you should or should not divide words at the end of lines.

a. Place the hyphen at the end of the line, not at the beginning of the next line.

The bill passed through Congress, but the President vetoed it.

b. Do *not* divide words of one syllable, numbers expressed in figures, contractions, or abbreviations.

>   thought   width   give   prayer (*not* pray-er)
>   3,416,521 (*not* 3,416-521)
>   shouldn't (*not* should-n't)
>   UNICEF (*not* UNI-CEF)

c. Do *not* divide a word if either part of the hyphenation is a word by itself and the hyphenation could cause confusion.

>   piety (*not* pie-ty)   tartan (*not* tar-tan)

d. Divide the word as it is pronounced. But do not divide one-letter syllables or unpronounced *ed* from the rest of the word.

amend-ment (*not* a-mendment)
at-tached (*not* attach-ed)

e. Divide a word after a prefix or before a suffix. But do not carry over a two-letter suffix to the next line.

trans-portation *or* transporta-tion (*not* transpor-tation)
mostly (*not* most-ly)

f. Divide compound words between their main parts. And divide hyphenated compounds at the hyphen.

home-coming (*not* homecom-ing)
self-respect (*not* self-re-spect)

g. Divide between double consonants. But divide after double consonants if the root word ends in the double consonant.

bab-ble   run-ning   mis-sion
pull-ing   miss-ing

Be aware that there are some exceptions to some of the rules for hyphenating prefixes and compound words. Check your dictionary whenever you are unsure about hyphenating words—whether dividing a word at the end of a line, adding a prefix, or using a compound word.

Quotation marks are used—

1. To enclose all parts of a direct quotation.

"I think you should condense this," said the editor, "because we're running out of space."

2. To enclose quoted words or phrases within a sentence.

My father always told me to "get a good night's sleep and eat a hearty breakfast."

Enclose a quotation within a quotation in single quotation marks.

"When I asked my father for advice, he said, 'Get a good night's sleep and eat a hearty breakfast,' " Jane explained.

3. To enclose the titles of short works of music and poetry.

"The Yellow Rose of Texas"
"O Captain! My Captain!"

4. Around the titles of lectures, sermons, pamphlets, chapters of a book, and magazine articles.

"The Way of the Just" in *The Self-Made Man in America* deals with social responsibility.

5. To enclose a word or phrase explained or defined by the rest of the sentence, a technical term in nontechnical writing, and slang, irony, or well-known expressions.

To "blue-pencil" an article is to edit it.
The "pagination" in this book is out of order.
The "joy of motherhood" is not found in doing diapers.

6. Before the beginning of each stanza of a quoted poem and after the last stanza.

7. Before each paragraph of continuous quoted material and after the last paragraph. They are not used at the end of intermediate paragraphs. Often quotation marks are not used with indented, single-spaced quotes set off from the text.

8. Commas and periods are placed *inside* closing quotation marks.

"I will go now," she said, "and be back in an hour."

9. Semicolons and colons are placed *outside* closing quotation marks.

She said, "I'll go to the store"; but then she stayed home.
"To be or not to be": this is one of Shakespeare's most famous lines.

10. Question marks and exclamation points are placed *inside* the closing quotation marks if they belong to the quotation.

"What book are you reading?" he asked.
"Go now!" she ordered.

But if they are *not* part of the quotation, question marks and exclamation points go *outside* the quotation marks.

Did they sing "America the Beautiful"?
I was shocked when she said, "I've been fired"!

Parentheses are used—
1. To enclose explanatory material in a sentence when this material has no essential connection with the rest of the sentence.

George Washington (1732–1799) was our first President.

2. To enclose sources of information within a sentence.

Cain was jealous of his brother Abel and killed him (Genesis 4:5–8).

3. Around numbers or letters that indicate subdivisions of a sentence.

There are three wedding promises: (1) to love, (2) to honor, and (3) to cherish.

4. Around figures which repeat a number.

I wrote the check for twenty-one dollars and five cents ($21.05).

Brackets are used—
1. To enclose parenthetical matter within parentheses.

Shakespeare's most difficult tragedy (*Hamlet* [about 1600]) has been performed numerous times.

2. To correct a mistake in a direct quote.

"The chocolate mous[s]e was delicious," wrote the gourmet.

3. To indicate your own explanations or comments within direct quotations.

Kathy said, "When I get older [about six years old], I'm going to buy a dog."

4. To indicate stage and acting directions in plays.

MARY [seated, with face in her hands] I am so depressed!

Ellipses are used—

With direct quotations to indicate that a word or words have been omitted. Use three spaced dots to indicate that words have been omitted at the beginning or within the quotation.

> The plants were healthy because Roger ". . . took care of them devotedly."
> "The gardener . . . took care of them devotedly."

(Both these quotes omit words from the complete quote "The gardener loved the plants and shrubs and took care of them devotedly.")

To indicate words omitted at the end of a sentence, use four spaced dots (the first dot is the period).

> "The gardener loved the plants and shrubs. . . ."

The virgule (slant line or slash) is used—

1. Between two words to indicate that the meaning of either word could apply.

> My son and/or my daughter will be home.

2. As a dividing line in dates, fractions, and abbreviations.

> 5/29/68   5/8   c/o (in care of)

3. With a run-in passage of poetry to indicate where one line ends and another begins.

> "All the world's a stage,/ And all the men and women merely players./ They have their exits and their entrances;/ And one man in his time plays many parts,/ His acts being seven ages."

Italics or underlining is used—

1. For the titles of books, plays, long poems, magazines, and newspapers.

> *Gone with the Wind*   *Hamlet*   *Paradise Lost*
> *Newsweek*   *The Tuscaloosa News*

2. For titles of paintings and other works of art.

> *The Blue Boy*   *Venus de Milo*

3. For names of specific ships, planes, trains, and satellites.

Titanic   *Spirit of St. Louis*   *Orient Express*   *Sputnik*

4. For any foreign word that is not commonly used in English. These words have labels (such as *Latin, French,* or *Italian*) in the dictionary.

Jimmy was an *enfant terrible*.
The commencement speaker went on *ad infinitum*.

5. For any words, letters, or numbers considered as words.

A, an, and *the* are articles.
Cross your *t*'s and dot your *i*'s.
The *7*'s in multiplication were hard, but the *10*'s were easy.

Remember that these words appear in italics when set in type (as in books or magazines); they are underlined when writing by hand or typing.

Review exercise

Rewrite the following sentences, adding all necessary punctuation. Underline all words that should be in italics.

Example: Its only 615 AM said Jean May I sleep a little longer Mother
Answer: "It's only 6:15 A.M.," said Jean. "May I sleep a little longer, Mother?"

1. Dr Emma Abram my best friends mother has occupied an office on Harlem Blvd in Rockford Illinois for twenty five years
2. Land sakes exclaimed Aunt Molly Arent those the largest sweet potatoes youve ever seen
3. Before going to bed Dan packed his book bag laid out his clothes and read two chapters in Mark Twains book The Adventures of Tom Sawyer
4. We will need to purchase some things before beginning this once in a lifetime trip a first aid kit a waterproof lantern and some good hiking boots
5. Ralph Ortez PhD has been researching the fatal voyage of the Titanic which occurred in April 1912
6. Dear Sir Enclosed is a check in the amount of five dollars $5.00 to cover the cost of ten 10 copies of the pamphlet Teaching Your Dog New Tricks Sincerely David R Olson

7. Driving along the highway we saw plush green fields quaint farm houses and peacefully grazing animals however after crossing the bridge nothing but gaudy billboards met our eyes
8. First we will visit Great grandmother Dieball in the hospital and then of course we will stop for lunch

Answer key

Page 140

1. Dr. Emma Abram, my best friend's mother, has occupied an office on Harlem Blvd. in Rockford, Illinois for twenty-five years.
2. "Land sakes!" exclaimed Aunt Molly. "Aren't those the largest sweet potatoes you've ever seen?"
3. Before going to bed, Dan packed his book bag, laid out his clothes, and read two chapters in Mark Twain's book *The Adventures of Tom Sawyer.*
4. We will need to purchase some things before beginning this once-in-a-lifetime trip: a first aid kit, a waterproof lantern, and some good hiking boots.
5. Ralph Ortez, Ph.D., has been researching the fatal voyage of the *Titanic* which occurred in April, 1912.
6. Dear Sir: Enclosed is a check in the amount of five dollars ($5.00) to cover the cost of ten (10) copies of the pamphlet "Teaching Your Dog New Tricks." Sincerely, David R. Olson
7. Driving along the highway, we saw plush green fields, quaint farm houses, and peacefully grazing animals; however, after crossing the bridge, nothing but gaudy billboards met our eyes.
8. First, we will visit Great-grandmother Dieball in the hospital, and then, of course, we will stop for lunch.

Bending the rules

English grammar and usage rules provide guidelines for clear communication. No language can exist without rules. Just try to imagine a language where "anything goes"—where there are no patterns of sentence structure, no set ways to form descriptions or make comparisons, no methods of establishing time frames for action, no principles for talking about people, places, or things. Impossible, isn't it? Every language must have rules, or people would not be able to understand one another.

In every age, grammarians, teachers, and others concerned with the structure and use of language have codified and explained the rules of English grammar and usage. But those rules do not remain completely unchanged from age to age. The English of a hundred years ago (or even of last year) is not exactly the same as the English of today. Just as we may look back at a line from Chaucer or Shakespeare and find the language quaint or old-fashioned, future generations will surely find "oddities" in the language we use today.

It is not only the passage of time that affects what is considered "right" and "wrong" in English. In any given period, different ways of expressing the same thought may be considered correct. Today, for instance, neither of the following two sentences would raise many eyebrows:

"Is that the man about whom you were talking?"
"Is that the man you were talking about?"

Most English speakers would say that both sentences express the same question clearly and correctly. But despite the fact that the two sentences clearly communicate the same meaning, there is little question that they have different tones: the first sentence is formal, the second, informal. The first sentence follows all strict grammatical rules; the second breaks the rule against ending sentences with prepositions.

What, then, is correct usage? What is incorrect? When the question is posed this way, definite answers may be hard to come by. Instead of asking if a particular usage is right or wrong, it is better to ask: When is a particular usage or rule appropriate? When is it inappropriate? The answers will depend on the situation rather than on any hard-and-fast rules. Some considerations are: Who will be reading or hearing what you have to communicate? Is the situation formal or informal? What is the purpose of your communication?

Different audiences have different expectations and call for different degrees of formality. An English teacher, for instance, may expect—and even require—that you follow every grammar rule to the letter. You may give a speech on graduation night or submit an application to a college or technical school or enter a report on a scientific experiment for first-prize consideration at a local science fair. In these kinds of situations, the people reading or hearing what you have to say will probably expect you to follow grammar and usage rules strictly to indicate your overall knowledge. This does not mean, however, that they expect you to be stuffy or boring. It is entirely possible to follow grammar and usage rules and still communicate vividly.

However, formal expression is not always appropriate. Highly formal language used in a highly informal situation may give your readers or listeners the impression that you feel superior to them. Sometimes, writing that is close to normal speech patterns communicates best, and in those cases you will choose to bend the rules of formal grammar and usage.

But even when you bend the rules, it is important to consider your readers' and listeners' expectations. For instance, there may be a great difference between the language in a letter you write to your Great Aunt Harriet and a letter you send to your friend Judy. These letters are both examples of informal writing, but they will differ because of your knowledge of the intended reader. Your Great Aunt Harriet may not care to read slang expressions that she may or may not understand. Judy, on the other hand, might feel you were being stiff and unfriendly if you did not express yourself as you do when you are talking to her in person. You may bend the formal rules in both letters, but you may bend them in different ways.

> Dear Aunt Harriet,
>
> Thank you so much for my beautiful birthday present. It's my first cashmere sweater! I love it, and it matches my tan skirt and my plaid skirt. Three people have already asked to borrow it.
>
> Love,
> Zelda

> Dear Judi,
>   You'll never guess what my aunt sent me. A cashmere sweater! Couldn't you just die! I wish I could wear it everyday. It's so cool. Annie Biggs turned green.
>   Write soon,
>   Zelda

Aside from the rule bending that occurs naturally in informal communication, rule bending is also a device used intentionally in various kinds of creative writing such as poetry, drama, and advertising.

For instance, writers who wish to create their own individual styles sometimes ignore certain rules completely. Newspaper columnist Don Marquis claimed that his column was written by a cockroach who could not operate the shift key on the typewriter. Thus, his entire work, compiled as *archy and mehitabel,* was written with no capital letters. The poet e.e. cummings disregarded many rules of grammar and punctuation in his search for a fresh and spontaneous approach. He made up words, ran words and sentences together, and rarely used capital letters. That is why he always spelled his name e.e. cummings.

Rule bendings are common tools of authors seeking to be original or to attract attention. Writers have a problem that speakers do not. Writers cannot whisper or shout. They cannot gesture or use body movement to catch their readers' attention. Writers must use the tools of writing to make the reader sit up and take notice. And, sometimes, the best way to attract the reader is to present material in a strikingly different way.

Advertising is an example of a kind of writing where little attention is paid to rules. For example, standard rules of capitalization are often abandoned. Whole sentences may appear in capital letters. This is one way that a writer can shout.

FREE!
PRIZES! TRAVEL! MONEY! ONE DAY ONLY!

Some advertising is designed to whisper. But since writers want the whisper to get our attention, they bend some rules.

preferred customer only...
conroy studio invites...
the selby gallery announces...

Advertising writers also frequently make use of sentence fragments, those nonsentences that students are warned to avoid. When every word counts (and costs) in an advertisement, the writer may "economize" by including only the essentials:

A real opportunity! Unbelievable savings! The chance of a lifetime!

Even if you are not an advertising writer, a dramatist, a novelist, or a poet, you will frequently bend the rules in response to the audience, the situation, and the tone you wish to communicate. Following are examples and explanations of some of the most commonly bent rules.

Rule 1. Do not end a sentence with a preposition.

This rule is often quoted but, except in examinations and highly formal usage, it is rarely followed. Some sentences sound fine when they are composed to follow the rules:

Mr. Johnson is the county official to whom we sent our complaint.
To what do you owe your great success?

Other sentences, however, sound unnecessarily stiff and unnatural when they follow the rule:

Of what could the coach be thinking?
That is the fence over which we climbed.

Your best guideline for breaking this rule is to listen to how the sentence sounds. Unless a teacher insists that you never end a sentence with a prepo-

145

sition, use your judgment and opt for the version of the sentence that seems most natural. Remember Winston Churchill's complaint against rigidly following the rule forbidding end prepositions. "That," he snorted, "is the kind of nonsense up with which I will not put!"

Rule 2. Do not split infinitives.

A split infinitive occurs when an adverb comes between "to" and the stem of a verb.

Jack and Walter decided to simply stay home.
(The infinitive "to stay" is split)

The recipe says to thoroughly mix the batter.
(The infinitive "to mix" is split)

In the past, there was a hard-and-fast rule against splitting infinitives and some teachers still insist on this rule. Most sentences can be written to avoid split infinitives. For example, the two sentences shown above can also be written as follows:

Jack and Walter decided simply to stay home.
The recipe says to mix the batter thoroughly.

However, it is now increasingly common to avoid split infinitives only when they create an awkward sentence, as in the following example:

Awkward: She wanted to quickly paint the kitchen.
Better: She wanted to paint the kitchen quickly.

In most other situations, it is now considered acceptable to split infinitives.

Jack seems to gladly take on projects nobody else wants to handle.

In some cases, it may actually be preferable to split infinitives rather than to create awkward or unclear sentences.

Awkward: I was unable fully to appreciate the program.
Better: I was unable to fully appreciate the program.

Unclear: To chew gum constantly ruins your image.
(does *constantly* modify *chew* or *ruin*?)

Better: To constantly chew gum ruins your image.

Rule 3. Use *who* in the nominative case, *whom* in the objective case.

While this rule is still followed in formal speech and writing, the use of the relative pronoun *whom* is growing less and less common when the word appears at the beginning of a sentence or a clause.

Whom will you invite to the party? (formal)
Who will you invite to the party? (informal)
That is the man *whom* my father wanted to meet. (formal)
That is the man *who* my father wanted to meet. (informal)

Whom is still frequently used even in informal speech when it directly follows a preposition

Is that the girl to whom you wrote a note?
Mr. Johnson is the grocer for whom I work.

Note, however, that such sentences can avoid the *who/whom* question by a slight slight rewrite that bends the rule against ending sentences with prepositions. Then the relative pronoun can be dropped entirely.

Is that the girl you wrote the note to?
Mr. Davis is the grocer I work for.

Rule 4. Use "It's I"; not "It's me."

Formal rules hold that the predicate nominative always takes the nominative case and that "It's I" is therefore the only correct construction.

Most grammarians, however, believe that it is perfectly acceptable to say "It's me." The more formal construction is still advisable when the subject and verb are not contracted: "It is I."

Alert: It is not considered proper to use the objective case for third person pronouns.

Incorrect: "It's him"; "It's her"; "It's them"
Correct: "It's he"; "It's she"; "It's they"

Rule 5. Use the subjunctive for statements that are doubtful, conditional, unreal, or improbable.

In formal usage, the subjunctive is still used for such statements:

If I *were* five years younger, I would sign up for that roller skating class.
If Sally *were* able to sew, she would help make the costumes for the play.

In informal usage, the indicative mood is frequently used in place of the subjunctive.

If I *was* five years younger, I would sign up for that roller skating class.
If Sally *was* able to sew, she would help you with the costumes for the play.

Rule 6. In the future tense, use *shall* for the first person and *will* for the second and third person conjugations. To show special determination, use *will* for the first person and *shall* for the second and third person.

According to formal grammar rules, "I *shall* go" means "I plan to go," and "I *will* go" means "I am determined to go and nothing will change my plans." Likewise, "you *will* go," "he or she *will* go," and "they *will* go" indicates intention to go, while "you *shall* go," "he or she *shall* go," and "they *shall* go" indicates special determination.

In informal use, all these distinctions have been fading. First, second, and third person all use the auxiliary *will* in the future tense, and special determination is seldom indicated. When it is, *shall* is used to indicate determination for all three persons.

Rule 7. Do not begin sentences with conjunctions.

Formal grammar rules state that sentences should not start with coordinating conjunctions. However, many sentences can be made to communicate extra force and interest when they bend this rule, as in the following examples:

Sandra thought she knew everything there was to know about her friend Jackie. But she was wrong.
Ralph predicted that everyone would show up just when the hardest jobs were already finished. And that's exactly what happened.

Rule 8. Do not use sentence fragments.

A sentence fragment is a group of words that do not contain both a subject and a predicate. Although it is generally wise to follow the rule forbidding sentence fragments, fragments can sometimes be used effectively for special impact.

> Johnny thinks Marsha doesn't like him. Not so!
> Will the Allentown Alligators beat the Bordentown Bears tonight?
> Hard to say.

Review exercise

Some of the sentences below follow formal grammar rules, while others bend the rules. First, identify each sentence as a rule follower or rule bender, and tell what rule is being followed or bent. Next, rewrite each sentence so that the rule benders become rule followers, and vice versa.

Example: I shall see you tomorrow morning.
Answer: *Rule follower*—Use shall for first person future tense.
Rule bender—I will see you tomorrow morning.

1. That is an idea with which I agree.
2. Our driving teacher told us to carefully check for oncoming traffic.
3. For whom did you bake that cake?
4. If it was up to me, I'd choose the red sweater over the blue one.
5. Who's that knocking on the door? It's I.
6. Alice swore she would never speak to Richard again. Later, however, she relented.
7. I could not see the area we were flying over.
8. Whom do you like best?
9. I wish George were able to come to the dance.
10. My younger brother Frank wants me to lend him my favorite cap. There is not a chance that I will do so.

Answer key

1. *Rule follower*—Do not end a sentence with a preposition.
   Rule bender—That is an idea I agree with.
2. *Rule bender*—Do not split infinitives.
   Rule follower—Our driving teacher told us to check carefully for oncoming traffic.
3. *Rule follower*—Use whom for the objective case; do not end a sentence with a preposition.
   Rule bender—Who did you bake that cake for?
4. *Rule bender*—Use the subjunctive for statements that are unreal or improbable.
   Rule follower—If it were up to me, I'd choose the red sweater over the blue one.
5. *Rule follower*—Use "It's I"; not "It's me."
   Rule bender—Who's that knocking at the door? It's me.
6. *Rule follower*—Do not begin sentences with conjunctions.
   Rule bender—Alice swore she would never speak to Richard again. But later she relented.
7. *Rule bender*—Do not end a sentence with a preposition.
   Rule follower—I could not see the area over which we were flying.
8. *Rule follower*—Use *whom* in the objective case.
   Rule bender—Who do you like best?
9. *Rule follower*—Use the subjunctive for statements that are unreal or improbable.
   Rule bender—I wish George was able to come to the dance.
10. *Rule follower*—Do not use sentence fragments.
    Rule bender—My younger brother Frank wants me to lend him my favorite cap. Not a chance!

Writing well

People write for many reasons. They write to express their feelings and to share their thoughts. They write to tell about what they know and to persuade others to agree with what they believe. They write to communicate facts and to create imaginary worlds.

Sometimes people write because they wish to write. They may keep a diary or journal, compose poems or editorials, or write short stories or novels. Other times, people write because they are required to write. If they are students, their teachers may give written exams and assign essays or term papers. If they are already out of school and working at jobs, they may need to write business letters or prepare weekly memorandums or monthly reports.

Whatever the reasons or the occasions for writing, the results may be good writing or bad. Of course, "good" and "bad" are relative terms. Every individual has different tastes, and your favorite novelist may leave your best friend absolutely cold, while the columnist your friend favors may be the writer whose essays you hate to read. But, despite these differences in taste, there are certain general standards that can be applied to just about any kind of writing. Teachers apply them to the writing of their students; employers apply them to the writing of their employees; and (perhaps most important!) careful writers apply them to their own compositions even before they submit them to the judgment of others.

This chapter will explain some of the standards by which writing is usually judged. It will outline the factors you should take into consideration before you set pen to paper and give you some pointers about writing clear and effective sentences and paragraphs. Finally, it will alert you to some of the pitfalls and problems you should avoid if you wish to make your compositions as interesting, convincing, and well-written as possible.

Preparing to write

Before you begin the actual process of composing, there are two important questions you should ask yourself.

The first one is: What do I know about the subject I plan to write about? There are many subjects about which you are an expert simply because you are who you are. Your thoughts, your feelings, your experiences, your friends, your family—nobody knows more about these topics than you do. It is possible to write fascinating essays, poems, short stories, and autobiographical sketches using this personal information as a basis.

Other subjects will require some degree of study if your writing is to prove interesting to others. For instance, your history teacher may assign an essay on shuttle diplomacy, or your biology teacher may ask you to submit a report on photosynthesis in plants. In such cases—even if you are a history buff or the president of your science club—you will most likely need to do some additional research before you begin your composition.

The second question you should ask yourself is: Who will be reading what I write? Different reading audiences will require that you treat your subject with different emphases and in different tones. Suppose, for instance, that you visited the Rocky Mountains last summer and have decided to write an essay about your trip. If the essay will be published as an article in your Scout troop's newsletter, you will probably wish to emphasize the adventures you had while camping: how you managed to pitch your tent in the midst of a raging rainstorm, how you got that blazing fire going in spite of high winds, and so forth. If the essay will be submitted to your science teacher, you will want to discuss what you learned on the trip: facts about the wildlife in the region, how you learned to identify poisonous and nonpoisonous fruits and berries, and other similar topics.

The tone of your writing will also vary with the reading audience. For the newsletter article, your audience would probably respond best to an informal essay chock full of personal anecdotes that recapture the excitement of the trip. For the science report, your teacher would probably expect a more formal approach, complete with detailed explanations and descriptions of what you saw and learned.

Remember: The purpose of writing is to hold the attention of your readers. Whenever you write, bear in mind the expectations and the interests of the people for whom you write.

Getting down to basics: grammar and punctuation

No matter what your topic or who your readers may be, it is important to follow the rules of grammar and punctuation.

This is important for two reasons. First, it helps you communicate your thoughts and feelings more clearly. Second, it lets your readers know that you care about writing accurately and well.

Grammar and punctuation rules are not cast in concrete and can be bent from time to time for special effect or to create a particular tone (see Bending the rules). But rule-bending is only effective when it is clear that you know the rules and have bent them *for a reason*. Compositions that are full of grammar and punctuation errors create an overall impression of sloppiness and carelessness and create a barrier between the writer and the reader. After all, if you have not taken enough care and time to follow the basic rules of writing well, how can your readers feel confident that you are really serious about wanting to communicate your thoughts, feelings, and ideas? And if your readers suspect that you have not taken your composition seriously, they may wonder why they should do so.

It's very simple: Following the rules of grammar and punctuation will help you get your message across.

Sentences: small building blocks

If you think about your composition as a building, then you will see that sentences are small building blocks in the structure as a whole. And just as a building depends on the quality of its basic materials, so does your composition depend on the quality and grace of its sentences.

Well-crafted sentences express ideas clearly. People sometimes make the mistake of thinking that long, complicated sentences are always more effective or more interesting than shorter ones. But that is not so. Do not try to express too many ideas in one sentence, or you may end up expressing none of them well.

Clarity is far more important than length. It is often more effective to write several shorter sentences than one long complicated one, as the following example shows:

Complicated: Everyone in our class was happy that the weather had turned fine because that meant that we would be able to go on our field trip after all.

Better and less complicated: Everyone in our class was happy that the weather had turned fine. Now we would be able to go on our field trip after all!

Variety of sentence structure is just as important as clarity. Too many similar sentences strung side by side will sound dull, while varied sentences will catch the reader's interest and make him or her eager to read on.

There are many ways to vary your sentences. You may vary them by length, sometimes using short sentences and sometimes longer ones. You may vary them by structure, using simple, compound, complex, and compound-complex sentences as appropriate (see pages 113–114). You may vary them by function, using declarative, interrogative, imperative, and exclamatory sentences (see pages 115–116). And you may vary them by the way in which you present ideas, using loose, periodic, and balanced sentences (see pages 116–117). The following passages illustrate how sentence variety can spice up writing.

Unvaried Sentences:
The little dog was lost. He trotted down the streets in search of his master, Billy. He rushed through the alleyways looking for a clue. Nothing looked familiar. He was about to give up. Suddenly he saw a white fence. It surrounded a yard with a doghouse. He recognized his home. He pushed his nose against the fence gate and it opened. He entered his doghouse and curled up inside. He was glad to be back where he belonged.

Varied Sentences:
The little dog was lost. Trotting down the streets, he searched for his master, Billy. Nothing looked familiar as he rushed through the alleyways looking for a clue. The pup was about to give up. Suddenly, he saw a white fence surrounding a yard with a doghouse. There was his home! He pushed his nose against the fence gate and it opened. As he entered his doghouse and curled up inside, he felt how good it was to be back where he belonged.

To show how sentences can be varied in many ways, let's take a look at one basic sentence and some of its possible variations.

Basic sentence: We laid out our picnic lunch on a checkered cloth when we reached the top of the hill.

Variations: When we reached the top of the hill, we laid out our picnic lunch on a checkered cloth.

We reached the top of the hill and laid out our picnic lunch on a checkered cloth.

The picnic lunch was laid out on a checkered cloth when we reached the top of the hill.

Reaching the top of the hill, we laid out our picnic lunch on a checkered cloth.

On a checkered cloth we laid out our picnic lunch when we reached the top of the hill.

Having reached the top of the hill, we laid out our picnic lunch on a checkered cloth.

Review Exercises

A. Rewrite the following sentence at least five different ways in order to create variety:

Example: The explorers crawled into the cave to search for interesting icicle formations.

Answer: Searching for interesting icicle formations, the explorers crawled into the cave.

B. Rewrite the following paragraph using a variety of sentence formations.

I will never forget how nervous I was when I arranged a surprise party for my brother Robert. I bought many kinds of food. I bought soft drinks, cookies, chips, dips, and three different cake mixes at the store. Then I rushed home to bake the cakes and arrange all the other food on Mother's best trays. One of the cakes fell. I had to run back to the store and buy another mix and bake another cake. Then I got busy working on the decorations. I strung crepe paper streamers all across the basement rec room. I also made two big signs to hang over the doorways. One said "Happy Birthday, Robert." The other simply said "Surprise!" Finally I changed into my best dress. I was all ready by the time the guests arrived. The party was a success. I don't know who was more surprised, Robert or I!

Paragraphs

Paragraphs are groups of sentences that form a unit. The start of each new paragraph is signaled by indenting the first word of the paragraph, so that a small space appears in the left-hand margin of the page.

Why are compositions divided into paragraphs? For one thing, paragraphing makes writing easier to read. Just imagine trying to read a book that had no paragraph divisions! Very soon, your eyes would get tired and start to roam all about the page.

But paragraphing does more than make it easier for the reader to follow the words on a page. Even more important, effective paragraphing helps the reader understand the author's message by providing him with signposts along the way. A paragraph indicates that the writer has finished one thought and has shifted to another. Sometimes that shift in thought will be very obvious, while other times it will be more subtle.

Good paragraphs are unified around a central idea, thought, or feeling, called the *topic* of the paragraph. Every sentence in the paragraph should be related to this main topic.

Topic Sentences

Many times, paragraphs contain a *topic sentence* that states the topic of the paragraph. Often, the topic sentence is the first sentence in a paragraph. This is true in the paragraph that follows:

Every member of our family wanted to do something different for our summer vacation. Dad wanted to go up to Willow Lake to catch fish. Marge dreamed of hiking in the mountains. Mother had her heart set on visiting a tropical island, while Bill just wanted to stay home and practice with his musical group, the Sunbeams.

Each sentence in the paragraph above adds information about the idea expressed in the first sentence, which is the topic sentence.

Sometimes, topic sentences appear at the very end of a paragraph where they sum up or underline the main idea of the paragraph. This is true of the following paragraph:

The day was sultry, with a deep and ominous silence that intensified as grey clouds covered the sky. At first the air was calm, the leaves of the trees standing almost motionless. As the day progressed, the wind began to rise. Gentle breezes became strong gusts. At last the gusts became a furious onslaught, bringing with it torrential rains. The hurricane had arrived.

In the paragraph above, every sentence but the last presents details that create a dramatic picture of events as they occurred. The final sentence shows what all those events were leading up to. It is the topic sentence of the paragraph.

Occasionally a paragraph will not have a topic sentence. But that does not mean that the paragraph does not have one central thought, feeling, or idea around which all the sentences hover. It simply means that the topic is implied, but never stated outright, as in the following example:

The sea sparkled in the distance, beckoning us to plunge into its cool blue freshness. As we ran toward the beach, we felt the hot sand crunch between our toes, and we stopped occasionally when a weed or a bramble threatened to trip us. But we never stopped long, for the heat of the sun and the pleasant anticipation of a midday splash made us eager to reach the water's edge. The closer we came, the more the soft sea breezes tantalized us, and the faster we ran.

In the paragraph above, there is no topic sentence, yet the entire paragraph is unified around a central topic: the recollection of a run toward the sea on a warm summer day.

A paragraph is not well-written simply because it has a topic sentence. If all the other sentences in the paragraph do not relate to the topic sentence, then the paragraph as a whole will lack unity and cohesiveness. Look at the two paragraphs below:

Paragraph #1:   The baseball game had reached a crucial point. A large crowd had been at the park all afternoon. The weather had been muggy. Vendors were selling hot dogs and cold drinks.

Paragraph #2:   The baseball game had reached a crucial point. It was the bottom of the ninth inning and the score was tied. Two batters were out. The third was at the plate, and the pitcher had already thrown him two strikes and three balls.

In paragraph #1, the topic sentence leads the reader to expect an explanation of *why* the game had reached a crucial point. But the reader's expectations are disappointed. Instead of following through on its promise, the paragraph proceeds to present a number of facts and details unrelated to the game itself.

In contrast, paragraph #2 follows through on its promise. All the sentences that follow the topic sentence give additional information about why the game had reached a crucial point.

Paragraph types

There are as many different paragraph types as there are writers. Every writer has a different style, a different tone, a different way of thinking, and a different way of expressing his or her ideas. These individual differences will be evident in the paragraphs each person writes.

However, it can be helpful to break paragraphs down into some general categories. That way, it is possible to learn more about how paragraphs are organized and how they express a unity of thought, idea, or feeling. We will look at four kinds of paragraphs: expository, narrative, descriptive, and argumentative.

Expository paragraphs

Exposition means explanation, and an expository paragraph is a paragraph that explains something—usually by means of examples, illustrations, details, or definitions. Following is an example of an expository paragraph:

Some people go to museums to learn about art, but I go to learn about people. In the course of my years as a gallery-hopper, I've run into just about every kind of person you could possibly imagine. There are the earnest young art students who come, sketchbooks in hand, to search out the secrets of the great masters. There are the bored vacationers who feel obligated to put in half an hour at the local Temple of Culture. There are the amateurs who stand before a painting for hours, lost in reverie. And then there are the people like me, who come to study what's in *front* of the canvas, not what's painted *on* it.

Expository paragraphs usually present one or more general statements, and then back them up with specific information. In the paragraph above, for example, the first two sentences present general statements: the writer goes to museums to learn about people, and over the years he or she has learned about many different kinds of people. The remaining sentences present specific examples of the kinds of people the writer has observed at museums.

Narrative paragraphs

Narrative paragraphs narrate, or tell about, events that happen. Narrative paragraphs are generally written in chronological order. That is, they follow the event step by step as it happens. Following is an example of a narrative paragraph:

> At 3 A.M. on the day of the space shuttle launch, the astronauts arose. After eating a hearty breakfast, they were driven out to the launch pad in a van. They emerged from the vehicle smiling broadly and giving the thumbs-up sign to indicate their excitement and their confidence in the mission. Quiet settled over the launching area as the astronauts entered the space ship and strapped themselves into their seats. The final countdown began. Then there was a giant blast, and the booster rocket rose powerfully. Observers barely had time to thrill to the take-off; the space shuttle was traveling so fast that soon it was merely a bright speck high in the sky.

You probably noticed that the narrative paragraph above has no topic sentence. The lack of a topic sentence is fairly common in narrative paragraphs since much of their unity comes from the natural relationship of the events being narrated. New narrative paragraphs often begin when a new character is introduced, when the action shifts to a different place or time, or when the narrative is interrupted for exposition or description.

Descriptive paragraphs

Descriptive paragraphs provide the reader with a picture of people, places, or things. Following is an example of a descriptive paragraph:

> The house was what is politely called a "handyman's special." The exterior was a patchwork of peeling paint that told the story of the house's many coats of color. Here was a dab of blue; there a spot of yellow; and out on the sagging back porch, where the sun beat hardest and the feet of many generations had worn down the surface, the clapboard was faded to an undistinguished grey. Inside, gouges scarred the wooden stairway treads and the ancient wallpaper peeled in strips from the cracked walls. The kitchen was enough to frighten even the most optimistic of remodelers: the cracked linoleum curled back to reveal wood ruined by some long-ago burst pipe; most of the wall tiles had fallen off; and the fawcet leaked into the rusty sink with a mournful drip.

A well-written descriptive paragraph is more than just a compilation of details. In writing a descriptive paragraph, it is important to identify the most important feature or features of your subject and then choose the details that best highlight those features. Always make sure you know just what it is that is interesting, impressive, or worthwhile about the subject. Then you will be able to share your impression with your readers.

Argumentative paragraphs

Argumentative paragraphs present an argument. That is, they are paragraphs that attempt to persuade the reader to agree with a particular idea, belief, or statement. Argumentative paragraphs are very similar to expository paragraphs in that they present general statements and details to back up those statements. But they differ from expository paragraphs in that they present statements that express a definite opinion or a point of view, rather than a simple fact. Following is an example of an argumentative paragraph:

> Older college students are revitalizing the Halls of Academe. While most people still enter college at the age of 17 or 18, many older adults are registering for Freshman English and Basic Biology at age 40, 50, or even 90! And while the younger students may have brute physical energy on their side, the elder scholars often can draw on a more impressive energy—the energy of experience and determination. After years or even decades in the workplace, older students usually know exactly what they want from a college degree. And they are willing to go to almost any length to obtain it. They will juggle job and family responsibilities to make it to class on time, and, once there, will often contribute with an enthusiasm rare in those youngsters who need merely to stroll leisurely from the dorm to the classroom.

Notice how all the details in this argumentative paragraph work to support the main opinion: that older college students are breathing new life into higher education.

Review exercises

The following exercises are self tests. Do your best writing based on the explanations of paragraph types on the previous pages. Then have someone read your work and make comments.

A. Write an expository paragraph about one of the following topics, or choose a topic of your own. Be sure to narrow your topic.

Your favorite sport	Planning a picnic
A definition of friendship	The value of a microcomputer
	Your leisure activities

B. Write a narrative paragraph about one of the following topics, or choose a topic of your own.

An unusual dream	A first-time airplane takeoff
An embarrassing moment	A funny experience in a foreign city
Your last birthday celebration	

C. Write a descriptive paragraph about one of the following topics, or choose a topic of your own.

A favorite room in your house
A musical composition
A forest scene in winter
Your favorite literary character
The view from the top of a skyscraper

D. Write an argumentative paragraph about one of the following topics, or choose a topic of your own. Be sure to narrow your topic.

The positive or negative aspects of TV viewing
Urban vs. rural living
The consequences of cigarette smoking
The value of vegetarianism
Jogging: good or bad?

Paragraph organization

As stated before, good paragraphs have cohesiveness and unity. All their parts contribute to developing the central thought, idea, or feeling.

There are many different ways of achieving cohesiveness in a paragraph. In expository paragraphs, you can move from a general statement to a series of specific facts that illustrate the statement, or you can start with the specifics and lead up to the general statement. In narrative paragraphs, you will probably follow a chronological order, telling each event as it occurs. In descriptive paragraphs, you will most likely draw a picture of your subject by using a spatial technique: describing a scene from left to right, near to far, or top to bottom. In argumentative paragraphs, you will marshall facts, details, and examples to support your opinion. You may start with the most convincing point and go to the weakest one or vice versa.

In organizing your paragraphs, it is important to develop your material so that it moves logically or smoothly from one point to another. Certain kinds of words help you make those connections within paragraphs. In expository paragraphs, words and phrases such as *thus, at the same time, similarly,* and *likewise* are often used to show the logical relationships among various points. In narrative paragraphs, time words and expressions such as *then, next, before, as soon as,* and *now* show the progression from one event to another. In descriptive paragraphs, spatial words such as *in, out, here, where, beyond,* and *above* help to create the picture you wish to describe. In argumentative paragraphs, words and phrases such as *of course, as everyone knows, contrary to popular opinion,* and *therefore* can help you argue persuasively.

Transition paragraphs

In long compositions that contain a number of separate but related sections, it will sometimes be necessary to use transition paragraphs. These paragraphs sum up what has been said before and alert the reader's attention to what will be discussed next. Following is an example of a transition paragraph:

> We have seen that the days of the early settlers were filled with toil. They faced the challenges of clearing the land, planting the crops, and building the homes that would shelter them from the frigid northern winters. But occasionally the settlers put down their hoes and their hammers for a day or two of celebration, and out of their meager resources they created holidays of great spirit and joy. Let us look now at how they celebrated one of their most joyous holidays, Thanksgiving.

The paragraph above moves the reader along from one subject to another. It tells the reader that the discussion of the settlers' work life has ended, and that now a discussion of their holidays will begin.

Logic within the composition

All writers want their works to be taken seriously. They hope that their audiences will be moved by their feelings, convinced by their arguments, and impressed by their knowledge. But writers cannot hope to be taken seriously unless their thinking is clear and their arguments are fair.

Following are some common errors in thinking and arguing that should be avoided in good writing.

False causality

There may be many different kinds of mistakes about causality. One of the most common mistakes is to confuse cause and effect. A simple example of confusing cause and effect would be to say, "Sunday is a holiday because people don't go to work then." Obviously, this statement confuses causality. It is more accurate to state, "People do not go to work on Sunday because Sunday is a holiday."

Another common mistake about causality is to assert that something is a cause without being able to provide sufficient proof. For instance, you might assert, "Sally caught a cold because she stayed up too late Friday night." Such causality would be very difficult to prove. Perhaps Sally caught the cold from her sister! Beware of making absolute statements of causality when you cannot prove for certain that they are true.

One type of causality error has a special Latin name: *post hoc ergo propter hoc* ("after this, therefore because of this"). In this kind of error, the writer assumes that because one event happened after another, the first event caused the second. An example of this kind of mistake would be to state, "It rained Saturday evening because we washed our car Saturday afternoon."

False analogy

An analogy compares one thing to another thing. A false analogy results when the comparison is not based on any real similarities between the items being compared, or when the similarities are only superficial and not related to the main point the author is trying to make. Following is an example of the first type of false analogy:

> Taking a test is just like flipping a coin. Sometimes
> you win and sometimes you lose.

This is a false analogy because there is no actual similarity between the two actions described—taking a test and flipping a coin. The author of the analogy is attempting to show that there is no point in studying because success at school is just a matter of chance. Those who have studied for tests know that the author is basing this argument on a false analogy.

Following is an example of the second type of false analogy:

> Sugar is white. Salt is white. Sugar is sweet. Therefore, salt must be sweet, too.

In this example, the author has found one significant similarity between sugar and salt: they are both white. From this similarity, the author reasons by analogy that both sugar and salt are sweet. Anyone who has accidentally poured salt over his cereal knows that this is a false analogy!

Begging the question

"Begging the question" means arguing in a circle. People who beg the question assume the truth of the assertions they are trying to prove. Following is an example of a statement that begs the question:

> My cocker spaniel Rusty should win first prize at the dog show. He is the best
> dog entered.

The argument would be much more convincing if it were written as follows:

My cocker spaniel Rusty should win first prize at the dog show. His coat is silky and shiny; he knows a lot of tricks; and he is very obedient.

Overgeneralization

Most statements that use words such as *all, no, always,* and *never* are overgeneralizations. It is rare indeed that absolute statements can be proven true. Many times, such statements turn out to be some type of definition, such as "all dogs are mammals" or "fires are always hot."

It is usually better to qualify your statements with such words as *usually, generally, most, some, often,* and so forth.

Writing essays on tests

An essay item is a test question that asks you to explain, discuss, summarize, outline, or otherwise examine a topic and assemble the information in a coherent pattern that you create. On essay tests, you often have an opportunity to express your own ideas or to reach your own conclusions about the subject being discussed. Your answers can demonstrate your understanding of the subject matter in both broad terms and detail.

There are several types of essay-test questions. These can be roughly grouped into two categories—extended-response and restricted-response items. Extended-response items are the type that allow you to organize your answers to best express your understanding of the subject. For example:

Discuss the role of the U.S. fleet in extending the political influence of the United States in Asia in the early years of the 20th century.

A restricted-response, or short, essay question puts limits on your answers. The limits might apply to length, topics that may be included, or specific numbers of items to be listed. For example:

Define *manifest destiny*. Give two examples of territorial acquisition credited to followers of this credo.

Essay types

Essay tests measure your ability to recall, organize, and blend ideas. They also demonstrate how well you can express yourself in writing—not only in supplying facts, but in interpreting and applying information.

The following examples illustrate types of extended-response questions.

A. *Making general comparisons*
—comparing things on a comprehensive basis, including many characteristics

Compare the battle tactics of the British-led troops with those of the French and Indian fighters.

B. *Cause and/or effect*
—lengthy discussion of why events happen and resulting events

What events led to the United States' entrance into World War I?

C. *Summarizing*
—bringing together the major points in an area of discussion

State the plot of *Star Wars* in about 100 words.

D. *Classification*
—explaining the reasons why things belong in a particular category

What do four of the five titles named below have in common?
"The Pasture"
"The Road Not Taken"
"Fire and Ice"
"The Bells"
"Mending Wall"

E. *Discussion*
—presenting information in essay form

Discuss the significance of the Magna Carta to modern political thought.

F. *Recognizing author's purpose*
—understanding why material is presented as it is

Why was this character introduced in a fantasy scene?

G. *Criticism*
—judgments based on knowledge

How is the Keane family's meal unbalanced?

Restricted-response items are useful in testing your understanding of specific situations. Some examples of the kinds of knowledge these items can measure follow.

A. *Giving evaluations*
—stating and justifying your opinions

Which do you think are the three most important technological advances in the field of communication since 1900? Why?

B. *Limited comparisons*
—comparing two things in only one area

Compare the naval strength of the North and South during the Civil War.

C. *Making decisions* (pro and con)
—forming a position for or against an idea

In your opinion, was it correct to lower the voting age to 18 years?

D. *Cause and/or effect*
—recognizing the causes of events and also the effects these events may have on a situation

What economic factor in 1981 was most responsible for the low volume of sales for single-family homes?

E. *Giving an exact explanation*
—detailed coverage of an operation or event

Explain one way of demonstrating capillarity.

F. *Analysis*
—an exploration of a situation

How have forest fires caused erosion in the Northwest?

G. *Recognizing relationships*
—understanding how things relate

Why should an exercise program accompany a reducting diet?

H. *Examples of rules and concepts*
—understanding the basic principles behind ideas

Give an example of the incorrect usage of a personal pronoun in a prepositional phrase and explain why it is incorrect.

I. *Applying principles*
—explaining or using rules and principles correctly

Explain the function of the tiles that are attached to the underside of the space shuttle.

J. *Outlining*
—listing main ideas and supporting details

Outline the reasons behind Japan's aggression in the 1930s and 1940s.

Answering essay questions

The most important thing to know about an essay question is what is expected in the answer. Exactly what is wanted should be clearly stated in the directions. While you are reading the directions, underline all the important words and phrases that tell you how the question should be answered and what should be included. Some of the words might be: *explain, state, summarize, outline, compare, contrast, prove,* and *illustrate.* Once you have identified these instructions, you must be careful to follow them in your answers. Here are explanations of ways to follow specific direction words.

Explain	Tell about and show how, using an illustration, if possible.
State	Briefly express ideas, but do not go into much detail or illustration.
Summarize	Bring together the main points without going into a lengthy discussion or presenting much detail.
Outline	Present the information in outline form that shows the relationship of broad topics (major heads) to specific information (details).
Compare	Show similarities and differences in given topics.
Contrast	Show the difference in given topics by discussing them side by side.

Prove   Write a discussion of arguments that favor the statement. At times it is helpful also to discuss those arguments that take the opposite point of view.

Illustrate   Give the best example you can think of. Do not define or discuss.

Remember how important it is to keep your writing focused on the specific words that tell you how to answer the essay question.

When you are sure that you understand the directions, it is time to begin your answering strategy.

1. Outline your answer or organize your ideas in a numbered list. Jot your ideas down lightly in the margin or somewhere on your paper. This helps your work to be well organized.
2. If your teacher permits, underline important names or ideas as you write. This will point out that you recognize their importance.
3. Use original illustrations as examples. Try to avoid using the same ones that were used in your classwork.
4. Do not clutter up your answer with unnecessary information.
5. Emphasize quality rather than quantity. Do not "pad" your answers unless you are adding important material.

If permitted, use scratch paper for your outline and to make notes. As you are writing, ideas may begin to come to you too fast for you to get them all down in detail. Quickly jot the main points down elsewhere so you will not forget them.

In each paragraph try to discuss only one main idea. This should be easy to do if you have made an outline. Write your main idea as the topic sentence and then finish the paragraph with details, examples, illustrations, and other information that supports the main idea.

Throughout your essay answer, use the vocabulary you have learned in the course to express yourself. Each subject has its own special terminology. Make a point of using the words that best communicate the subject matter.

When expressing opinions, give reasons for them. An opinion should be backed up by your reasons for arriving at it. Writing with examples telling why you like or dislike or agree or disagree with something is much more convincing than merely stating that yes, you agree with or like something, or no, you do not agree with or like something. Besides, your reasons are probably the most important part of your answer.

Stick to the question. If you do not know the answer, do not try to bluff by writing about something else. If you are unsure of an answer but have a hunch about it, try writing out your hunch instead of giving no answer at all. You may get some credit, which is better than getting no credit.

167

Write all the information that is needed to answer the question. Do not leave something out because you assume that the teacher is aware that you know it. Even if your teacher is aware that you know something, you should show how well you can relate it to other material.

If you are running out of time and have not finished, quickly outline answers for the rest of the items you are working on and the remaining required questions still unanswered. You may not receive full credit, but you will probably get some. It is possible that your teacher may like your outlined answers and give you full credit. Some teachers actually prefer outlines to long-winded discussions.

Leave some space at the end of your answer to each question. If something occurs to you while answering another question, then there will be room to write additional material.

You should present all your work in the best possible manner. Take pride in how your papers look. Your answers make a much better impression if they are written neatly with attention paid to correct spelling and punctuation.

When you are finished writing your answers, go back and read them again. Watch for careless errors such as skipped words or misspellings. You also may find that you have left out important information that you wanted to include.

Style stumbling blocks

Whether you are writing for school exams or essays, for your job, or for your own enjoyment, you will want to make sure that you avoid some common stumbling blocks that can mar the power of your writing. Listed below are some stumbling blocks to avoid.

Run-on sentences

A run-on sentence consists of two or more independent clauses connected only by a comma or by no punctuation at all.

> **Run-on sentence:** The tour group visited the chapel, they were interested in the stained glass window.
> **Run-on sentence:** A shipment will arrive tomorrow, it has been expected for the last ten days.
> **Run-on sentence:** The class spent $90.00 for the trophy they liked the design.

Run-on sentences can be corrected in several ways.

—Make two separate sentences:

The tour group visited the chapel.
They were interested in the stained glass window.

—Use a semicolon between the clauses:

A shipment will arrive tomorrow; it has been expected for the last ten days.

—Connect the two clauses with a conjunction:

The class paid $90.00 for the trophy because they liked the design.

Repetition of words and meanings

Sometimes it can be effective for a writer to repeat words or ideas for special emphasis.

The new department store is big. The new department store is huge.
In fact, the new department store is absolutely monumental.

Usually, however, repetition of words and meanings tends to dull the power of writing rather than enhance it. The following examples show repetitious sentences and paragraphs that have been rewritten for better effectiveness.

Repetitious: A large, big, huge ship sailed into the harbor.
Effective: A large ship sailed into the harbor.

Repetitious: The tiny, small, petite poddle sat on the woman's lap.
Effective: The tiny poodle sat on the woman's lap.

Repetitious: The clown was funny. Everyone laughed at the clown. Dimsey was the name of the character who brought so much laughter. Dimsey played tricks to make the crowd laugh. The clown did many humorous things.
Effective: A clown named Dimsey was the favorite of the crowd. His actions, his tricks, his jokes—everything combined to make Dimsey a very funny man.

Wordiness

The architect Mies van der Rohe was famous for his maxim, "less is more." The same maxim generally applies in writing. Try to avoid unnecessary words. They clutter up a sentence or a paragraph and get in the way of clear and simple expression of thoughts and ideas.

Wordy: The reason why the snow fell was because the temperature dropped.
Better: The snow fell because the temperature dropped.

Wordy: There were seven people who attended.
Better: Seven people attended.

Wordy: The patient was near a state of shock
Better: The patient was near shock.

Wordy: It was during the day that the candidate learned that he won.
Better: During the day the candidate learned he had won.

Wordy: No one came with the exception of Jane.
Better: No one came except Jane.

Wordy: I cannot find the time to talk to you now.
Better: I cannot talk to you now.

Wordy: It is a good idea to inspect your house for termites every now and then.
Better: It is a good idea to inspect your house for termites occasionally.

Wordy: I regret very much that I have to inform you that the decision is final.
Better: Unfortunately, the decision is final.

Wordy: I only met him on one occasion.
Better: I only met him once.

Wordy: It snows in April once in a great while.
Better: It rarely snows in April.

Wordy: In the event that he comes, we will be prepared.
Better: If he comes we will be prepared.

Wordy: Father is of the belief that practice makes perfect.
Better: Father believes that practice makes perfect.

Wordy: The commission conducted an intensive study of the transportation problem.
Better: The commission studied the transportation problem intensively.

Wordy: The speaker told his audience that he had the intention of running for Congress.
Better: The speaker announced that he would run for Congress.

Review exercise

Rewrite each of the following sentences, eliminating the repetition or wordiness.

Example: The funny play was hilarious.
Answer: The play was hilarious.

1. Everyone who was attending the party had a great time.
2. The spectacular, amazing view from the mountain top was breath-taking.
3. Bob was so nervous, worried, and upset that he couldn't get the crying baby to calm down.
4. The old, run-down, decaying warehouse was ready to be torn down.
5. A telephone call from Aunt Martha came yesterday during the day.
6. John and Leah will probably be late, the reason being that they had a flat tire.
7. My teacher recommended a book that was exciting, absorbing, and hard to put down.
8. Our employee who just started working yesterday lives very near to me.

Trite expressions

Trite expressions (also known as clichés) are expressions that have lost much of their original impact due to overuse. No writer deliberately sets out to use clichés, yet they are difficult to avoid entirely because they have become so firmly established in the language.

People use trite expressions without thinking. By increasing your awareness of clichés, you will be able to cut down on their use. Following is a list of some of the most commonly used clichés:

abreast of the times	all in all	as luck would have it
aching void	along the same line	at a loss for words
acid test	among those present	at one fell swoop
after all is said and done	ardent admirers	avoid like the plague

bated breath
bathed in tears
better half
bitter end
blood is thicker than
    water
bolt from the blue
budding genius
burn the midnight oil
busy as a bee
by and large
by leaps and bounds
calm and collected
captain of industry
center of attention
checkered career
clear as a bell
clinging vine
conspicuous by its
    absence
cooked his goose
cool as a cucumber
crack of dawn
deadly earnest
depths of despair
discreet silence
doomed to disappoint-
    ment
drastic action
each and every
easier said than done
epic struggle
equal to the occasion
every fiber of his being
fair sex
festive occasion
few and far between
finer things of life
first and foremost
fly off the handle
footprints on the sands
    of time
force of circumstances
free as the breeze
generous to a fault
get down to brass tacks
goes without saying

goodly number
green with envy
heartfelt gratitude
heart's content
heated argument
holds promise
holy bonds of matri-
    mony
humble opinion
in (at) one fell swoop
in terms of
in the bag
in the last analysis
in this day and age
iron will
irony of fate
it stands to reason
last but not least
last straw
life of the party
like a bull in a china
    shop
like an old shoe
looking for all the world
    like
method in his madness
more than meets the
    eye
mother nature
needless to say
needs no introduction
nipped in the bud
no one in his right mind
none the worse for wear
paramount issue
pending merger
picturesque scene
pleasing prospect
powers that be
pretty as a picture
promising future
proud possessor
pure and simple
raving beauty
reigns supreme
relatively new to the
    field

revolutionary develop-
    ment
right and proper
riot of color
ripe old age
sad to relate
sadder but wiser
safe to say
sea of faces
self made man
sigh of relief
significantly reduced
skeleton in the closet
smart as a whip
strong as an ox
strong, silent type
struggle for existence
stubborn as a mule
sturdy as an oak
sweat of his brow
take my word for it
tale of woe
talk is cheap
tempest in a teapot
the bottom line
the happy pair
the plot thickens
the thrill of victory
the time of my life
the weaker sex
the worse for wear
thereby hangs a tale
thunderous applause
time marches on
tired but happy
to all intents and
    purposes
too funny for words
too numerous to men-
    tion
untold wealth
unvarnished truth
upset the applecart
venture a suggestion
view with alarm
walk of life
wedded bliss

wends its way	without further delay	wrought havoc
wheel of fortune	wit's end	wry smile
widespread use	words fail to express	yesterday's darling

Answer key

Page 154 (Exercise A)
Possible sentence rewrites:
1. Into the cave crawled the explorers, searching for interesting icicle formations.
2. To search for interesting icicle formations, the explorers crawled into the cave.
3. The explorers, searching for interesting icicle formations, crawled into the cave.
4. Crawling into the cave, the explorers looked for interesting icicle formations.
5. The search for interesting icicle formations led the explorers to crawl into the cave.

Page 155 (Exercise B)
Possible paragraph rewrite:
Boy, was I nervous as I arranged a surprise party for my brother, Robert. At the store, I bought many kinds of food: soft drinks, cookies, chips, dips, and three different cake mixes. I rushed home to bake the cakes. Unfortunately, one of the cakes fell. I had to run back to the store, buy another mix, and try again. Then I arranged all the other food on Mother's best trays. Next, I worked on the decorations, stringing crepe paper streamers across the basement rec room. Over the doorways, I hung big signs. One said "Happy Birthday, Robert," another, simply "Surprise!" By the time the guests arrived, I was finally ready, wearing my best dress. The party was a big success! I don't know who was more surprised, Robert or I!

Page 171
Possible sentence rewrites:
1. Everyone at the party had a great time.
2. The view from the mountain top was breathtaking.
3. Bob was so nervous that he couldn't calm the baby.
4. The decaying warehouse was ready to be torn down.
5. Aunt Martha telephoned yesterday afternoon.
6. John and Leah will be late because they had a flat tire.
7. My teacher recommended a very exciting book.
8. Our newest employee lives near me.

Kinds of writing

Normally when you write, you probably give little thought to the kind of writing, or discourse, you are doing. You explain your thoughts and ideas, narrate the progress of events, describe scenes, and express your opinions as they come to mind.

As long as your writing is well organized and coherent—as long, that is, as it communicates your meaning and intention clearly—there is no reason for you continually to analyze the kind of writing you are doing. But to better understand the fundamentals of good writing and clear expression, it is helpful to learn the definitions and the procedures of the four basic methods of writing: expository, descriptive, narrative, and argumentative writing.

Expository writing

Expository writing is writing that explains. It answers implied questions such as:

**Who or what is the person or thing (animal, object,
    idea, event, for example) under discussion?
Why is the person or thing important?
What does the person or thing do?
How does the thing work?
What is its origin?
How did it develop?**

Expository writing is usually organized to show the logical relationships among the various points being discussed. That is, expository writing shows the connections between one fact and another fact, one idea and another idea, one event and another event. Expository writing contains both general statements and the specific details or illustrations to back up those general statements.

Following is an example of expository writing:

Most Paris neighborhoods these days are a striking blend of the old and the new. Narrow nineteenth-century buildings still dot the residential streets, but they now coexist with towering modern apartment complexes. Down in the commercial areas, small decades-old shops specializing in one commodity—cheese, perhaps, or fish or fruit or baked goods—stand side by side with huge new supermarkets carrying every food imaginable.

Like the surreal paintings of the French masters, contemporary Parisian neighborhoods present a striking juxtaposition of contrasts: modern chrome and mottled wood, poured concrete and ancient stone. But, unlike the Surrealists' creations, Paris' transformation is far from fanciful. It is based on cold, hard economic facts.

Real estate prices are soaring in Paris, just as they are in most modernized countries. A lot that ten years ago would have sold for the equivalent of $500,000 in American dollars now goes for at least three times that price. Rents, too, have increased accordingly, echoing the rising property values.

The increase in the price of land has affected both residential and commercial patterns. Owners of older, smaller residences, tempted by the high prices offered by developers, sell their properties to the highest bidders. Often, neighbors sell *en masse,* thus opening up the large lots necessary for development of high-rise apartments.

Shopkeepers who own their property find themselves in the same situation. Often, the prices offered for their shops are more than they could ever dream of making as proprietors; so they sell and go into retirement or open up a small shop on the outskirts of town, where property values are lower. And shopkeepers who rent can no longer afford the rates charged by owners who realize the value of their property.

The passage above employs some of the most common techniques of expository writing. Refer to the passage and reread it, if necessary, as you examine these explanations of the techniques.

Using examples

Throughout the passage, examples are used to support main statements. For example, in the first paragraph, the opening sentence makes a general statement and all the other sentences in the paragraph give examples that support the first sentence. The third, fourth, and fifth paragraphs also use this technique.

Using analogies

The second paragraph uses an analogy, a statement of the similarities between two or more different kinds of things. Expository writers often use analogies and comparisons (statements of the similarities and differences between two or more related things) to help explain their points. A related technique, contrast, points out the differences between two or more things.

Explaining cause and effect

Expository writing frequently explains its topic by demonstrating cause-and-effect relationships. Two examples would be: "The price of sugar

175

rose because the sugar crop was bad, creating a scarcity" and "The plane veered off course because its automatic navigation control broke down." This kind of explanation is used in the third and fourth paragraphs of the passage, where the increase in land price is used to explain the changing nature of Parisian neighborhoods.

The expository techniques you use will, of course, vary with the purpose and intention of your writing. Not every technique will be used in every expository piece. For example, the passage above uses only some of the most common techniques of expository writing. Following are a few more:

Defining

A *definition* explains something by telling what it is or how it works. Definitions may be quite straightforward, or they may be incorporated into the flow of the writing so that they are barely noticeable.

Straightforward: Every well-equipped kitchen should contain at least one meat cleaver. A cleaver is a large, wedge-shaped knife that can cut through almost any kind of bone and gristle.

Incorporated: One of my favorite Italian foods is manicotti, those fat noodles stuffed with cheese or meat and smothered in a pungent tomato sauce.

Explaining a process

Many times, exposition explains how something operates or works. Following is an example of this type of expository writing:

> Threading a needle demands a sharp eye and a steady hand, but it is not a difficult task to accomplish. A right-handed person should hold the needle with the left hand; a left-hander should hold the needle with the right hand.
>
> Many people dampen the end of the thread before placing it through the needle's eye; this reduces friction and smooths out any loose ends. It is important to use a fairly high-quality cotton or nylon thread so that the strands do not unravel as the thread is inserted in the needle's eye.

As the passage above illustrates, process explanations take the reader through a process step by step. The present tense is usually used for this type of expository writing.

Descriptive writing

Descriptive writing attempts to recreate the impression evoked by a person, place, or thing. Descriptive writing appeals to the reader's emotions and senses. It concentrates on how things look, smell, taste, feel, or sound and—indirectly—on what effect the thing described may have produced on the observer. That observer may be the writer or a fictional character of the writer's creation. Following is an example of decriptive writing:

> We reached the top of the hill, dropped our backpacks, and stretched out on the soft grass that covered the cool earth. The air was filled with the fragrance of hundreds of brilliant wildflowers, their dense patterns and colors—purple, pink, red, orange, and blue—spread out like Oriental carpets laid at a bazaar. The air was still around us, and where we rested not a sound filled the air. But from down below in the valley came the sharp, clear chime of a church bell and the duller clank of cowbells.

Effective descriptive writing is characterized by a number of factors, including the following:

Concrete detail

In attempting to recreate an impression, it is important to emphasize the specific and concrete, as opposed to the general and abstract. Since descriptive writing attempts to describe a person or thing, its vividness depends greatly on how clearly that person or thing is delineated through use of the telling detail that appeals to one or more of the five senses. In the passage above, for instance, generalities are avoided and details are stressed: for example, soft grass, cool earth, fragrance, brilliant wildflowers, dense patterns and colors.

Point of view

To ensure unity and cohesiveness, descriptive writing is generally organized from a particular point of view—a vantage point from which the observer (the writer) describes the person, place, or thing. This point of view may be fixed or moving.

With a *fixed point of view,* the observer "stands" at a fixed point and describes the things that come into view in some kind of spatial order: left to right, front to back, bottom to top. The passage above, for example, employs a fixed point of view. It starts with what is close at hand to the observer and then moves farther away.

With a *moving point of view,* the observer "moves" through space and describes the people, places, and things that appear in the course of the motion. Following is a brief example of a moving point of view:

Near the forest's edge, the sparse foliage barely sheltered us from the sun's intense heat. But deeper into the forest, thick umbrellas of leaves gave protection from the sweltering rays, and lush ferns cooled our feet.

Selection of details

There are an infinite number of details that could be mentioned about any person, place, or thing. But not every detail is equally important for each descriptive passage. For example, think about your neighborhood. There are many details you could mention about it. If you wanted to describe the architecture of the neighborhood, you would concentrate on a description of what the houses and shops look like. If you wanted to describe your neighbors, you would concentrate on their personal style and their physical appearance.

Effective description calls for a selection of the most significant details. It is often better to tell less about a subject but to tell it well. Do not overload your descriptive writing with irrelevant or uninteresting details.

Narrative writing

Narrative writing tells about events that happen. Following is an example of narrative writing:

> I had an important appointment in town yesterday, and I had planned to take the 2:15 train into the city. I drove to the station with plenty of time to spare but then discovered I had no coins to drop into the parking meter. I raced into the drugstore, hoping to get quick change for a dollar; but there was a long line at the cash register due to a special two-for-one sale. Next, I went into the hardware store two doors away, where the cashier gladly changed my dollar.
>
> By the time I got back to the parking lot, it was too late. The train was just pulling out of the station. So, although I usually hate to drive into the city, I backed out of the lot and headed for the expressway. I made it into town by 3:00 and managed to arrive at my appointment on time.

As the passage above shows, most narrative writing follows chronological order, starting at the beginning of a sequence of events and following those events step by step until the conclusion. Occasionally, however, writers employ flash-forward or flashback techniques in narrative writing. This is done for special emphasis, as in the following passage:

> When I stepped onto the stage at the age of six to give my first violin recital, my heart was racing and the blood was pounding in my throat. I walked timidly to the center of the stage, made a stiff bow, brought the instrument up to my shoulder, and started to play.
>
> Had I been able to anticipate the thunderous applause that would greet me at the end of my performance, I would have been less nervous.

My mother shouted "bravo," my father leapt to his feet and cheered, and my grandmother led the audience in a rousing display of appreciation. There were calls for an encore, which I gladly granted.

But all that adulation had been far from my mind as I made those first scratchy noises on my half-size violin. At the start of the recital, all I had wished for was its conclusion.

By interrupting the natural sequence of events to show what happened at their end, the narrative passage above emphasizes the pathos and charm of the child's initial nervousness.

Argumentative writing

People usually think of an argument as a quarrel, but in writing, arguing has nothing to do with quarreling. Rather, argumentative writing attempts to convince the reader to agree with the writer's ideas, opinions, or attitudes. Argumentative writing can appeal to the reader's intellect, emotions, or both. Following is an example of argumentative writing:

Driving a car with a manual transmission is much more interesting than driving a car with an automatic transmission. Driving an automatic car is boring; all you have to do is put the car in "drive" and steer. There's no variety, no challenge, no skill involved in that kind of driving.

But when you drive a car with a stickshift, there's always something to do. You have to downshift whenever you see a red light ahead or when traffic slows down or when a dog suddenly shoots across the road. Then, as you start up again, you move up through the gears until you reach your cruising speed. Your mind is always alert and active, and even a simple drive around the block calls on your skill and deftness.

Notice how this argumentative passage combines facts (you don't have to shift with an automatic transmission; you do have to shift with a manual transmission) and claims (driving a car with a manual transmission is more interesting than driving a car with an automatic transmission). Notice, too, how the argument combines both neutral tones (when you drive a car with a stickshift you have to downshift) with emotional tones (driving an automatic car is boring). While some argumentative writing makes no appeal to the reader's emotions, basing its argument entirely on reason, much argumentative writing does attempt to affect the reader's emotions as well as the mind.

Effective argumentative writing sometimes voices potential criticisms of its position in order to blunt those criticisms. For instance:

Opponents of the proposed construction claim that it will destroy the natural flood plain and create hazards for property owners in the older sections of town. This simply is not true. Engineering reports have shown conclusively that the proposed industrial parks and housing developments will utilize the city's largest and newest storm sewers, and these pose no threat.

By admitting the objections to the argument in advance, the passage above enhances the credibility of its line of argument.

Merging of methods

It is possible to give clear definitions of the four kinds of writing and to provide pure examples of each kind. But in most writing, the four methods merge. Expository writing may contain passages of descriptive, narrative, and argumentative writing; descriptive writing may include passages of exposition; argumentative writing may make its point through narration of events, for example.

Writing is really a reflection of thinking and feeling, and thinking and feeling know no artificial boundaries. The mind works in various ways to solve problems, answer questions, interpret experience, recall events, and record impressions of the world. While it is a useful exercise to analyze the various ways thinking is reflected in writing, it is important to aim for as natural and fluid a writing style as possible. Do not worry if your expository writing contains some passages of narration or if your narration includes some descriptive elements. Anything is possible as long as the writing is clear, unified, and coherent.

Nonfiction

Looking at writing as expository, descriptive, narrative, and argumentative is one way of understanding writing. Another way is to divide writing into nonfiction and fiction. Fiction, which will be discussed later in this chapter, is writing based on the author's imagination. Nonfiction, which will be discussed immediately below, is writing based on factual experiences and occurrences. The main forms of nonfiction include diaries, biographies, autobiographies, histories, and essays.

Diaries

Diaries are notebooks filled with a writer's personal experiences recorded day by day. *Journals* are expanded diaries that comment on the writer's ideas and personal experiences. Diary writing is popular with all kinds of writers. Teenagers often keep diaries to record their turbulent emotions and the hustle and bustle of their active lives. Adults often keep diaries to keep track of the passing years. Poets and novelists frequently keep journals to serve as the source of much of their published writing.

Although diaries are mainly a private form of writing, professional writers sometimes keep diaries with the intention of publishing them. In addition, some diaries, originally meant only for the eyes of the writer, eventually are published because of their great interest and relevance for the reading public.

Some of the most famous diaries include those of Samuel Pepys (1633–1703), an English government official; Jonathan Swift (1667–1745), an English satirist; and Anne Frank (1929–1945), a German girl who perished in World War II.

Biographies

A *biography* is the story of a person's life written by someone other than the subject. It may tell the story of a living person or of a person deceased for decades or centuries. Biographies may be "authorized"—that is, written with the consent of the subject or the subject's family—or unauthorized.

To compile biographies, writers spend thousands of hours reading documents, letters, diaries, newspapers, books, and other written sources that contain information about the subject. In some cases, authors of biographies are also able to interview the subject or people close to the subject.

In addition to presenting the facts of their subjects' lives, biographers interpret those facts for their readers. In the process, they often devote many pages to historical, sociological, and psychological explanation and interpretation.

Biographers write about those people who were important in their own lifetimes or whose importance became recognized after their deaths. For example, Eleanor Roosevelt and George Washington were important subjects for biographies while they were still alive. But the importance of someone like Samuel Pepys, the English diarist and government official mentioned earlier, became obvious only after his death, when the influence of his diaries was felt. In subsequent years, several biographies were written about him.

Autobiographies

An *autobiography* is a person's self-told life story. In writing their autobiographies, people may draw on a number of sources including their diaries, the letters they wrote and received, and their memories. Public figures such as presidents, members of Congress, and Cabinet members often keep detailed daily notes of their activities while in office so that they will have a record of events and thoughts when it comes time to write their autobiographies.

181

Many different kinds of people write autobiographies. Some are politicians, artists, or scientists. Some are less well-known people who write their autobiographies because they believe their personal experiences are relevant and interesting to others.

Histories

Histories recount the stories of the human past. Historians base their writing on many kinds of evidence including folk tales, works of art, archaeological objects, and written documents. Historians rely mainly on the latter kind of evidence, written documents, for their information.

Histories cover all aspects of human experience. Some of the major topics of histories include social, cultural, political, and economic trends and events.

Essays

The term *essay* covers a fairly wide range of writing. In the most general sense, an essay can be defined as a composition on a specific subject. Examples of essay topics would include, "My Summer Vacation," "The Importance of Speaking Well," or "The Charms of the Sea."

Essays that are written in an informal style and that strongly reflect the author's personality are sometimes called personal, or familiar, essays. People enjoy reading these essays because of the glimpses they often give into human problems and joys and because of the easy, natural way in which the essays are written.

Essays can also be formal, impersonal, and direct. For instance, most articles in magazines are actually essays. In them, authors usually analyze and interpret information rather than simply present their own opinions and attitudes.

Michel de Montaigne, a sixteenth-century French writer, was the first person to use the term *essai* (which means "attempt" in French) to refer to his written reflections on various ideas. The sixteenth-century English writer Francis Bacon composed the first works in English to be called essays. These consisted of a collection of compact bits of worldly wisdom, organized under general topics such as truth, marriage, travel, fear, and wealth. British magazines and newspapers began publishing essays in the early 1700s.

In the nineteenth century in America, Washington Irving's essays were the first to develop along the European pattern. Critics often cite Ralph Waldo Emerson as the greatest American essayist. But many other American authors of the time contributed to the form's popularity. Those writers include Edgar Allan Poe and Henry David Thoreau. Twentieth-century essayists of note include James Thurber, E. B. White, Norman Cousins, and Susan Sontag.

Fiction

Fiction is writing based on the author's imagination. The word fiction comes from the Latin word *fictio,* which means a *making* or a *fashioning.* The forms of fiction include the novel, the short story, drama, and poetry.

Throughout the centuries, critics have debated whether the chief function of fiction is to divert and amuse readers or to present them with various judgments on moral, philosophical, psychological, or social problems. This debate will probably continue as long as fiction is written. Sometimes fiction entertains by diverting the reader's attention; sometimes it instructs by stimulating the reader's mind; and sometimes it performs both functions simultaneously or at different times in the same work.

Some of the most important elements in a work of fiction are characters, setting, plot, and theme.

Characters are the people or animals represented in fiction. Characters make up the central interest of many dramas, novels, and short stories. Even a poem is concerned with characters. The speaker, actually the poet, is often the main character of a poem.

Much of fiction is concerned with the characters' motivation. *Motivation* means the reasons for a character's actions. A writer must be sure that the motives of the characters seem realistic. This does not necessarily mean that the motivations will be logical, but they must appear believable, or plausible, to readers.

Setting is the place in which a character's story unfolds. It may be a real place, one that exists now or existed in the past, or it may be an imaginary place on the earth or even in outer space.

Plot tells what happens to the characters. Plots are built around a series of events that take place within a definite period of time. Critics have generally believed that plots should be unified. This means that a plot should have a beginning, a middle, and an end. That is, an author leads the reader from one point (for instance, a character is shown to have a problem) to another point (the character is shown facing the problem) to an end point (the character overcomes the problem or is overcome by it).

This *plot movement* is often described by the terms exposition, rising action, climax, and denouement. The *exposition* gives the background and situation of the story. The *rising action* carries the situation further, creating suspense and enhancing the reader's desire to find out what happens next. The *climax* is the highest point of interest, when all the incidents and relationships are fully spelled out in their greatest complexity. The *denouement,* or outcome, ends the story.

The *theme* is the basic idea expressed in the work of fiction and develops out of the interplay of character and plot. A theme may warn the reader to lead a better life or a different kind of life. It may declare that life is profitable or unprofitable, or that crime does not pay.

Novels

Novels are long works of fiction that tell about events in the lives of real or imaginary persons. Novels can provide an escape from everyday life, but they also appeal to the most serious concerns of living. For instance, many novels encourage the reader to think about moral, social, or philosophical problems. Some novels point out injustices or other evils in society and challenge the reader to seek social or political reforms.

The form of the novel is highly flexible. Novelists can arrange incidents, describe places, and represent characters in an almost limitless variety of ways. They also may narrate their stories from different points of view. In some novels, for example, the story is told by one of the characters. In others, the events may be told from the viewpoint of a person outside the story. Some novels present different points of view in different sections of the story.

Novels also vary in their portrayal of time. They may devote hundreds of pages to the description of the events of a single day; or, in the same number of pages, they may cover centuries.

There are many kinds of novels. *Detective novels* (also called *mysteries*) are novels about a puzzling crime (often a murder), a number of clues, and the detective (professional or amateur) who solves the mystery. *Gothic novels* tell about mysterious events that often take place in gloomy, isolated castles. They have suspenseful, action-filled plots. *Historical novels* recreate the atmosphere of a past period and sometimes include actual characters and events from history. *Naturalistic novels* portray people who are trapped by circumstances beyond their control. Many of these novels deal with grim subjects. *Novels of manners* detail the customs of a particular social class or group. *Realistic novels* attempt to portray life as it is actually lived. These novels do not shy away from the painful or the ugly. *Romantic novels* emphasize emotion and the imagination. They present a rosy vision of life where there is little trouble, ugliness, or pain. *Science fiction* novels include subjects such as space and time travel and marvelous discoveries or inventions. Most science fiction stories are set in the future, but some take place in the present or the past.

Some of the most famous English-language novelists of the nineteenth century include Jane Austen, Charles Dickens, George Eliot, Thomas Hardy, Nathaniel Hawthorne, Herman Melville, Mark Twain, and Henry James. In the twentieth century, well-known English language novelists include Virginia Woolf, James Joyce, Ernest Hemingway, F. Scott Fitzgerald, William Faulkner, Saul Bellow, and James Baldwin.

Short stories

A *short story* is a work of fiction that is shorter than a novel. A short story may range in length from a short, short story of 1,000 to 1,500 words to a *novelette,* or short novel, of 12,000 to 30,000 words. Because of its shorter length, the short story has fewer and less complicated situations and characters than does a novel.

Short story writers have developed a number of literary techniques including the surprise ending and epiphany. A *surprise ending* usually involves an unexpected event or a revealing explanation. Such endings were the specialty of O. Henry, an American short story writer of the late 1800s and early 1900s. *Epiphany,* a sudden revelation or perception, can be used at any point in a story to explain the meaning of a complex event. The epiphany can come in the form of a sudden comment, incident, or symbol. James Joyce, who wrote in the early twentieth century, created this technique.

Some short stories concentrate on the events of ordinary life instead of emphasizing dramatic action. Anton Chekhov, a Russian writer of the 1800s, used such an approach in many of his stories. A number of later writers followed his style, including twentieth-century American authors John Cheever, John O'Hara, and John Updike.

Drama

A *drama* is a story written to be presented by actors on a stage. It usually includes stage directions describing the appearance and actions of the characters. A drama takes the form of a *dialogue,* or conversation, between two or more persons. The major forms of drama are tragedy and comedy.

Tragedy is a form of drama that deals with serious human actions and issues. Tragedy explores questions about morality, the meaning of human existence, relationships between people, and relationships between human beings and God. The most famous tragedies were written during three periods—the 400s B.C. in Greece; the late 1500s and early 1600s in England, and the 1600s in France.

The greatest writers of Greek tragedy were Aeschylus, Sophocles, and Euripides. They took most of their plots from Greek mythology. William Shakespeare was the most important tragic playwright of the English period. His tragedies, such as *Hamlet* and *Macbeth,* are noted for their suspenseful plots, their insights into human nature, and their poetic dialogue. Jean Racine dominated tragic drama during the French period. His tragic heroes and heroines are victims of violent passions they cannot control.

Critics disagree about whether any true tragedies have been written in modern times. Some believe that several playwrights have created works that can be considered tragedies, such as *The Death of a Salesman* (1949) by Arthur Miller.

Comedy is a form of drama that deals with humorous or ridiculous aspects of human behavior. Most comedies have a playful mood and end happily.

There are many types of comedy. The three most common types emphasize character, ideas, or situation. In *comedies of character,* the humor comes from the major traits of the characters. *Comedies of ideas* deal primarily with social issues. *Situation comedies* rely on comic actions and events. Other important types include *comedies of manners* and *romantic comedies.* Most comedies of manners are humorous treatments of the social codes of the upper classes. Most romantic comedies concern people in love. An exaggerated kind of comedy called *farce* is sometimes considered a separate type but may be treated as a form of situation comedy.

The first important comic playwright was Aristophanes, who lived in Greece from about 445 to 385 B.C. During the Middle Ages, farce was the major type of comedy. In the late 1500s and early 1600s in England, William Shakespeare wrote plays that included almost every type of comedy. In the 1900s, George Bernard Shaw was especially well known for his comedies of ideas; and in the twentieth century, Edward Albee and Harold Pinter became well known for their bitter comedies, known as *dark comedies.*

Because drama has been written and performed since ancient Greek and Roman times, it would be impossible to describe all the kinds of plays that have been written since then. Instead, following is a brief glance at some of the major trends of twentieth-century drama.

Epic theater

The discontent of the post–World War I era appeared in many of the plays written in the 1920s. Dramatists of this period believed that the theater should focus attention on political and social evils. One experiment growing out of this philosophy was epic theater, developed by the German playwright Bertolt Brecht. Brecht condensed the action and mixed narrative with dialogue in his plays. He tried to make his audience think critically so that they would relate what they saw to real situations.

Theater of the Absurd

This was the most influential drama movement in the post–World War II years. Absurdist playwrights emphasize the illogical and confusing elements in life. Most absurdist drama is concerned with the anxieties of individuals trying to survive in an essentially hostile world. Samuel Beckett and Eugène Ionesco are two of the best-known absurdist playwrights.

Happenings

Happenings achieved their greatest popularity in the early 1960s. They often combined improvised acting, motion pictures and slide projections, music, and painting. They emphasized spontaneous actions by everyone present, although the situation may have been planned in advance.

Environmental theater

In this type of drama, audiences and performers occupy the same area so that the spectators actually become part of the production.

Poetry

Poetry is language used in a special way. Its words form patterns of sound and of thought that appeal strongly to the imagination. There are three main types of poetry: lyric, narrative, and dramatic poetry.

Lyric poems are usually short and may have a songlike quality. In lyric poems, the poet expresses personal reactions to things—to what the poet sees, hears, thinks, and feels. Following are two examples of lyric poetry.

Who has seen the wind?
  Neither I nor you:
But when the leaves hang trembling
  The wind is passing through.

Who has seen the wind?
  Neither you nor I:
But when the trees bow down their heads,
  The wind is passing by.

Christina Rossetti (1830–1894)

Beginning My Studies

Beginning my studies, the first step pleas'd me so much,
The mere fact consciousness, these forms, the power of motion,
The least insect or animal, the senses, eyesight, love,
The first step I say awed me and pleas'd me so much,
I have hardly gone and hardly wish'd to go any farther,
But stop and loiter all the time to sing it in ecstatic songs.

Walt Whitman (1819–1892)

Narrative poems tell a story and are usually rather long. In narrative poems, the poet suggests the setting, characters, and events and gives them meaning. Epics and ballads are among the foremost kinds of narrative poetry.

Epic poems are long narrative poems. Almost all epics tell about the heroic deeds of gods and people who participate in wars or voyages. Many epics tell how a nation or race began. Some of the most famous epic poems in western literature are the *Iliad* and the *Odyssey*, believed to have been written by the ancient Greek poet Homer.

Ballads are songs that tell a dramatic story in verse. Most ballads are either folk songs or imitations of folk songs. The English poet Samuel Taylor Coleridge (1772–1834) imitated the ballad style in the opening lines of his "Rime of the Ancient Mariner":

> It is an ancient Mariner,
>   And he stoppeth one of three.
> "By thy long grey beard and glittering eye,
>   Now wherefore stopps't thou me?"

Dramatic poems resemble narrative poems because they tell a story and are fairly long. But the poet tells the story through the speech of one or more of the characters in the story. "My Last Duchess," a dramatic monologue by Robert Browning (1812–1889) is a famous example of a dramatic poem. Through what the duke says in his monologue while supposedly speaking to a visitor, Browning shows the duke's character and reveals much about the duchess. Here are the opening lines of the poem:

> That's my last Duchess painted on the wall,
> Looking as if she were alive. I call
> That piece a wonder, now: Frà Pandolf's hands
> Worked busily a day, and there she stands.
> Will't please you sit and look at her? I said
> "Frà Pandolf" by design, for never read
> Strangers like you that pictured countenance,
> The depth and passion of its earnest glance,
> But to myself they turned . . .

Verse

Poets who write in modern English can use either bound verse or free verse. *Bound verse,* as in the poem by Christina Rossetti, is the older and more common form. It is *bound to,* or based on, a rhythmic pattern. A poem that is written in *free verse,* such as the one by Walt Whitman, has no regular rhythmic pattern.

It is usually fairly easy to tell which verse system a poet has used. By reading a few lines aloud, you will discover how the poem goes. If you become conscious of a fairly regular beat, the poem has a rhythmic pattern and is therefore in bound verse. If you do not, the poem is in free verse.

Metrical patterns

Each poem in bound verse is based on a metrical (rhythmic) pattern. This pattern can be described in terms of its basic foot, its meter, and its rhyme scheme.

People tend to hear the syllables of a line in poetry in groups of twos or threes. Each of these rhythmic units is called a *foot.*

In English poetry, the rhythm is based on the natural accents placed on words. For example, the first syllable of the word *heavily* is stressed but not the last two syllables. The rhythm of the word goes DUMM-de-de and, in a line of poetry, it could be marked ´ ˘ ˘ .

The four basic feet in English verse are:

> *iambic* (de-DUMM)
> *anapestic* (de-de-DUMM)
> *trochaic* (DUMM-de)
> *dactylic* (DUMM-de-de)

The number of feet in a line sets its *meter.*

> *monometer,* one foot   *pentameter,* five feet
> *dimeter,* two feet   *hexameter,* six feet
> *trimeter,* three feet   *heptameter,* seven feet
> *tetrameter,* four feet   *octameter,* eight feet

When the ends of words at the ends of two or more lines of poetry sound alike, they are said to rhyme, as in "lore" and "door." "Napping" and "tapping" form double rhymes, and "mournfully" and "scornfully" form triple rhymes.

The arrangement of rhymed lines forms the *rhyme scheme* of the poem. A *stanza* is a repeated pattern of lines with a fixed rhyme scheme. A two-line stanza is called a *couplet,* and a three-line stanza is called a *tercet.* A stanza of four lines is called a *quatrain.*

To summarize a rhyme scheme, you can use one letter (A, for instance) for the first rhyme sound, another letter (B) for the second, and so forth. For example, the rhyme scheme of the Shakespearean sonnet that follows can be summarized as ABAB; CDCD; EFEF; GG.

Sonnet 116

Let me not to the marriage of true minds	(A)
Admit impediments. Love is not love	(B)
Which alters when it alteration finds,	(A)
Or bends with the remover to remove.	(B)
Oh no! It is an ever-fixed mark	(C)
That looks on tempests and is never shaken.	(D)
It is the star to every wandering bark,	(C)
Whose worth's unknown, although his height be taken.	(D)
Love's not Time's fool, though rosy lips and cheeks	(E)
Within his bending sickle's compass come.	(F)
Love alters not with his brief hours and weeks,	(E)
But bears it out even to the edge of doom.	(F)
If this be error and upon me proved,	(G)
I never writ, nor no man ever loved.	(G)

Reports and research papers

Organizing for effective writing

In all kinds of schooling, at all levels, you are asked to complete many different kinds of writing assignments. Some writing assignments are based on your own ideas, opinions, experiences, and imagination—such as essays, themes, and stories. Other writing assignments are based on reading and research—such as book reports, short reports, and term papers.

No matter what kind of writing assignment you receive, you—the writer—must have a plan to achieve a finished piece of writing. In this chapter, you will be given some guidelines for organizing an effective piece of writing. These guidelines for choosing, analyzing, researching, and outlining a topic are necessary steps for most kinds of writing. Although some of the guidelines apply specifically to writing based on research, the suggestions given will help you to organize any kind of writing assignment more effectively.

Choosing a topic

For most writing assignments you are asked to choose a topic. Your instructor might give you a list from which to choose. Or you might be asked to choose a topic that relates to the material you are studying in class. Choosing a topic wisely is one of the more important steps in writing.

How then do you choose a topic? You learned in "Writing Well" that your topic should be something that interests you, something that you want to know more about, or something that you know well and want to inform others about. If you're not interested in your topic, it will be difficult to make the topic interesting to your readers. Your best papers will come when you have a genuine interest in your topic and believe that it is important enough to learn more about or to inform others about.

Consider the time factor

When you are choosing your topic, you must also consider how much time you have before your paper is due. The amount of time will determine how much research you will be able to do. You might have two days to write a theme or an essay; two weeks to read a book and write a report on it. A short report of 300 to 500 words could have a three-week deadline. And you might have as much as a whole quarter or semester in which to prepare a term paper.

The topic you choose should be appropriate for the amount of time you have for reading, researching, and writing. If your time is short, don't choose a topic that is too broad or that is too complex to learn about in a short time. Save the broader topics, and topics you know nothing about, for longer assignments when you have more time.

Consider available materials

It is also important to know the different kinds and amount of reference materials that are available on your topic. When you have decided on a general topic, go to the library and find out if there is enough information readily available for your research. The fastest way to do this is to check both the card catalog and the most recent issues of the *Readers' Guide to Periodical Literature*.

The card catalog contains cards for all the books that your library has. For each book, cards are entered under the subject, the title, and the author's name. All these cards are arranged alphabetically. If you were writing a paper about ecology, you would look in the card catalog under "Ecology." The sample cards from the card catalog show the kinds of information such cards contain. Look carefully at the subject card, since this is the kind of card you will look for first when seeking available material on your topic.

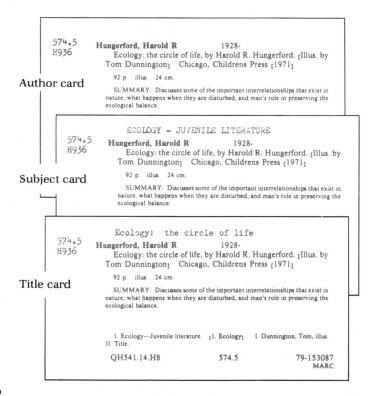

The *Readers' Guide* helps you find information about available articles in magazines and journals. It is arranged alphabetically by author, subject, and sometimes by title for plays and books. Look at the sample *Readers' Guide* entry to see the kinds of information such entries include.

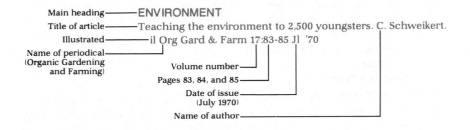

Main heading——————ENVIRONMENT
Title of article————Teaching the environment to 2,500 youngsters. C. Schweikert.
Illustrated——————il Org Gard & Farm 17:83-85 Jl '70
Name of periodical—————┘
(Organic Gardening
and Farming)   Volume number——┘
                 Pages 83, 84, and 85————┘
                      Date of issue—————┘
                       (July 1970)
                   Name of author————————┘

Limiting your topic

When you have decided that there is enough material available in your area of general interest, it is then time to limit your topic. You must decide whether your topic is too broad or too narrow. Establishing suitable limits for your topic is a crucial step in organizing an effective paper. You should remember that you want to focus on one main idea or event. Any information that you use should be related to that one idea or event.

Let's look at some possible general topics and some ways to limit them. In an American history class you might be studying the Constitution; in biology, systems of the human body; and in English, the drama. You first might choose broad topics, such as "The Constitutional Convention," "The Circulatory System," or "Shakespeare's Comedies." After looking through the card catalog and the *Readers' Guide*, you would realize that these topics are too broad. If your topic is a main heading in these guides, your topic is probably too broad for one paper.

For a workable paper, those topics must be narrowed down. The following are examples of more limited topics:

Compromises Made in the Constitutional Convention
The Function of White Blood Cells
The Purpose of Disguise in *The Merchant of Venice*

These topics could be limited even further; you could, for example, write about only *one* of the compromises made in the Constitutional Convention. How much you limit your topic depends on the length of your paper. The shorter your paper, the more you need to limit your topic.

193

But in any length paper, the more specific your topic is, the better your paper will probably be. A mistake students frequently make is to choose a subject that is too large to cover thoroughly. A paper that presents detailed ideas on a smaller topic is almost always preferable to a paper that presents only general ideas on a larger topic. If you are unsure whether you have limited your topic appropriately, you might ask your instructor if the topic is narrow enough (or broad enough) for the paper assigned.

Now that you have chosen a topic, determined if you have enough time and materials available for your research, and limited your topic accordingly, you are ready for the next step.

Analyzing a topic

In this step of the writing process, you should do some background reading and make a preliminary outline. Your preliminary outline might simply be a list of ideas that you might include in your paper. Or your preliminary outline could be done in the form of a series of questions about your topic.

If you are doing background reading for a book report, look through the table of contents, read the preface or introduction, and find out something about the author. Then, ask yourself some questions and write them down. Leave enough space so that you can jot down answers or notes as you read. For a book report, you might start with questions like these: Who are the main characters? What are their relations to one another? What is the main plot or story that the author is telling? How does the setting influence the characters or the mood of the story? What message is the author getting across? Along with these general questions, jot down any other specific questions you might have about the book.

If you are doing a short report or term paper, you should do background reading to become generally familiar with the topic. Encyclopedia articles dealing with your topic would be good sources for background reading. Getting a general idea of what the topic is all about should help you decide what parts of the topic you will include in your paper—and what parts you'll leave out. After you've finished your background reading, ask yourself some questions that you hope to answer in your paper. If your topic is "Compromises Made in the Constitutional Convention," you might ask yourself questions like these: What were the compromises? Why were compromises necessary? Who were the leaders in the debates? How were the compromises reached? Use such questions to guide you in your research. You will probably be able to use these questions later when you prepare the actual outline of your paper.

Researching a topic

Research is a two-step process consisting of locating information and reading and taking notes.

Locating information

First, you must locate the sources for your research. You probably found some sources when you were deciding whether or not there were enough reference materials available on your topic. Now you must gather together all the books and articles that you think will aid you in researching your topic.

You should make a bibliography card for each source. By making a complete bibliography card for each source at this point, you will avoid a lot of trouble when it is time to prepare the bibliography for your paper. A bibliography is required for most papers that require research.

Besides the card catalog and *Readers' Guide,* there are other places in which to find information. The *New York Times Index* and *Facts on File* are sources of information on current events. Materials that are hard to store on a shelf are found in the vertical file. The *vertical file* is a set of file cabinets in which pamphlets, pictures, and maps are filed alphabetically by subject. Other sources of information might be personal interviews and radio or television programs. No matter where you get your information, be sure to make a bibliography card for each source.

Reading and taking notes

Now that you have gathered your sources, you should begin reading and taking notes. The single-note system works best. In the *single-note system,* you write only one idea or quotation per note card. In that way, your note system remains flexible. You can rearrange your notes as you develop a logical order for your topic.

Your note cards should be different in size or color from your bibliography cards. By doing that, you can easily keep your two sets of information—bibliography and notes—separate.

What information should your note cards contain?

1. *A heading.* A heading briefly identifies the material on the note card. It should be placed at the top of the note card. The heading might be an idea listed in your preliminary outline (and might later become a main heading or a subheading in the actual outline) of your paper.
2. *The source.* Below the heading you should record the author's last name, a shortened form of the source's title, and the page number in the source where the material was found. This makes it possible to recheck your information quickly, if necessary. It also makes it easy for you to write your footnotes, if you quoted or paraphrased the author.
3. *The body of the note.* There is no one way to write a note. The note could be a few words, a summary, or a direct quotation. But your note should be written clearly and legibly, and it should be exact and complete.

It's a good idea to write the note in your own words. Don't copy word for word from your source, unless you want to use a direct quotation. Use direct quotations only if they are significant or if they support your position. Be sure to put quotation marks around any direct quotations so that you remember to give the author credit for the quote.

Look at the sample note card for a paper on the British parliament to see how a note card should be set up.

Sample note card

Heading ———————— *The power of the House of Lords*

Source ———————— *Bagehot, The English Constitution, p. 141.*

Body of note ———— *Although the House of Lords was always respected, it never was as important as the House of Commons.*

Outlining a topic

After you have finished taking notes but before you write the first draft, you should make an outline. An outline will help you organize your notes and thus make it easier for you to write the first draft. You will not be required to submit an outline with every writing assignment. But you should make at least a working outline for your own use—as a guide for writing your first draft.

Take the preliminary outline that you prepared and all your note cards. Lay them out on a large desk or table. Arrange the note cards according to the headings. Once you have your note cards arranged under the headings, then decide what topics belong together under main headings. Organize your cards under main headings and subheadings. If you are writing about the compromises made in the Constitutional Convention, for example, your notes might indicate that these should be your main headings:

The three-fifths compromise
Trade compromises
The Great Compromise

Now decide on a logical order in which to present your information. Put the main headings in order and number each one with a roman numeral.

I. The Great Compromise
II. The three-fifths compromise
III. Compromises about trade

Your note cards will also help you determine the subheadings for your outline. The subheadings go below the main headings and begin with a capital letter.

I. The Great Compromise
  A. Created a Congress of two houses
  B. Pleased both large and small states

You may or may not have subheadings under the other main headings. But never have just one subheading under a main heading. If, for example, you had "No taxes on exports" as the only subheading under "Compromises about trade," you should change the main heading to read:

III. Compromise about trade
or:
III. Trade compromise: no taxes on exports

A topic outline

The kind of outline about which you have just been reading is called a *topic outline*. A topic outline is perhaps the easiest kind of outline to prepare. It consists of brief phrases or short clauses for all the headings. The first word of each main heading and subheading is capitalized. But periods are not used after the phrases and clauses.

All headings in a topic outline must have parallel construction. That is, all main headings must be similar in form. If you used parallel construction, the main headings for the outline on "Compromises Made in the Constitutional Convention" would look like this:

I. The Great Compromise
II. The three-fifths compromise
III. The trade compromises

All subheadings under one main heading must be similar in form, also.

I. The Great Compromise
  A. Created a Congress made up of two houses
  B. Pleased both large and small states

A sentence outline

In a *sentence outline,* each heading is a complete sentence. This kind of outline takes more time to write, but it does have some advantages.

1. You are forced to state your thoughts clearly and completely.
2. You can usually transfer the sentences from your outline directly to your first draft.
3. You can use the main headings (and some subheadings) as topic sentences for the various parts of your paper.

Like the topic outline, the sentence outline is divided into main headings *(I, II, III)* and subheadings *(A, B, C)*. The following is an example of a sentence outline. This outline is also divided into sub-subheadings *(1, 2, 3)*.

WHY STUDENTS SHOULD HAVE A JOB AFTER SCHOOL

I. A job provides students with a way to earn money.
  A. Some students need extra money to pay for clothes, hobbies, and car expenses.
  B. Some students use their earnings for high school or college tuition.
II. A job gives students more responsibility.
  A. Students must budget their time for school, work, and leisure.
  B. Students learn to fulfill certain duties on the job.
    1. They must arrive at work on time.
    2. They must follow the directions of a supervisor.
    3. They must carry out certain procedures in doing their jobs.
III. A job after school helps students prepare themselves for a long-term job or career.
  A. By trying a variety of after-school jobs, students can discover what kind of work they like best.
  B. Through contact with adults at work, students find out what training or education is needed for certain jobs.

Outlining a theme or an essay

Up to this point, you have been given examples of outlining for a research-related paper. Outlining is also helpful before you write the first draft of a theme or an essay. It will help you sort out your thoughts and ideas so that you can arrange them in logical order. A good outline will make your final paper more interesting and easier to read. The following is an example of a topic outline for an essay.

WHY I LIKE SPORTS

    I. A way to improve my health
      A. By exercising indoors
        1. Weight training
        2. Swimming
      B. By being outdoors in the fresh air
        1. Jogging
        2. Bicycling
   II. A form of competition
      A. As an individual
        1. Tennis
        2. Golf
        3. Handball
      B. As a member of a team
        1. Softball
        2. Basketball
        3. Soccer
  III. A way to relax
      A. Going to a sports event
      B. Watching a sports event on television

Writing a short report

During a school year, you will usually write several short reports for various courses you take. A short report presents ideas on one particular subject, based on research from one or more sources. Your job in a short report is to clearly present the information from the sources. You should write the report in your own words. And you should make the report interesting and informative for your reader.

A short report is usually between 300 and 500 words long and runs from 1½ to 3 typewritten pages. Your instructor will usually tell you how long the report should be. If you're to write a 400-word report, don't count the words as you are writing. Cover the topic thoroughly, and don't worry if you are a little over or under the 400 words. Your instructor is not going to count them. Do not, however, turn in a one-page or a twenty-page report when you were assigned 400 words.

Planning a short report

If you have not read "Organizing for effective writing" (pages 191–199), you should do so now. That section gives you suggestions for choosing, analyzing, researching, and outlining a topic. After you have completed the steps explained in that section, you are ready to move on to the next steps described in this section. Here you will find out how to plan the actual writing of a short report. You have chosen a topic, done your research, taken useful notes, and written an outline. Now you are ready to plan the writing of your report.

Keep your reader in mind

The reader is usually your teacher. But sometimes reports are read aloud or distributed to all members of the class as the basis for class discussion. Decide how you will keep the reader's attention. Give clear, complete descriptions and brief summaries to help the reader understand your ideas.

You must convince the reader that the statements in your report are accurate. Be sure that you have enough facts to back up the main points in your outline.

Keep your purpose in mind

There are two kinds of short reports: summary reports and critical reports. Each has a different purpose. In a *summary report* you present the information you have found. You do not make any judgments about the information or give your opinions. Say, for example, that you have been assigned to write a summary report on the boycott of the 1980 summer Olympics. In such a report you could (1) tell what events led up to the boycott; (2) compare and contrast the views that various groups of people had about the boycott; or (3) explain why other countries joined the boycott.

In a *critical report,* you are called upon to evaluate what you have read. You take a position, make judgments, and justify your ideas. This time, for example, you have been assigned to write a critical report about the boycott of the Olympic games. You could (1) evaluate the effect the boycott had on foreign relations; (2) judge whether or not the boycott was an adequate or appropriate response; or (3) justify the boycott.

Your instructor will usually tell you to write either a summary report or a critical report. If the choice is left to you, the material itself might suggest which kind of report you might write. Material that lends itself to being listed or put into categories might be presented in a summary report. Material that you strongly agree with—or strongly disagree with—could be given in a critical report.

Write a thesis sentence

What does all the information you have gathered seem to say? What does it all relate to? In other words, what main idea has your research uncovered? Decide what your main idea is and summarize it. This statement of your main idea is your *thesis sentence.* It should be placed near the beginning of the report. It will help both you and your reader focus on the main thought and message of your report. As you write the report, make sure that everything in it relates to the thesis sentence.

Here are some examples of possible thesis sentences for a report about the Olympic boycott:

The decision to boycott the 1980 Olympics in Moscow received a mixed reaction from the American people.
The boycott of the 1980 Olympics changed the careers of many American athletes.
Many Third World nations supported the boycott of the 1980 summer Olympics.

After you have written your thesis sentence, be sure you have enough facts to support the statement. You must use facts, examples, and details to convince your reader that your thesis sentence is true and accurate.

Check your outline

Now that you have written a thesis sentence, you should reread your outline. Your thesis sentence might indicate that you should emphasize some ideas and delete others. Perhaps you should organize your material differently. If that is the case, revise your outline. Remember: The outline is a writing tool. You don't have to stay with the original outline. Change it to meet the needs of your report. The following example shows how the title and outline for a report were changed.

Original: The Olympic Boycott and United States Foreign Policy
I. With the Soviet Union
II. With its allies
III. With the Third World

Corrected: The Olympic Boycott Affected Relations with the Soviet Union
           I. An end to detente
          II. A stall on the SALT treaty
         III. A slowdown in trade

Writing the first draft

Put all your sources away; don't be tempted to look at them while you are writing. If you do, you might start to copy from them. Rely on your notes instead. Your report is supposed to show in your own words what you think or what you have found.

Now you are ready to write the first draft of your report. Put your outline in front of you, and keep your notes close by for reference. Use wide-lined paper; it will make revising easier. And leave wide margins so that you can make notes to yourself in the margins as you write.

Start writing! When writing the first draft, don't worry about mistakes in spelling, grammar, or sentence and paragraph structure. Put question marks or notes in the margins if you are unsure of a spelling or think you've made some other error. You will correct these errors in the revision stage.

In the first-draft stage, you want to get all your thoughts and ideas down on paper. Use your outline as a guide. Refer to your note cards when you need more examples to support a major point. Be sure to use footnotes if you use a direct quotation or someone else's opinion or idea.

Put your thesis sentence in the first paragraph. Then get the reader on your side with convincing evidence and arguments. State your ideas clearly. Bring all the facts, examples, and details together. Define and describe your ideas. Make comparisons and contrasts between ideas when appropriate.

You want the reader on your side, but you don't want to write only what the reader wants to hear. Your job is to inform or to persuade your reader. Therefore, be straightforward and honest in your writing.

Revising the first draft

Try to plan the writing of your report so that you have a day between writing the first draft and revising it. The literal meaning of *revise* is "to look again." You should put some time and distance between the first draft and this second look. By doing that, you will see your writing with a fresh eye. It will be easier to see if you actually said what you meant to say—and if you said it clearly and correctly.

Know the mechanics of revising

When you revise your report, use a colored pencil or a different color of ink. Make your corrections right in the copy. If there are big corrections—a sentence that should be added—put them in the margin. Use an arrow to show where they belong in the report. That way, when you write your final copy, you won't forget these corrections and additions.

Reread your report

First, read the thesis sentence. Then go through your report and take out all the parts that do not relate to the thesis sentence. Circle those parts rather than crossing them out. You might be able to rephrase them so they fit with the thesis sentence. If an idea relates to the thesis sentence but doesn't seem to fit in its paragraph, see if it belongs in a different part of the report.

Emphasize major points

Be sure that you have emphasized the major points of your report. Treat each major point in a separate paragraph. Provide the facts and evidence to support your major points. You can't make statements without backing them up. The following statements could not stand alone in a report:

The oil shortage is a myth.
A draft during peacetime is illegal.
The decision to boycott the 1980 summer Olympics unified
the American people.

The first statement needs support from facts and figures. The second statement would require mentioning specific laws or the opinions of legal experts. And the third statement would have to be backed up by the results of public opinion polls and interviews.

Improve weak points

Clear up any parts of the report that seem unclear or that could be confusing to your reader. Here are a few suggestions for clearing up confusion:

1. Reword the sentence.
2. Rearrange the sentences in the paragraph if a different order would be clearer.
3. Give a more complete explanation by adding related details.

Add description to parts of the report that seem uninteresting but are important to your thesis. You don't want to lose your reader. The following paragraph isn't very exciting:

> Many people wrote to the President. Some of them felt that the United States should not send a team to the Olympics. Others believed that athletics and politics should not be mixed.

By adding some concrete details and descriptive phrasing, the paragraph takes on new life:

> Thousands of people flooded President Carter's office with letters. Many of the people strongly agreed with the President and said that the United States definitely should not participate in the 1980 summer Olympics. Another vocal group, however, strongly felt that the President and Congress had no business mixing politics with athletics.

Maintain coherence

Cohere means "to stick together." Make sure that the parts of your paragraph "stick together." The material in each paragraph should be related to one idea. Also check to make sure that the paragraphs "stick" to each other. Are they presented in a logical order? Does one paragraph flow into the next? Finally, "stick" to the main subject. Don't get sidetracked by interesting but unrelated material. But keep in mind the material that sidetracked you; it could be used in another report.

Check for weakness in writing style

At this point of the revision process, you delete any unnecessary words or phrases—words and phrases that add clutter but not meaning to your report.

Also correct any faults in sentence structure. Make sure every sentence is a complete sentence. If you have many short, choppy sentences, you can occasionally combine the ideas of two sentences into one sentence. If some sentences seem too long, you can break some of them into shorter sentences.

Check your word choices. Avoid repeating the same word or using words with the same root word. For example, "The information informed us . . ." should be changed to "The facts in the report informed us . . ." or "The information explained that. . . ."

Correct grammatical errors

You may have already corrected major grammatical errors as you were revising for ideas and writing style. After you have completed those other parts of the revision process, however, it's important to read through the report once more to catch the "little" mistakes. These are errors in spelling, punctuation, capitalization, and word usage.

Check your verb tenses and point of view. Generally you should stay primarily with one verb tense in a paper. Some reports are written primarily in the past tense, particularly when relating past events. But some are written primarily in the present tense.

Decide which *person* you are going to use: *I, you, he, she, it.* In some formal writing, *I* and *you* are avoided and the third person is used. For example:

> *This report* proves that . . . *(third person)*

rather than:

> *I* will prove in this report that . . . *(first person)*

or:

> *You* will understand that . . . *(second person)*

Some formal writing, however, uses *I* and *you*. You might check with your instructor to see what person is appropriate for your paper.

When you have decided which person you are going to use, don't change persons or point of view. Maintain the same point of view throughout the report.

Now you are ready to prepare the final copy of your report.

Preparing the final copy

Learn to type if you don't know how. Reports that are typed look neater and are easier to read than handwritten reports. And typing can take less time than writing by hand. Use high-quality typing paper, a clean typewriter, and a fresh ribbon.

If you have not learned how to type yet, write in your best handwriting. Use a good pen and wide-lined white paper.

Write or type the final copy from the revised first draft. Be sure to include all corrections and additions in the final copy. When your report is in its final form, read it once again. Check for any typing errors and neatly correct them. And look for any errors in spelling and punctuation.

Now submit your report!

Writing a term paper

The term paper, like the short report, is a research paper. But it differs from the short report in many ways. Term papers have broader topics and are longer than short reports. Many term papers are eight to fifteen pages in length, but some are even longer. The research for a term paper requires more sources than that for a short report. And term papers have more parts—a title page, an outline, footnotes, and a bibliography.

Term papers serve many purposes. Some students think that the only purpose a term paper has is to crowd into their leisure time. Researching and writing a term paper, however, have several positive purposes that are both immediate and long-range. First, you have a chance to explore in depth a topic that interests you. Second, you can practice developing research skills that you will need throughout your school years and in many careers and professions. Here are some of those research skills.

1. Using a library to find information. Learning how to use the card catalog, periodical indexes, and microfilm readers.
2. Selecting information and using it to answer questions.
3. Taking notes.
4. Analyzing information and putting it in your own words.
5. Organizing information so that it is understandable and useful.
6. Documenting the sources of your information.
7. Preparing footnotes and a bibliography.

Planning a term paper

If you have not read "Organizing for effective writing" (pages 191–199), you should do so now. That section presents suggestions for choosing, analyzing, researching, and outlining a topic. You should follow the steps explained in that section. This section offers some additional suggestions that apply to preparing a term paper.

Make a schedule

As soon as you receive an assignment to write a term paper, make a schedule. By making a schedule you will realize the amount of time and work needed to prepare a term paper. And you will see that you cannot put off starting your work until the week before the paper is due.

Mark the due date for the term paper on your calendar, and start counting backward from that date. This is one time you put last things first. Start by allowing time to type the final copy. Next figure out how much time you will need to revise the first draft. Third, decide how long it will take you to write the first draft. And allow time to organize your note cards and to construct a final outline. The amount of time left before you organize the note cards will be used to gather information and take notes.

Let's say, for example, that you have between 6 and 8 weeks to prepare a 10-page term paper. Since you need to attach a final outline and a bibliography, we'll build a schedule that allows for preparing about 12 full pages of material.

1. Allow at least an hour per page to type the final copy. This includes time for last minute corrections, proofreading each page after you have typed it, and placing footnotes correctly. That means 12 hours for typing the final copy. You will not do this in one 12-hour stretch. Type about 3 hours a day over 4 days.
2. Count on at least 2 hours per page to revise the first draft, or 24 total hours. If you work 3 hours each day, plan on taking 8 days for revising.
3. Give yourself at least an hour to write each page of the first draft, or 12 total hours. This again should be written over 4 days.
4. Allow 1 day to organize your note cards and 1 day to construct the final outline.

This means you will spend 18 days—about three and a half school weeks—organizing, writing, revising, and typing your paper. You have the rest of the available time to do your research and take notes. And if you know you won't be able to work as many as 3 hours every day, you'll have to adjust your schedule accordingly.

Choose a topic

Your instructor will often let you choose your own topic for a term paper. Therefore, choose something that interests you—something you will enjoy learning more about. Pick a topic that you can easily find information about. But don't choose what is considered a traditional term paper topic. Topics such as "The Causes of the Civil War" or "How to Dissect a Frog" are no longer interesting because they have been done so frequently.

When you have chosen your topic, decide how you are going to present it. Try to take a fresh approach to your topic; view it from a new or different angle. For example, instead of simply telling what happened at the time of the Boston Tea Party, you could show how John Adams, Thomas Paine, and a recent historian viewed the Boston Tea Party.

Get started

As for any effective writing, begin by asking yourself questions that you want to answer in your term paper. Write these questions down, and use them as the basis for a preliminary outline. The questions and outline should guide your reading.

At first, read widely to gain a broad background about your topic. You may not be able to use all the information in your paper, but you will be able to write a better paper. While you are doing this background reading, you should be adding to your preliminary outline, noting ideas you might decide to include in your paper. If you don't have time for background reading, limit your reading to your specific topic.

Find sources of information

You will find most of the sources for your paper in the library—books, articles, and pamphlets. You may also find films, filmstrips, records—even TV—helpful. There are, however, additional useful sources of information. Depending on your topic, you might want to use some of these other sources.

1. *Personal interviews* allow you to get firsthand information from people. You can find out their opinions, ideas, or special knowledge about a topic. Before you interview anyone, prepare a set of questions to guide you during the interview.
2. *Questionnaires* and *surveys* give you a chance to ask a large number of people the same questions. These sources will help you determine general trends in opinion.
3. *Family records* are also good sources of information—records of births, marriages, deaths, and ownership of property. Bills, receipts, and check registers that cover a number of years could be used to show a family's buying trends or to illustrate how prices have increased. Other family sources are scrapbooks, photographs, home movies, a family Bible, and tape recordings.
4. *Government record offices* and *historical societies* are also good sources of information.

Compiling the final outline

The sample outlines shown in "Organizing for effective writing" were outlines that you would use as writing tools. The outline discussed here is the final outline you may be required to include with your term paper. The final outline contains the title of your paper, your thesis sentence, and the outline of your paper. You should use your rough, preliminary outline and your note cards to prepare the final outline.

The title

The title of your term paper should tell the reader exactly what the paper is about. You must carefully word the title so that it specifically and accurately reflects the topic of your paper. If your paper is about the battle of

Vicksburg, don't title it "Battles of the Civil War" or even "The Battle of Vicksburg." Be specific. Here are some examples of more specific titles:

Military Strategies Used at the Battle of Vicksburg
The Effects of the Battle of Vicksburg on the South
The Battle of Vicksburg: Turning Point of the Civil War

The thesis sentence

The thesis sentence of your term paper is like the thesis sentence of a short report. In the thesis sentence, you state the main idea of your paper. You must write your thesis sentence carefully so that your reader has a clear understanding of the paper's main idea. Here is a thesis sentence for a paper about the battle of Vicksburg:

By cutting Arkansas, Louisiana, and Texas from the Confederacy and by reuniting the states of the Mississippi Valley, the victory at Vicksburg turned the Civil War in the Union's favor.

The outline

Three to five main headings (roman numerals) are usually enough for a term paper's outline. If you have more than five, check to see whether or not two or more headings are about the same idea. If they are, put the ideas together and write a new heading. Although you won't often use all these levels of subheadings in your outline, here is the correct form for subheadings:

Remember that you should not have single subheadings. For every *A* you must have a *B;* for every *1,* a *2.*

Here is an example of a final outline page. It is in the form that yours should be when you submit your term paper.

NATIONAL SERVICE: ALTERNATIVES TO THE DRAFT IN PEACETIME

Outline

Thesis sentence: A program of national service that would enable all Americans to actively serve their country should be considered as an alternative to the military draft in peacetime.

 I. Purposes of national service
   A. Unite Americans in a common goal
   B. Create positive aspects of patriotism
   C. Give citizens opportunities to solve their country's problems
 II. Kinds of national service
   A. VISTA
   B. Peace Corps
   C. Conservation programs
   D. Research and development programs
III. Requirements of national service
   A. Two years of service
   B. No deferments
 IV. Pay for national service
   A. Based on minimum wage
   B. Not taxed

Writing the first draft

Writing the first draft of a term paper is similar in many ways to writing the first draft of a short report. Keep your final outline and note cards in front of you. Your note cards should contain all the information you will need for your paper. They should have the quotations set off in quotation marks. The cards containing summaries of information should be written in your own words.

Put your thesis sentence in the first paragraph. Develop each heading and subheading of your outline to support the thesis sentence. You will usually need at least one or two paragraphs to present the information from each subheading *(A, B, C)*. Conclude your paper with a paragraph that sums up the main points and arguments.

Direct quotations

When you use a direct quotation, introduce the quotation and relate it to the idea that it is supporting. Be sure to provide a transition between the quotation and your own words. In that way, your paper will read smoothly. It won't lurch along from quotation to quotation.

Use direct quotations sparingly. Most of the paper should be in your own words. The quotations should emphasize, agree with, or support the points you are making.

If the quotation is less than four lines long, use quotation marks and keep it in the text of the paper. If it is longer than four lines, set off the quotation by indenting on both sides and single-spacing it like this:

> Footnotes serve a variety of purposes. In addition to documenting sources, a footnote may also (1) explain a point more fully, (2) make an editorial comment, (3) add an interesting sidelight, (4) be a cross reference to another part of the report, or (5) offer a difference of opinion.[1]

[1]"How to Do Research," *The World Book Encyclopedia,* Vol. 22, p. 27.

Notice that quotation marks are usually not used with indented, single-spaced quotations. For the correct use of ellipses (. . .), single quotation marks (' '), and brackets ([]) with direct quotations, see "Punctuation," pages 136–139.

Footnotes

As the sample direct quotation stated, "Footnotes serve a variety of purposes." The main purpose—and usually the only purpose—for footnotes in your school papers is to document sources. To *document sources* is to give credit to the author whom you are quoting or whose ideas you have used. If you do not use quotation marks and footnotes where they are required, you are guilty of *plagiarism.* This means that you have stolen someone else's words or ideas and have passed them off as your own. If you are very careful when taking notes, you can avoid accidentally plagiarizing. Put quotation marks around those notes that will be used as direct quotations; write all other notes in your own words. In that way, you will avoid the problem of plagiarism.

When you write your first draft, keep a separate sheet on which to list the footnotes. Put the footnote number in the text of your paper. On the separate sheet, record the footnote number and the information about the source—author's name, source title, and page number. By recording this information now, it will be ready when you type the final copy. For more information about correct footnote form and some examples of footnotes, read "Preparing footnotes" on pages 213–215.

Bibliography

When you have finished writing the first draft, prepare the bibliography for your paper. The bibliography should list all the sources that you used and consulted during the preparation of your paper. By correctly preparing the bibliography at this point, you will only have to type it when you do the final copy of the paper.

Revising the first draft

You follow the same basic procedures in revising the first draft of a term paper that you would for a short report (see pages 202–205). But you must check a few more things. Here are some additional tips for revising the first draft of a term paper:

1. Allow several days for revising.
2. Be sure your thesis sentence is in the first paragraph.
3. Check your footnotes. Are they in the correct order? Do the numbers in the text of your paper correspond with the numbers on the separate sheet? Do you have all the required information in each footnote?
4. Check the direct quotations in your paper against your note cards. Be sure the wording in your paper is accurate.
5. Check the bibliography. Is it alphabetized correctly? Do you have all the required information for each entry? Have you included all the sources that you used or consulted?

Preparing the final copy

Term papers should always be typed. If you do not know how to type, pay someone to type it for you. Use high-quality paper, a clean typewriter, and a fresh black ribbon. Read each page after you have typed it. You can catch most of your typing errors in this way. And it is especially important to make sure you have not skipped any sentences or paragraphs *before* you type the next page.

Most instructors and schools have an established format for term papers. If yours does not, follow these suggestions for typing your paper:

1. Leave a margin of 1½ inches on the left, and margins of 1 inch on the right, the top, and the bottom of the paper. But start the outline page and the title on the first page 2 inches from the top.
2. Indent all paragraphs 5 spaces.
3. Double-space the text of your paper.
4. Single-space the outline, but double-space between the main sections.
5. Single-space each footnote and bibliographic entry; double-space between footnotes and between bibliographic entries.
6. Single-space and indent quotations that are set off from the text.

Find out if you should put your footnotes at the bottom of each page or on a separate page at the end of the paper. If you put them at the bottom of each page, be sure to leave enough space for them. All footnote numbers on a page must have a corresponding number and note at the bottom of that page.

Number the pages starting with the first page of the paper and ending with the last page of the bibliography. If you number the pages in the outline, use lower case roman numerals *(i, ii).* Center the number at the bottom of the first page of the paper and the first page of the bibliography and outline. Center the number at the top or right-hand corner of all the other pages. Do not put a number on the title page.

Assembling the final paper

Your final paper should be assembled in the following order:

1. The *title page* with the title of the paper, your name, the date, and sometimes the course title and the instructor's name.
2. The *outline,* which includes the title of the paper, the thesis sentence, and the final outline.
3. The *text* of the paper. The title of the paper is repeated in all capital letters on the first page of the text.
4. A page titled *NOTES* that lists the footnotes if you did not put them at the bottom of the pages.
5. A page titled *BIBLIOGRAPHY* that lists the bibliographic entries.

Reread your paper once more to check for typing errors and mistakes in spelling and punctuation. Check the accuracy of the information in your footnotes and bibliography. Now you can put your paper in a binder or in a manuscript-sized folder and submit it to your instructor.

Preparing footnotes

Footnotes are important in any writing that uses information from various sources—books, magazines, newspapers, pamphlets, or encyclopedias. Footnotes give credit to your sources and establish the authority for your statements. Always use footnotes when you use direct quotes from sources, when you rephrase someone's opinions or ideas, and when you present facts or figures that might be questioned.

The word *footnote* comes from the appearance of footnotes at the *foot,* or bottom, of the page. In this style, the footnotes are numbered consecutively throughout the paper. The number of the footnote appears slightly above the line after the sentence, fact, or quotation you are presenting in the paper. Then that same number appears at the bottom of the page, slightly above the line, before the footnote itself, which gives the source of the information.

Another footnote style has all the footnotes appearing in one list. These *endnotes* may be so entitled and would appear at the end of the paper immediately before the bibliography. Except for position, there is no difference in how these footnotes are presented, with the only exception being that the numbers preceding the footnotes themselves may not be raised and may appear with a period following them (1.).

Footnotes should follow a consistent format and style. Commas appear between the parts of a footnote, and a period is placed at the end. The first line of each footnote is indented; the second and following lines are flush with the left margin. The content of footnotes varies somewhat depending on the type of source you are citing. In the following paragraphs, the raised numbers refer you to sample footnotes for various kinds of sources.

When the source is a book, the footnote includes the author's name, the book title, and the number of the page(s) on which the information can be found.[1] The author's name is written first name first, and the book title is underlined.

[1]Theodore M. Bernstein, *Bernstein's Reverse Dictionary,* pp. 37–39.

When the source is a magazine article, the footnote includes the author's name (if it is given), the title of the article, the magazine, the volume number, the date of the issue, and the page number(s).[2] The article title is in quotation marks, and the magazine name is underlined. If no author is given, begin with the title of the article.[3]

[2]Rudolf F. Graf, "Build an Electronic Guard to Foil Car Thieves," *Popular Science Monthly,* vol. 193, October 1968, p. 140.
[3]"The Righting of Writing," *Time,* vol. 115, May 19, 1980, p. 88.

For a later reference to a previously cited source, shorten the form of the footnote. A shortened form may contain only the author's last name and the page number.[4] (If you have used more than one book by the same author, you'll need to include the title in the shortened footnote.) If the source is the same work and page as the immediately preceding footnote, use *Ibid.* in place of a full footnote.[5] If the source is the same work but a different page from the immediately preceding footnote, use *Ibid.* followed by a comma and the page number.[6] Underline *Ibid.* and place a period after it.

[4]Bernstein, p. 41.
[5]*Ibid.*
[6]*Ibid.,* p. 52.

The following are examples of footnotes for an encyclopedia article,[7] a newspaper article,[8] a work by more than one author,[9] and an edited work.[10]

[7]"How to Do Research," *The World Book Encyclopedia,* Vol. 22, p. 27.
[8]"Mayors Seek Greater U.S. Effort Against Drugs," *The New York Times,* May 6, 1971, p. 19.
[9]William Strunk, Jr., and E. B. White, *The Elements of Style,* p. 64.
[10]Thomas S. Kane and Leonard J. Peters, eds., *Writing Prose: Techniques and Purposes,* p. 220.

Citations placed together at the end of a paper, article, chapter, or book are called *end notes.* They are constructed in the same way as footnotes except the number preceding the source is on the line and followed by a period.[11]

11. "The Righting of Writing," *Time,* vol. 115, May 19, 1980, p. 88.

Be aware that there are several more standard footnote formats that have slight variations from one another. A common and often used "footnote" technique, for example, is to insert source information directly into the text by enclosing authors' names, titles, and page numbers within parentheses. The reader then refers to the bibliography for additional information, if necessary.

The detailed formats given here will be appropriate in most kinds of writing you will do. If your instructor, school, or place of work requires a particular format, use it. Whatever format you use, be sure to use it consistently throughout your paper or report.

Preparing a bibliography

Your bibliography lists all the sources—books, magazines, encyclopedias, newspapers—that you used in preparing your research paper or report. The bibliography shows your reader the number and types of sources you used. It also shows your reader where to find more information on your topic.

Bibliographic entries have standard forms. The information included differs somewhat from that in footnotes. Like footnotes, a bibliographic entry contains the author and title, but it also includes facts about the publication of a source. The style of bibliographic entries differs from footnotes in that authors are listed last name first, and periods separate the three main parts of the entry (author, title, and facts of publication).

Following are examples of the content and format for various types of entries. Notice the information included and the punctuation used in each type of entry; then follow those formats in your own bibliography.

A bibliographic entry for a book contains the author, title, and facts of publication. The facts of publication include the city of publication (followed by a colon), the publisher (followed by a comma), and the year of publication. Here is an example of an entry for a book, along with sample entries for an edited book and a second (or third, etc.) edition of a book.

A book:
Bookchin, Murray. *Our Synthetic Environment.* New York: Harper & Row, 1974.

An edited book:
Kane, Thomas S., and Peters, Leonard J., eds. *Writing Prose: Techniques and Purposes.* New York: Oxford University Press, 1965.

A second edition:
Fowler, H. W. *A Dictionary of Modern English Usage.* 2d ed. New York: Oxford University Press, 1965.

Following are examples of entries for articles from a magazine, a newspaper, and an encyclopedia. The page numbers given are the pages for the entire article.

A magazine article:
Ellis, William S. "Canada's Highway to the Sea." *National Geographic,* vol. 157, May 1980, pp. 594–623.

A newspaper article:
Romero, Jack. "Panthers Finish First." *Prairie Gazette,* May 18, 1980, sec. 3, p. 4.

An encyclopedia article:
"How to Do Research." *The World Book Encyclopedia* (1976), Vol. 22, pp. 27–29.

Sometimes information—date, publisher, place of publication—cannot be found because a book is quite old. In that case, place an abbreviation in brackets—such as [n.d.] for "no date"—to show that the omission was not an oversight on your part. You do *not* need to make such a notation when no author is given for a newspaper or magazine article. It is generally understood that often no author is mentioned for articles in newspapers and magazines.

Bibliographic entries are arranged alphabetically according to the last names of the authors—or according to the titles when authors are not listed. If a bibliography has more than one work by the same author, list those entries together and order them alphabetically by title. Use a long line where the author's name would appear in any entries following the first one.

Bibliographic entries are not numbered. Start each entry at the left margin. Indent any additional lines. Single-space within each entry, and double-space between entries.

Here is a short sample bibliography:

Bernstein, Theodore M. *Bernstein's Reverse Dictionary.* New York: Quadrangle/The New York Times Book Co., 1975.

———. *The Careful Writer: A Modern Guide to English Usage.* New York: Atheneum, 1978.

Ellis, William S. "Canada's Highway to the Sea." *National Geographic,* vol. 157, May 1980, pp. 594–623.

"The Righting of Writing." *Time,* vol. 115, May 19, 1980, pp. 88–91.

Strunk, William, Jr., and White, E. B. *The Elements of Style.* 2d ed. New York: Macmillan Publishing Co., 1972.

As with footnotes, there are several variations of format for bibliographies. The format here would be appropriate in most of your writing. If you are asked to use a different format, do so. Remember to use one format consistently in your bibliography.

Letters, business reports, and memorandums

Plan before you write

You probably have to do some kind of writing at least once a week, and maybe more often than that. This writing may be a letter, a school or business report, or maybe something as simple as a short note asking someone to do a chore or a favor for you.

If you are like most of us, you almost certainly feel a twinge of panic when you actually put pencil to paper. You may ask yourself, "Now, what am I going to say? How should I say it? Can I be sure a reader will understand my meaning?" These questions, and others like them, are a sure sign that you have not planned your writing.

How often have you heard someone say, "My project failed because I did not take the time to plan it out properly"? Well, a piece of writing can also fail to communicate its message if it was poorly planned, or not planned at all, to begin with.

Identifying your audience

The very first thing in any writing plan is to identify the audience. Before you begin to write, you must identify whom you are writing to.

This sounds simple enough. But it is one of the most frequently ignored writing rules. Most people write to please themselves. That is why sentences, letters, whole reports are often perfectly understandable to the people who wrote them but make little or no sense to the people who are trying to read them.

Because anything you write as a means of communication is directed at a specific audience, you should know as much about that audience as possible. You should know in general the age level, sex, educational background, occupation, and likely interests of your audience. This information will give you some understanding of the possible likes and dislikes of your audience. And this understanding will help you to adjust your writing style and content to your audience.

If you are communicating with a friend, relative, or business associate, part of your problem has been solved. You know these people. You probably communicate with them regularly. You should have a very good idea of the words you must choose and the style you must use to communicate your meaning.

But if you are communicating in writing to persons you have never met, how can you find out about them? What can you do to try to make sure that your meaning will be understood?

If you have already received some kind of written communication from the person, you have an advantage. Remember, most people write to please themselves. The content and style of almost every piece of writing is full of clues about its writer.

For example, the person's name may tell you the person's sex. The intent of the piece of writing may give you some clue about the person's occupation. Vocabulary, structure, and spelling may tip you off to level of education. The actual subject may help you to pinpoint some of the person's interests.

Once you have a feeling for *who* your audience is, you should begin to consider *what* your message is going to be. Is this a business communication or a personal communication? Do you wish to deliver your message in a formal or in an informal manner?

Make a list of the topics that you could cover. Now review the list and consider both who your audience is and what you wish your message to be. Eliminate the topics that you think would either not interest your audience or would be inappropriate. Of the topics that remain, decide in what order you wish to present them.

For example, you may be writing an informal letter to a close friend who lives in a distant city. You know your friend enjoys music but is bored by sports. If you have planned your letter, you would probably describe in detail any records or tapes you may have purchased recently but would probably not mention that extra-inning baseball game you attended. You have identified your audience and have planned your writing to suit the reader. In this way you have helped to guarantee that your message will be communicated.

Your mother might want to hear about your records and tapes, the baseball game, the weather, and the neighbor's new baby. If that is the kind of letter she likes to receive, that is the kind of letter you should write to her. In both cases, remember to arrange the topics into some logical order and try to make some connection between topics.

Another example of matching writing to the intended audience might be that of an engineer who is writing a formal report about a new automobile engine. If the report is to be sent to the stockholders of an automobile company, the engineer would not use technical language. Instead, the report would probably stress how the new engine would enable the company to make a larger profit. But if this report was to be read by other engineers at the company, the writer would probably describe in detail how the engine works.

Always keep in mind the fact that you are writing to communicate a message. If your writing fails to do this, the message may just as well not have been written. You must always have your audience in mind as you write if clear, concise communication is your goal.

Identifying your purpose

After you have identified your reader, you must determine *why* you are writing. You must identify the main purpose of the report or letter. Do you want to *complain* about a product, to *invite* your cousin for the weekend, or to *persuade* the board of directors to acquire another company?

When you have determined your main purpose for writing, ask yourself if the letter or report has other purposes. Another purpose in a letter of complaint might be to have a defective product repaired. A second purpose of a report to persuade might also be to present factual information. In almost every kind of written communication, an underlying purpose might be to motivate some kind of action on the part of the reader.

When you are planning the purpose of your letter or report, you should decide what *tone* your message will have. Will it be humorous, apologetic, sympathetic, informative, questioning, or urgent? The way you word your message is as important as the message itself. If you are humorous when you should be apologetic, your reader will probably be angry. If you are sarcastic when you should be understanding, your reader will probably be hurt.

Identifying your purpose before you start to write is as important as identifying your audience. Knowing what your purpose is will help you to choose exactly the right words and use exactly the right tone to deliver your message.

Personal letters

The personal letter is also known as the *friendly* letter. It is the kind of letter you might write to a member of your family or to an acquaintance. Even though the personal letter is written to someone you know, it has certain forms you should follow.

Format for personal letters

There are five parts to a personal letter: (1) the heading, (2) the salutation, (3) the body, (4) the complimentary close, and (5) the signature. An explanation of each part follows:

1. *The heading* is placed in the upper right-hand corner of your letter. The heading features information the reader needs to quickly identify the writer of the letter. The heading should include your street address; your city, state, and zip code; and the date. If you write to a person often, you may wish to omit your complete address from the heading. The use of either a block form or an indented form is equally acceptable in the heading of a personal letter.

Block form:

1011 East 28th Street
Minneapolis, MN 55401
March 28, 1983

Indented form:

1011 East 28th Street
Minneapolis, MN 55401
March 28, 1983

Do not use abbreviations in either the address or the date (except for the state abbreviation which the post office requests you use along with the zip code). Numbered street names should be spelled out if they are ten or less, but given in numerals if they are 11 or above (for example, *Fifth Avenue,* but *42nd Street*). Note that no punctuation appears at the end of a line.

2. *The salutation,* or greeting, is followed by a comma.

Dear David,   Dear Mom and Dad,   Dear Mrs. Smith,

It is placed at the left-hand margin of the letter, about four lines below the heading.

3. *The body* of the letter should begin two lines below the salutation. The body contains the message you wish to communicate to the reader. Paragraphs within the body of the letter may be set off in either one of two ways. The first line of each paragraph may be indented. In this case, the space between paragraphs should be the same as the space between lines within each paragraph. Or the first line of each paragraph may be aligned with the left-hand margin of the letter. In this case, extra space should be left between paragraphs.

4. *The complimentary close* should be placed two lines below the body of the letter and should be aligned with the heading. The complimentary close is followed by a comma.

Sincerely yours,   Your friend,   Love,

5. *The signature* is written below the complimentary close. It may be aligned with the first letter or the last letter of the complimentary close, or it may be centered below the close.

Sincerely yours,   Love,   Your friend,
Kevin   Kevin   Kevin

The envelope for a personal letter should follow the same style (block or indented) that was used in the heading of the letter. The writer's return address can be placed on the back flap or in the upper left-hand corner of the envelope. The name and address of the person to whom the letter has been written should be centered slightly below the middle of the envelope. Be sure to write out in full the name of the person to whom you are writing.

Now study the sample envelope below and the sample showing personal letter format on page 223. Both were prepared using block style. The numbers added to the letter correspond to the five parts of a personal letter just described.

Personal letter envelope

L. M. Jones
1174 Home Avenue
Oak Park, IL 60304

Mr. David Anderson
15 Nautilus Court
Pittsburg, CA 94521

Content of personal letters

The *content* is what makes up the body of a personal letter. It is what a letter is all about. Letters can center on one topic or on several. Some letters that concentrate on one topic are invitations, replies to invitations, thank-you notes, and sympathy notes.

However, some personal letters may revolve around several different topics. Such personal letters are usually the long, newsletter kinds of communications you may write to close friends or family members.

Even though long personal letters may contain many separate topics, these kinds of letters should not become collections of unconnected notes. It is very difficult to maintain a reader's interest if he or she must continuously jump from one topic to another. And if a reader's interest is not held, you are not accomplishing your main purpose—communication.

Personal letter format

1. 1174 Home Avenue
   Oak Park, IL 60304
   June 5, 1981

2. Dear David,

3. How surprised I was to receive your letter. I know you must be busy unpacking at home and settling in at your new job. The company that you work for has a division in Illinois. One of Joe's best friends is a sales manager for them.

   You asked when we could come out for a visit. Well, we don't have any vacation time left this year. Perhaps next February we could fly out and stay a week. Would you be able to take time from work then?

   We are all happy for you and would enjoy visiting you in California.

4. Love,
5. Linda

Make sure each separate topic is fully developed, sprinkled with the kind of rich detail you think your reader would find interesting. Try to create transitions between topics. Transitions will help one topic flow smoothly and evenly into the next and will make your letter much easier to read.

Remember, the thoughts in your personal letters should be well-organized and clearly presented. Your letter should use transitions to move smoothly from one idea to another. Do not abruptly break into one idea with "Oh, I forgot to mention before when I was saying. . . ." Put all your thoughts about one item together in the same paragraph.

The people to whom you write personal letters are probably the people who are closest and most important to you. Show that you truly care about them and value their friendship by taking time to plan and then write thoughtful, legible letters.

Business letters

You may have looked at the title of this section and thought, "Well, this is not for me. I don't work at a job that requires me to write letters." On the other hand, you may have thought, "I write many business letters every day. I don't need any advice on how such letters should be written."

Well, both attitudes should be reconsidered. The person whose job requires the writing of many business letters should always be searching for ways to make those letters clearer. And the person who believes that he or she never deals with business letters is in for a surprise.

Everyone both sends and receives business letters—not just business people. Business letters are sent from one company or organization to another, from companies and organizations to individuals, and from individuals to companies and organizations. You probably receive, either at work or at home, several business letters every week. Letters asking you to subscribe to magazines or apologizing for not properly crediting your checking account are some examples of business letters you receive at home.

You have many occasions to write business letters yourself. You might wish to cancel a subscription, to apply for a job, to complain about faulty merchandise, or to request a copy of a doctor's bill. All of these are examples of business letters. Whenever you write a business letter, you should follow the established format.

Format for business letters

A business letter always has six parts: (1) the heading, (2) the inside address, (3) the salutation, (4) the body, (5) the complimentary close, and (6) the signature. An explanation of these parts follows:

1. *The heading* is placed in the upper right-hand corner of your letter. It includes your street address; your city, state, and zip code; and the date. The heading should be arranged in block form. The block form is preferred because it is easier to set up and has cleaner lines.

Block form:

210 Park Boulevard
Glen Ellyn, IL 60305
April 12, 1983

Do not use abbreviations in either the address or the date (except for the state abbreviation that is used with the zip code). Numbered street names should be spelled out if they are ten or less, but given in numerals if they are 11 or above (for example, write *First Street,* but *12th Avenue*).

If you are using stationery with a printed letterhead, add the date two or three lines below it. The date may be placed flush with the right-hand margin or flush with the left-hand margin.

2. *The inside address* is placed four lines below the heading and flush with the left-hand margin. The inside address consists of the recipient's name and title; the name of the department or office, if any; the name of the company; the street address; and the city, state, and zip code.

When you write to an individual in a company or organization, use the person's personal, professional, or business title. For example, write *Ms. Jane Smith, President* or *Dr. James Bentley, Registrar.* If the person's business title is long, place it on the second line. Use the same form—block—for the inside address as you did for the heading. If your letter is short, you may add extra space between the heading and the inside address.

Block form:

Mrs. Ellen Smith
Editorial Vice-President
Mathematics Department
Read-It Publishing Company
120 East Adams Street
Chicago, IL 60635

3. *The salutation,* or greeting, is placed two lines below the inside address and is followed by a colon. When you write to an individual in a company, use the individual's name *(Dear Mr. Jones:).* If the person to whom you are writing has a professional title *(Doctor, Professor),* it should be used *(Dear Professor Smith:).* When you are addressing a woman, use the title *(Ms., Mrs.,* or *Miss)* that she prefers. When you write to a company or to an individual whose name you do not know, use *Gentlemen:, Dear Sir:,* or *Madam:.* If you do not know if the person reading the letter will be a man or a woman, you could use *Dear Sir or Madam:* or *Ladies and Gentlemen:* as a salutation.

4. *The body* of the letter begins two lines below the salutation. All the information that you wish to communicate to the recipient of your letter is placed in the body. It is recommended that block style be used throughout the body of a business letter. The body should be single-spaced; double-space between paragraphs.

5. *The complimentary close* is begun two lines below the body of the letter. You may align the complimentary close either with the left-hand margin or with the heading. Only the first word in the complimentary close is capitalized. The complimentary close is followed by a comma. Here are some suitable complimentary closes for a business letter arranged from the most formal to the least formal: *Respectfully yours, Yours truly, Very truly yours, Yours very truly, Yours very sincerely, Sincerely yours,* and *Cordially yours.*

6. *The signature* is handwritten below the complimentary close. Your name should be typed below your signature. Usually, your typed name appears four lines below the complimentary close, with your signature written between them.

7. If you *enclose* something with your letter—a check, a bill, or an article—you should call attention to it by writing the word *Enclosure* or *Enclosures.* This notation should be placed two lines below your typed name, flush with the left-hand margin.

8. If you are sending a *carbon copy* of your letter to someone, that person's name should be mentioned after the abbreviation *cc:,* which stands for "carbon copy." This notation should be placed flush with the left-hand margin, two lines below your typed name, or two lines below the notation *Enclosure* if that has been used.

The *envelope* for a business letter should follow the block style that you used in the heading and inside address of your letter. Place your full name and address in the upper left-hand corner. Center the recipient's full name and address slightly below the middle of the envelope. The recipient's name and address on the envelope should be the same as in the inside address.

Look at the samples of a business letter on page 228 and an envelope (below) which show the proper format. The numbers added to the letter correspond to the eight parts of a business letter just described.

Content of business letters

The *content* is in the body of a business letter; it is the subject matter that you wish to communicate. Business letters often deal with only one topic. And such letters are usually classified according to the content, or subject matter, that they contain. A few of the different kinds of business letters are letters of inquiry, application, introduction, and recommendation; order letters; complaint letters; and sales letters.

Your letters represent you. They should be brief, to the point, clear, and courteous. The message you wish to communicate must be the main, most obvious part of the letter. When your letter is received, you will not be present to explain what you really *meant* to say. You must state your message clearly in the letter. Much time and money will be wasted—by both you and the recipient—if other letters must be written to clarify the message of the first letter.

Your letters should be arranged in a logical, orderly manner. To do this you should gather all the facts you need *before* you write the letter. Know to whom you are writing, why you are writing, and what the order of importance is of your ideas.

Business letter envelope

```
Joseph F. Wesley
784 Chatham Place
Elmhurst, IL  60126




                    Ms. Pamela Marsh, Director
                    Office of Admissions
                    Marquette University
                    1380 West Wisconsin Avenue
                    Milwaukee, WI  53233
```

Business letter format

1. 784 Chatham Place
Elmhurst, IL 60126
January 5, 1981

2. Ms. Pamela Marsh, Director
Office of Admissions
Marquette University
1380 West Wisconsin Avenue
Milwaukee, WI 53233

3. Dear Ms. Marsh:

4. Thank you for sending me the brochures and the application
forms for the College of Journalism. I also appreciated
your suggestion about writing to Dr. Jones. He has arranged
for me to visit with some journalism professors and students
in March.

I have enclosed the application forms and the $20.00
application fee.

Would you please send me another brochure? My counselor
would like one to show to other interested students.

5. Sincerely yours,

Joseph F. Wesley

6. Joseph F. Wesley

7. Enclosures

8. cc: Dr. Albert Jones

For example, you see an advertisement in a magazine for a product that none of the stores in your town carry. You decide to write to the manufacturer to find out more about the product and where you can purchase it. In your letter, put first things first:

1. Tell where you saw the advertisement.
2. Tell why you need more information.
3. Ask for the information.

Your letters should be written in a straightforward, natural manner. Which of the following statements would you use in a letter?

1. The matter has been attended to by my office.
2. My office has taken care of some matters.
3. Mr. Jones, my assistant, has solved your problem.

If you chose the third statement, you chose a statement that is specific. It shows a person *(Mr. Jones)* doing *(has solved)* a definite task *(your problem)*. The first statement is written in the passive voice and shows a thing *(office)* doing the action. In the second statement, a thing *(office)* is doing an indefinite task *(some matters)*. You should, therefore, use the active voice and show people doing the action in your letters. As much as possible, you should write your business letters to read as if you were present and speaking to the receiver.

There is no special language for business letters. You should avoid stiff, stilted, or stuffy words and phrases. Above all, avoid the use of clichés. The list at the right shows a few of the many clichés you should avoid in business letters. You would not use such clichés if you were talking to someone on the telephone or face-to-face; don't use them in your letters either.

Your letters should also be courteous. You are entering another person's home or office through your letter, so maintain a friendly tone. By choosing your words carefully, you can even express displeasure or register a complaint without making an enemy. If you want some positive action to result from your letter, avoid annoying the intended receiver.

Clichés to avoid in business letters

according to our records
answering yours of
anticipating your favor/order/reply
as per
as regards
beg to advise/assure

check to cover
duly noted
enclosed find
for your files
for your information
hereby advise

hoping your order
I am [ending last sentence]
I have your letter of
in due course
in receipt of
in reference to
kind order
kindly advise
looking forward to
may we suggest
of the above date
our records show
permit us to remind
please accept/find/note/rest assured
recent date
referring to yours of

regarding the matter
regret to advise/inform/state
take pleasure in
take the liberty of
thanking you in advance
trusting to have
under separate cover
valued favor/order
we are [ending last sentence]
we are pleased to advise/note
wish to advise/state
with reference to
your kind indulgence
your letter of recent date
your Mr., Mrs., Miss _____
your valued patronage

Business reports and memorandums

Writing (and reading) reports and memorandums are often considered necessary evils in the business world. They are necessary, but they need not be evils. Poorly written, hard-to-read reports and memorandums are often the result of either one or a combination of problems. The next time you write a report or memorandum, it may be poorly understood if:

1. The subject is unfamiliar to you and you do not know how to obtain necessary facts that would clarify the communication.
2. You do not fully understand the subject.
3. You are not able to communicate your meaning clearly because you are unsure of the purpose or audience.
4. You are not able to organize your information clearly because you are unsure of the form—report or memorandum—your communication should follow.
5. Your reader has not been given enough background information to understand the subject.
6. The form selected—report or memorandum—might not be suitable for the length of the communication.

Business reports and memorandums can be effectively written, however, when you, the business writer, understand their purpose, audience, form, and content.

Purpose of business reports

All business reports should have one *general* purpose: *to present information in an orderly, objective manner.* Your reports should be based on facts, not opinions; they should show a fair and true picture of whatever situation you are attempting to deal with. The purpose of your reports is to communicate a message to your reader; therefore, do not bury your message under ambiguous words and phrases.

Each business report also has a *specific* purpose. Some reports—progress reports and annual reports—merely *state facts.* Progress reports tell how far along a project is. Annual reports show the stockholders how well or how poorly an organization has performed during the year. Other reports *explain* or *interpret* the facts. For example, a report might be written primarily to explain a new method which could be used to make motors. Besides telling what the method is and how it works, such a report might also explain how the company could use this new method to make production more efficient.

The most complex types of reports are those that *analyze* a subject. For example, your company is considering building a plant in Brazil. You have been asked to study the situation in Brazil to find out whether or not building a plant there would be a good idea. Your report should analyze several elements, such as the political and economic conditions in Brazil, and the availability of raw materials and skilled workers. When your analysis is completed, you should be able to make your recommendations: to build or not to build.

The purpose of your report will usually determine whether the report should be informal or formal. *Informal reports* usually deal with the smaller parts of large projects. A monthly progress report would be an example of an informal report. An informal report could be contained in a letter or memorandum.

Formal reports are usually long; they may be many pages long, even book length. Such reports are sometimes published. However, this does not mean that any less care should go into the creation of a short, informal report. A large part of the way in which an organization views you may depend on how well you are able to communicate. So careful planning and execution should be your goal at all times. And careful planning begins with establishing a format that is logical and easy to follow.

Format of informal business reports

The format of short, informal business reports may vary considerably, depending on the purpose of the report. The various sections of a short report should have headings. These headings may be placed on a separate line at the left-hand margin and underlined; or they may simply be underlined at the beginnings of paragraphs. Headings help you organize the information and help your reader understand the information. Organizations often have their own standard formats for reports that are frequently written, such as sales reports, progress or status reports, budget reports, and production reports. The first time you are asked to do a particular kind of report, ask if there is a standard format. Whether or not the format is standard, you might look at previously written reports, if possible, to get ideas for setting up your report. If you have to set up your own format, use brief, clear headings that will help you put your information in a logical order.

Format of formal business reports

There are six main parts to most long, formal business reports: (1) the introduction, (2) the summary, (3) the body, (4) the conclusions, (5) the recommendations, and (6) the appendix. Most companies have their own established structure for formal business reports. Some structures place the conclusions and recommendations before the body of the report; others put the summary before the introduction. There are, however, specific kinds of information that make up each part of a long, formal report.

1. *The introduction* presents a clear statement of the problem or problems that will be covered in the report. It gives the purpose and aim of the report and tells why the report was compiled. The methods used to gather and analyze the facts are often described in the introduction.

2. *The summary* is a brief overview of the main points of the report. The results, conclusions, and your recommendations should be emphasized in the summary. Executives and managers sometimes receive only the summaries of reports. They want to know what should be done to solve problems; they do not want to be bothered with the details. The summary is sometimes called a *synopsis,* an *abstract,* or an *executive summary.*

3. *The body* of the report presents the facts, explains what, if any, action was undertaken, and analyzes the results. The body of a report could be contained in one or two paragraphs, or it could involve many pages.

4. *The conclusions* tell what the results of the study mean. The conclusions are always based on the facts that were presented in the body of the report.

5. *The recommendations* are suggestions for what should be done to solve the problem or to clarify the situation that prompted creation of the report. The recommendation may be that action be taken or changes be made, or the recommendation might be that nothing should be done, or that additional study of the subject is required before a decision can be made.

6. *The appendix* is further information for the reader. Maps, charts, graphs, and tables that would break into the text of a report are usually placed in the appendix. If the report is lengthy, an index might be included in the appendix. A bibliography could also be added to an appendix.

Extremely long reports sometimes include one or more additional parts. These additional parts might be—

1. *A title page* which gives (a) the title of the report, (b) the name of the person or company who authorized the report, (c) the author's name, and (d) the date the report was submitted.

2. *A table of contents* which lists the major sections of the report and the page numbers on which each section is located.

3. *A letter of authorization* written by the person who authorized the report.

4. *A letter of transmittal* from the person who wrote the report to the person or persons who will receive the report.

Appearance of formal reports

Each part of a report has a heading—*Introduction, Conclusion, Appendix*. If the report is long, the heading should be centered at the top of the page on which the section begins. If the report is short, the heading can be placed at the left-hand margin and underlined. You may use the terms *Introduction, Summary, Conclusion, Recommendations,* and *Appendix* for headings. But you should devise a descriptive term or title for the heading of the body.

Maps, charts, graphs, and tables that are referred to in the report may be placed within the text if they are necessary to understanding the main points of the report. If these items just provide additional information, they should be placed in the appendix.

Use numbers or letters—(1), (2), (a), (b)—to set off items in a list. Such listed items are much easier to read.

Readability is also improved if you leave adequate white space in your report. Double-space the text of a long report, and single-space that of a short report. Leave additional space between the text and lists or between the text and illustrations.

Content of business reports

The content of a business report is what the report is all about. Whether you are writing a brief status report or a long analysis of a problem, the final judgment of a report's accuracy and effectiveness is based upon the report's content.

The facts

Facts are the foundation upon which you build your report. You must know where to find the facts and how to interpret them. You must decide which facts to emphasize and which ones to omit.

One central idea

Your report centers on one specific problem or idea. All your facts, results, conclusions, and recommendations must relate to this one central idea or problem. You want to keep the reader aware of the central idea. Do not introduce irrelevant material into your report, or get sidetracked by remotely related material.

Clear, concise writing

Your reports should be written in a straightforward, clear, and concise manner. Clear writing reflects clear thinking. Explain to the reader why you did or did not do certain things, and what procedures you used. Remember, the purpose of a report is to communicate information.

Unclear, ambiguous writing is what causes most business reports to fall apart. The writers are afraid to take responsibility. They hide behind ambiguous statements, use the passive voice, or show objects doing actions. Readers quickly lose interest in such vague writing.

Logical arrangement

The ideas in your report should fit together to create a clear, orderly picture of the problem. There are many different kinds of arrangements that you can use—chronological, spatial, simple to complex, or cause and effect. Before you start to write, make an outline. It will help you put your ideas in a logical arrangement.

Courteous tone

As is true for all forms of written communication, business reports should be courteous in tone. Do not assume that the reader has as much background in the subject as you have. You are the expert; you have done the research. Now you must write the report so that the readers can share, understand, and use the information you have gathered.

You should know exactly to whom the report will be sent—your immediate supervisor, the president of the company, all managers, the stockholders, or the plant's supervisors. When you know who your readers will be, you can choose appropriate language and reading level for your report. In general, the number of words containing more than three syllables should be kept low. Sentences should usually not be more than 25 words long. And the length of most paragraphs should be about 150 words.

Do not use business or technical jargon when it is not necessary. If you cannot explain in simple and clear language how a system or method works, you probably do not understand how it works yourself.

Many times reports are made to evaluate existing problems or situations. These problems and situations usually involve many people. Therefore, you should be diplomatic in your suggestions for making improvements.

Steps in preparing a report

Now that you know something about the format and content of business reports, you are ready to prepare a report. The following list suggests seven steps you should use in preparing a report:

1. Know the problem with which your report will deal, and set limits on the range of your study. Know who the readers of the report will be and to what use the report will be put.
2. Find out what already has been suggested or done to attempt to solve the problem.
3. Gather your facts from the files, from libraries, from laboratory experiments, or from interviews with people who are involved in the problem.
4. Make an outline that organizes your facts into logical groups of ideas. Arrange these groups of ideas into a logical sequence.
5. Write your report using the active voice, concrete nouns, and specific examples.
6. Have your report typed according to your organization's format.
7. Proofread your report, and ask an objective person to read and critique it *before* you submit the report.

Writing memorandums

Memorandums are used for communication within an organization whenever a written record of information or of a message is required. A memorandum can be sent from one department to another, from one person to another, or from a person to a department. Memorandums—memos—can be used for something as simple as notifying people about a department

Sample memo—first version

```
TO:  All department heads

FROM:  E. B. Jones, Personnel Director

DATE:  June 10, 1981

SUBJECT:  Vacation schedules


The personnel department is putting together the vacation
schedule for the period July 1981 to June 1982.  Please have
your employees fill in the attached forms indicating their
first and second choices for vacations to be taken during
the period July 1981 to June 1982.
```

Sample memo—improved version

```
TO:  All department heads

FROM:  E. B. Jones, Director of Personnel

DATE:  June 10, 1981

SUBJECT:  Vacation schedules for
          July 1, 1981 through June 30, 1982


Please distribute one of the attached forms to each of your
employees.  Ask them to follow the directions carefully so
that you can return the forms by June 20, 1981.

We need everyone's cooperation.  Thank you for yours.


Employee vacation preference forms
```

meeting, or as complex as reporting the results of a study to relocate the company.

Most companies have preprinted forms for memorandums. The forms usually have five parts.

1. *To:* (The name of the person to whom the message is sent. The names of several people, or of a department, could be listed here.)
2. *From:* (The name of the person or department who sent the message, sometimes followed by the initials of the person who authorized the message.)
3. *Date:*
4. *Subject:* (A brief phrase or a sentence that tells what the message is about.)
5. The rest of the page is for the message.

Sometimes other materials—letters, charts, pamphlets—are attached to a memo. In those cases, an *enclosure* or *attachment* line should be added toward the bottom of the memo sheet and all the attached materials should be listed.

The message in a memo is given briefly and concisely. Therefore, the writer must try a little harder to be accurate, clear, and complete. Do not repeat information that has already been given in another part of the memo. Read the first sample memo on page 236 and answer the following questions:

1. Is the title of the subject accurate?
2. Was anything repeated in the message that was already in a heading?
3. Was the memo complete?

Now look at the second version of the sample memo. Compare it with the first version. In what ways is the second version better?

As in business letters, there are clichés to be avoided in reports and memorandums. The final table below gives simple, direct equivalents for these clichés.

Clichés to avoid in reports and memos

Instead of	Use	Instead of	Use
ahead of schedule	early	a majority of	most
a large number of	many	are of the opinion	believe, think
almost never	seldom	at the present time	now, today

Instead of	Use	Instead of	Use
comes into conflict	conflicts	indigenous	native
costs the sum of	costs	initial	first
created the possibility	made possible	in the amount of	for
		in the event that	if
due in large measure to	due largely to	in the near future	soon
endeavor	attempt, try	make inquiry regarding	inquire
fabricate	build	maximum	most
for a period of a week	for a week	minimum	least
for the purpose of	for	of a confidential nature	confidential
give encouragement to	encourage	optimum	best
give rise to	cause	substantial portion	many, much
have need for	need	take into consideration	consider
in all cases	always	to conduct an investigation of	to investigate
in a most careful manner	carefully	utilize	use
inaugurate	begin		

Appendix

Table of roots

Root	Meaning	Root	Meaning
acro	height, high, tip, end	carn	flesh
		cav	hollow
agr	field, land	ced, ceed	go, yield
alg, algos	pain	cens	judge
ali	another	cept	take, receive, catch
alt	tall, high		
alter, altr	other	choreia, chorus	dancing
ama, ami	love	chron	time
ambul	walk	cide	kill
angle, angul	corner	circ	ring, around
annus	year	civ	citizen
anthropo	man, humankind	claim	shout
aqua	water	clam	shout
arch	chief	clar	clear
arch, arche	ancient, first	class	class, group
arm	weapon	clin	lean
aster, astro	star	clud	shut
athl, athlon	prize, contest	clus	shut
aud	hear	cogn	know
auto	self	colo, cult	cultivate, settle
avi	bird	commun	common
baro	weight	cornu	horn
belli	war	corp	body
bene	good, well	cosm	order, universe
bibl	book	cracy, crat	rule
bio	life	cred	believe
brev	short	crim	judge, accuse
bronch	windpipe	crit	separate, judge
bursa	bag, purse	crypt	secret
camera	vault, chamber	culp	fault, blame
cand	glow, white, pure	cum	pile up
		cumb, cub	lie, recline
cant	song	cur, cour	run
cap	head	cur	care
capt	take, receive	cycl	ring, circle
cardi	heart	dat	give

Root	Meaning	Root	Meaning
deb	owe	*flex*	bend
decor	proper, fitting	*flor*	flower
dei	god	*flu*	flow
demos	people	*fol*	leaf
dent	tooth	*form*	shape
derm	skin	*fort*	strong
dia, die	day	*fract, frag*	break
dic, dict	say	*frat*	brother
dign	worth	*fru*	enjoy
div	separate	*fug*	flee
do	give	*funct*	perform
doc	teach	*fus*	pour
dorm	sleep	*gam*	marriage
doxa	belief, praise	*gen*	race, birth
duc	lead	*geo*	earth
dur	hard	*gnos*	know
dyn	power	*gon*	angle
ego	I	*grad*	step
em, empt	buy, obtain	*gram*	letter, written
emia, hemia	blood	*gran*	grain
enni	year	*graph*	write
equ	equal, even, just	*grat*	please, thank
erg	work	*greg*	herd
err	wander	*gyn*	woman
esth	feeling	*hedr*	side, seat
fac	make, do	*heli*	sun
fall, fals	deceive	*hom*	man
femina	woman	*homo*	same
fer	carry, bear	*hum*	earth, soil
fic	do, make	*hydr*	water
fid	faith	*iatrik, iatro*	healing art
fili	son, daughter	*ident*	same
fin	end	*idio*	peculiar
firm	steady	*ign*	fire
fix	fasten	*imperi*	command
flam	blaze	*insul*	island
flect	bend		

Root	Meaning	Root	Meaning
integ	whole, untouched	*mand*	order
		mare	sea
ir	anger	*mater, matri*	mother, source
it	go	*med*	middle
ject	throw	*memoria*	memory
jocus	joke	*ment*	mind
journ	daily	*merg*	plunge, dip
ju, jud	law, right	*meter*	measure
junct	join	*metr*	measure
jur	law, right	*migr*	move
jus	law, right	*mil*	soldier
labor	work	*mim*	imitate
laps	slip	*miser*	wretched, pity
lat	side	*miss*	send, let go
lect	gather, choose	*mnem*	memory
lect, leg	read	*mob*	move
leg	law, contract	*mon*	advise, warn
lev	raise, lift	*mor*	custom
liber	free	*mort*	death
libr	book	*mot*	move
lingu	tongue	*mov*	move
litera	letter	*mut*	change, exchange
lith	stone		
loc	place	*nat*	born
locu	speak	*naus, naut*	ship
log, logue, logy	speech	*nav*	ship
lop	run, leap	*nes*	island
loqu	speak	*nom*	law, arrangement
lu	wash		
luc	light	*nomen*	name
lud	play	*nov*	new
luna	moon	*numer*	number
magni	great	*ocul*	eye
mal	bad	*onym*	name
man	hand	*op, opt*	sight

Root	Meaning	Root	Meaning
orare	speak, pray	*rota*	wheel, round
oss, osteo	bone	*rupt*	to break
ov	egg	*sacr*	holy
paed, ped	child, teach	*san*	healthy, sound
par	give birth	*sanct*	holy
par	equal, compare	*sat, satis*	enough
		saur	lizard
past	shepherd	*scend, scens*	climb
pater, patr	father	*schole*	leisure, school
path	feel, suffer	*sci*	know
ped	foot	*scope*	to watch
pel	drive	*scrib, script*	write
pen, pun	punishment	*sec, sect*	cut
pend, pens	hang	*sed, sess, sid*	sit, settle
petr	rock	*semin*	seed
phag	eat	*sen*	old
phil	love	*sens, sent*	feel
phobos	fear	*seps, sept*	decay
phon	sound	*sequ*	follow
phor	to carry	*serv*	save, keep
photo	light	*servus*	slave, server
plac	please	*sexus*	division, sex
pne	air, lung, breathe	*signi*	mark, sign
pod, pus	foot	*simil, simul*	like, same
poli, polit	city	*sol*	alone
port	carry	*solidus*	solid
porta	gate	*solu, solv*	loosen, free
pos	place, set	*somn*	sleep
pter	wing, feather	*son*	sound
puls	drive, push	*soph*	wise
quer, quest, quir	seek, ask	*spec, spect*	look
rect	straight, right	*spher*	ball, sphere
referre	carry back	*spir*	breathe, live
reg, regn	rule	*spond, spons*	answer
rid, ris	laugh	*sta*	stand
rod, ros	gnaw		
rogare	ask, request		

Root	Meaning	Root	Meaning
stru	build	vad, vas	go
studeo	be eager	vag	wander
surg, surr	rise	val	strong, worth
syllaba	take together	van	front, forward
tabl, tabula	board, tablet	vapor	steam
tact, tang	touch	vari	different, various, spotted
tain, ten	hold		
tact, tax	to arrange, order	ven	come
tele	distant	ven	sale
temp	time, season	ven	vein
tend, tens, tent	tend, stretch	ver	true
terrere	to frighten	ver, verer	fear, awe
testare	to witness	verb	word
thanatos	death	vers, vert	turn
the	god	vesper	evening
thermo	heat	vest	clothing
tom	cut	veter	old, experienced
topos	place, spot	via	way
tort	twist, turn	vict	conquer
tox	poison	vid	see
tract	pull, draw, drag	vis	see
trud	thrust	vit	live
tuitus	watch over	viv	live
turb	whirling, turmoil	voc, voke	call
ultimus	last	vol	wish, will
umber, umbra	shade, shadow	vol, volv	roll, turn
unda	wave	vor	eat
urb	city	zo	animal
vaca, vacu	empty, hollow		

Table of prefixes

Prefix	Meaning	Prefix	Meaning
a-	on	endo-	inside, within
a-, an-	not, without	epi-	upon, in addition
ab-	from		
ad-	to	eu-	well, good
ambi-	both, around	ex-	out
amphi-	both, around	extra-	outside, beyond
ante-	before	hept-, sept-	seven
anti-	against	hetero-	different
apo-	away from, from	homo-	same
auto-	self	hyper-	over, beyond
bene-	well, good	hypo-	under, too little
bi-, bin-, bis-	two, twice	il-	not
cent-	hundred	im-	into
circu-	around, about	im-	not
circum-	around	in-	into
co-	with, together	in-	not
col-	together, with	infra-	below
com-	together, with	inter-	between, among
con-	together, with	intra-, intro-	within
contra-, contro-	against	ir-	not
counter-	against, in return	iso-	equal, same
de-	down	kilo-	1,000
de-	away	macro-	large, long
dec-	ten	mega-	large
deci-	tenth	meta-	change
demi-, hemi-, semi-	half, partly	meta-	beyond
		micro-	small
di-	two	milli-	$\frac{1}{1,000}$
dia-	through, between	mis-	wrong
		mono-	one
dis-	not	multi-	many
dis-	apart from	neo-	new, modern
dis-	opposite	non-	not
du-	two	non-, novem-	nine
dys-	bad	ob-	against, opposite
e-	out		
en-	in		

Prefix	Meaning	Prefix	Meaning
octa-, octo-	eight	*quasi-*	seemingly, partly, as if
olig-	few		
omni-	all	*quin-*	five
pan-	all	*re-*	back
para-	beside	*re-*	again
pen-, pene-	almost	*retro-*	back
penta-	five	*semi-*	half
per-	throughout, thoroughly	*sept-*	seven
		sesqui-	one and a half
peri-	around, near, about	*sex-, hex-*	six
		sub-	under, below
poly-	many	*super-*	over
post-	after	*sym-*	together, with
pre-	before	*syn-*	together, with
pro-	before	*tetra-*	four
pro-	in place of	*trans-*	across, over
pro-	forward	*tri-*	three
pro-	in favor of	*ultra-*	beyond
pro-	in front	*un-*	not
proto-	first	*uni-*	one
pseudo-	false	*vice-*	in place of
quad-, quart-, quatr-	four		

Table of suffixes

Suffix	Meaning	Suffix	Meaning
-able, -ble, -ible	can be done	*-ence*	state, quality, condition of
-able, -ble, -ible	inclined to	*-ency*	quality of, state of
-acy, -cy	office, rank of, state of	*-er*	comparative degree
-ade	result, product, substance made	*-er, -or*	person connected with
-ade	process, action	*-ery, -ry*	place where
-ae	Latin feminine plural	*-ese*	derivation, language
-age	place of	*-esque*	in the manner, style of, like
-age	action, process	*-ess*	feminine ending
-al	relating to	*-et, -ette*	small
-an	relating to	*-eur*	agent
-ance	state of	*-ful*	enough to fill
-ancy	state of	*-fy*	make of, form into
-and, -end	to be done		
-ant	state of, condition of	*-hood*	state of, quality of, condition of
-ant, -ent	person who	*-ial*	characterized by, related to
-arian	person who, place where, object which	*-ian*	characterized by, related to
-ary	person who, place where, object which	*-ic*	of the nature of, characterized by
-ary	characterized by, relating to	*-ic*	to form nouns
-ate	to make, cause to be	*-ical*	of the nature of, characterized by
-ation	process, action	*-icle*	little
-ation	state of, quality of, result of	*-ier, -yer*	person who, place where
-atory	process, action, place where	*-ine*	like, characterized by, pertaining to
-cule	small	*-ine*	feminine suffix
-dom	state of		
-ectomy	surgical removal		
-en	to make		

Suffix	Meaning	Suffix	Meaning
-ing	present participle	-ly	characteristic of, in the manner of
-ing	material	-ment	action, process
-ings	noun associated with the verb form	-ment	state of
-ion	act, process	-ness	state of, quality of, condition of
-ion	state of	-oid	like, resembling
-ious	characterized by	-or	person who
-ise, -ize	subject to, make, carry on	-orium	place for, object used for
-ish	like, pertaining to	-ory	place where
-ism	action, process	-osis	abnormal condition, state of
-ism	state of, condition of	-ous	possessing the qualities of
-ism	doctrine, system	-ry	collection of
-ist	person who	-ship	state of
-itis	inflammatory disease	-ship	office, profession
-ity	state of	-ship	art, skill
-less	without	-ster	one belonging to, characterized by
-let	small		
-like	like		
-ling	small	-ule	little, small
-logy	science of	-wise	way, manner, respect

Index

the Electrodynamics of Moving Bodies the four-vector of force. Lorentz equation. e momentum equation in Electrodynamics Momentum. Physical Review, 14, 1962, 487.